RADICALISED BY FIFA

FOOTBALL, HISTORY AND FEMINISM

RADICALISED BY FIFA

FOOTBALL, HISTORY AND FEMINISM

Jean Williams

First published in 2025 by Fair Play Publishing
PO Box 4101, Balgowlah Heights, NSW 2093, Australia

www.fairplaypublishing.com.au

ISBN: 978-1-923236-05-9
ISBN: 978-1-923236-06-6 (ePub)

© Jean Williams 2025
The moral rights of the author have been asserted.

All rights reserved. Except as permitted under the *Australian Copyright Act 1968* (for example, a fair dealing for the purposes of study, research, criticism or review), no part of this book may be reproduced, stored in a retrieval system, communicated or transmitted in any form or by any means without prior written permission from the Publisher.

Design and typesetting by Leslie Priestley

Front cover photograph of Jean Williams and Sepp Blatter in 1999 by Simon Williams
Back cover photograph of Jean Williams at the 2023 World Cup in Brisbane by Alamy
All other photographs supplied by the author.

All inquiries should be made to the Publisher via hello@fairplaypublishing.com.au

A catalogue record of this book is available from the National Library of Australia.

CONTENTS

PROLOGUE — 1
Feminist

CHAPTER I: THE BARBIE WORLD CUP, 1999 — 12
Introduction: Thriller in Windhoek
Jeanola and Simone in LA
Conclusion: The Football Mothership Calling me Home

CHAPTER II: THE HANGOVER WORLD CUP, 2003 — 40
Introduction: Falling
The SARS Pandemic Disrupts Women's World Cup 2003
Conclusion: Falling for Marta

CHAPTER III: THE INVISIBLE WORLD CUP, 2007 — 60
Introduction: Lunch with Sir Bobby and Sepp Blatter
Marta's World Cup
Conclusion: The unseen GOAT and disappeared women players

CHAPTER IV: THE 'TIE IT UP WITH A BOW AND GIFT IT' WORLD CUP, 2011 — 71
Introduction: Free Lunch
Karla Kick, and Germany 2011
London 2012: The Second Austerity Olympics
Brittle Academic Masculinity
Defying Clarity

CHAPTER V: THE ARTIFICIAL WORLD CUP, 2015   99

    Jacqui and the Chocolate Factory

    Not Staying in My Lane

    Grass is a Gas in Canada 2015

CHAPTER VI: THE WAGE THEFT WORLD CUP, 2019   129

    Storied Objects

    Chicks' Football France 2019

    Different But Equal?

CHAPTER VII: THE INDUSTRIAL DISPUTE WORLD CUP, AUSTRALIA, 2023   159

    The Night Soilman's Granddaughter

    A Kiss is Just a Kiss: Australia 2023

Dedication

For Simon, always and forever.

With thanks

Mum and Dad, thank you. Apologies for the swearing and the name-dropping.
J, K and L, thanks for your comments on the early drafts.

In memory

In celebration of the revolutionary generosity of Grant Wahl.

PROLOGUE
Feminist

Growing up on a farm, I had seen a lot of sex, birth and death by the time I was nine. The mating animals were 'fighting', we children were told. Probably not the best preparation for a lifetime of balanced adult intimacy, but I have been happily married for 38 years at the time of writing, so I must have negotiated this particular maze OK at some point. The births were miraculous and messy, as is life. The deaths were unbelievably sad and final. Watching that spark leave the eye. I still prefer animals to human beings. Not you, of course. You are unique and wonderful. Do tell your friends about this book. But I am probably going to greet your dog before I notice you. For which, my apologies in advance. Your best friend, however, understands entirely. I loved spending my quiet time in childhood leaning against a ruminating cow, draped over a sleepy horse or nose to snout observing a piglet's complicated facial expression. Home is standing in a Leicestershire field, this heart-shaped county in the centre of England.

Mischief and mayhem came naturally. Still do. The local refuse collectors, aka 'bin men', were in accordance that my rendition of Sandy Shaw's 1967 Eurovision-winning *'Puppet on a String'*, complete with barefoot dance moves and an encore, was a triumph, if lacking any musicality. By way of rehabilitation, aged three, off I was sent to Mrs Dunbar's Academy for Young Ladies and Gentlemen. I went three times a week. Singing *'Puff the Magic Dragon'* in the car with my Dad or my Mum on the journey to and fro, I made up for in volume what I lacked in accuracy. Dad always had a nice car, most memorably a burgundy Daimler, and Mum drove a sporty banana yellow Escort MK 2.

The daily sticking point on arrival was that I liked the colour orange, and Mrs Dunbar had decided that the towels for girls in the bathroom should be lemon yellow. She was clearly influenced by the nursery rhyme, '*Orange and Lemons say the Bells of St Clements*' which we sang most days. Saint Clements-style, our towels were arranged in alphabetical order, boy-girl, orange and yellow. The boy before me was called Ian, so he had an orange towel; and the boy after me, Justin, did too. I just could not understand this illogical system where I got a yellow towel. So… I'd swap the towels. Every day.

Mrs Dunbar was keenly aware that I was a forceful child. It may have been a coping strategy as I am from a large family, but it could just have been my personality. The other Academy children had an hour's nap after lunch. This mystified me as being a complete waste of time. When Mrs Dunbar invited me to sleep after lunch, I replied that I'd rather keep her company. I suspected she would have preferred to nap herself, but instead we made cakes and I chatted to her in what I imagined was a companionable way. I could see that her facial expression was a little tired sometimes. She once kindly asked, would I like a little cookie dough from the bowl. I was offended as I had never heard of this abomination. 'No thanks, Mrs Dunbar I'd sooner wait until the cake is baked, like at home.'

The Dunbar Academy Christmas party was worse. We were each given a toy to take home about an hour before the party ended. Instinctively I could tell Justin would not like his—the shiny red sportscar, but I loved it. Instead of the car, Justin coveted a fashion book I was given, where the cardboard girl models could be dressed in paper mix and match items to make a full outfit. The clothes were pressed out of the book and fitted onto the dolls with little paper tabs at the back. Justin and I swapped toys and played happily until it was time to go home, when we were made to swap back again. The fate of the car remains a mystery, but my paper dolls lay unloved until they were used as kindling to light the coal fire at home.

Mrs Dunbar seemed relieved when I started school aged five, and baked me a cake to send me off. I still remember the little white picket fence of her house with great affection. It was rumoured she retired soon after and returned to the Highlands and Islands. Some folks said she went as far as the Isle of Skye. No forwarding address was ever forthcoming.

Infant school was a pointless blur of sticking, colouring and singing. Frankly, the other children seemed too easily distracted by playing house, making fuzzy felt pictures and other nonsense. I had that dreadful realisation at the end of Week One that I would have to go back. The horror! As someone who was down the farm by 6.30am each morning, I would reluctantly have my day interrupted to go to breakfast and then school about 8am, and then waited impatiently every day for three in the afternoon so I could return to the animals. Summer holidays were bliss! September still fills me with dread.

Potato picking in the freezing October rain of 1970s Britain instilled in me my first feminist sensibility. The middle child of five, 'Being Useful' on the farm was important. I prized icy tubers from mud so heavy with clay that it sometimes retained my wellie boot, and hurled them into the wire basket before dragging it to the sack where one of the men would lift and return it to me. And on, and on, and on. A wet sock, a dribbling

PROLOGUE

nose, hands with hot-aches, toes with chilblains, and a soaked anorak were the main rewards, along with the potatoes. I knew, even then, that people who were nostalgic about the nobility of unskilled manual labour probably didn't have to do much of it. Now, I am not pretending for a moment that, aged nine, I did a 37-hour working week. But I did do every day of the October half term for several hours, helped by sweets from neighbours, and the camaraderie of a joint task.

Until I went to university in 1982, October half term holidays consisted of brown mud, grey mist, and potatoes. At least on Thursdays there was *Top of the Pops*. Fridays there was the cheery children's programme on TV at five minutes to five called *Crackerjack*! As soon as I was in charge of my own destiny, I endeavoured to spend October half terms somewhere sunny, where the only potatoes I encountered had already metamorphosed into golden chips.

The feminist education came courtesy of assumptions about men's and women's work that saw my elder brother Michael, by then almost 18, not actually collecting the spuds but driving the tractor. Although he was my childhood hero, Michael found many creative ways to torture us. Glorying in being in a warm cab, with the radio on, a place for both the farm dog and hot coffee, Michael would gurn as he passed us with the 'tater device on the back of the David Brown. His tractor-work theoretically raised the King Edwards to the surface for our collection, but in icy ground this was only partially successful. Once bagged, the sacks of potatoes would be collected on the back of a trailer pulled by a Massey Ferguson. So, there was a lot of driving to do, and also a lot of opportunity for him to warm up in the sheds out of sight of the frozen souls in the field.

Michael was in absentia too often for my liking. At the end of the week, we children were each given 50p. Pretty good wages and probably worth the equivalent of £15 pounds now. But Michael got £5. It was plain economics so far as I was concerned, ignoring the age difference.

I resolved then and there to be the one who drove the tractor.

I soon got my wish and was steering the Land Rover around fields. This had begun about age 10 when Uncle Ted, who lived on the farm, would put the vehicle in a crawler gear, and get out, walking just behind the door so I couldn't see him in the mirrors. About 100 metres from a hedge, I'd shout— 'Ted, Ted we're going to crash!' and he would open the door, laughing, hop in and turn the wheel. Eventually, I could steer around corners, and Ted could stand on the tailgate at the back to throw feed to the animals who followed the truck. Not strictly legal, but very empowering. More perilously, Uncle Ron would tow us on sleds behind tractors, weaving around to try and throw us off into the snow. But we became very self-reliant. There was all kinds of kit to drive on the farm, with tractors legal on the fields, but not the roads, from age 13.

My friend June and I used to drive a Mini around fields on Sunday afternoons, using goats as slalom posts until one occasion when she failed to break in time and nudged a dozing animal over. The billy goat was more offended than hurt. He went on to live a very long life. I can assure you that no goats have been harmed in the writing of this book. I still love to drive, and would love a pale lavender Porsche Targa with colour coded ceramic brakes if this memoir takes off, so have tried really, really hard to make it good. As I said, it would make a great gift for your many, many friends!

Youth, and being young, were very politicised during the whole of the 1970s. Youth unemployment ran rife after the 1973 oil crisis, with yacht-owner and Prime Minister Ted Heath unsympathetic to families. I distinctly remember my Mum making complex dinners in the evenings followed by family board games during the power cuts in 1972 when the lights were off for nine hours at a time. The scale of the miners' strike which occasioned the electricity rationing, was the first such widespread industrial action for 50 years. In 1974 during the three-day working week Mum was cooking by candlelight on a Gaz-powered camping stove for seven people, and after with no television, we read books by candlelight. At least on a farm we had 'red' diesel with which to run generators, but fuel prices soared. The three-day week lasted for two months during January and February, meaning my tenth birthday was a very frugal affair.

Growing up in the 1970s was like that iconic chocolate brown Admiral football shirt design for Coventry City, with two thin vertical rails of white. There was 90% hard grind and 10% celestial hope.

Three things saved me: in chronological order they were reading, David Bowie, and Simon. My first big book I read on my own, aged 8, was Treasure Island, a pretty good one to start off. By the age of ten I had read all of the books in the village library and had moved on to Hinckley where I got my first identity badge, a library card, which entitled me to ten, TEN, books a week. What an absolute luxury! The library was warm, well-lit, quiet and stuffed with ideas. I loved it. Since this book is jam packed, (and consequently very good value) I am not going to go off on a tangent here about David Bowie who arrived in the drab 1970s in glorious technicolour with his arm around Hull's silver-haired Mick Ronson, so will save that for another project. Simon is just about to stroll in to make his entrance in a few pages.

Moving on to Barwell Junior School, my next significant memory as to my feminist education came aged 12. A great friend, Annette Astley, was a sporting all-rounder, and academic to boot. Annette was the leading striker for the school football team, until a ruling came down which I later learned was the Theresa Bennett case, which prevented girls at the age of 12 playing on a team with boys. This included school teams. More mature and faster than most boys her age, I had a sense of injustice that she was clearly discriminated against for being a girl. Annette excelled at many other sports and went on to study at Loughborough University where she picked up her football again. Years later this sense of being perplexed, when Annette was clearly the best player, would pop up out of my subconscious and motivate me to write a PhD. And then some...

PROLOGUE

I wasn't personally outraged, because my football was mainly social, and by then my chief pastime was a very old hand-me-down pony called Rocket upon whom I'd amble around. He was a wily old trooper. He would breathe out while I'd cinch up his saddle, then breathe in again when it was on to give himself plenty of breathing space. I'd have to be very determined to get him into the field, intending to jump hurdles, before he would get to the gate, turn of his own accord and Usain Bolt it back again, direct to the stable. If he got winded on his return, he'd lean up against a telegraph pole, making sure to crush my leg with his full body weight, to remind me not to kick him in future. Adoration was not even close to how much I loved him.

Being a farm kid, by the age of 14 the bullying on the school bus was so bad I would often prefer to walk the two miles home from Earl Shilton Community College—whatever the time of the year. This was risky. Both the short-cut through the park, and the last mile home were entirely unlit. Even with a torch, the lack of streetlighting left an all-enveloping blackness in October, November, December, January and February. So, some bleak winter nights the battle of the bus had to be borne. To avert my dread of two boys in particular, I would usually read books from the school library.

The boys in question, Big Kev and Jeffrey, would grab my school bag, take it to the back of the bus and empty it at the start of the journey. Jeffrey was in my year, sly and spiteful; Big Kev in the year above and about 13 stone. I was less than five foot tall and six stone wet through. I knew Big Kev's Mum was religious and ruled him with a rod of iron, literally. So, I understood he was clearly taking this out on someone else. Essentially a biddable bear. But Jeffrey delighted in tormenting others cruelly. He would wait to assault me as soon as we left the school gates, to avoid being reported, and encourage Big Kev to restrain me while he ceremoniously tipped up the bag. I was determined not to give them the bag voluntarily in spite of the consequences.

In what became a regular social contract understood by everyone on the bus, all my stuff would be kicked up and down the aisles for the entire journey by the other kids, who realised that as long as they participated in that game, they wouldn't be the object of bullying themselves. The driver was impervious, as he was just doing his job until the shift was over. Since my house was half a mile before the final destination in the next village, I would have to wait until everyone else got off at the last stop, pick up my stuff, say a wordless goodnight to the driver who sat with averted eyes, and walk home half a mile in the dark. My little brother was also on the bus, and while they were picking on me, they weren't hassling him. Well, quite so much anyway.

So, I didn't like the bus, and there was also the matter of the friendless half-hour wait between the end of the school day and the bus journey. Boredom. However, the school library was quiet, well lit and warm. So the obvious thing to do was to look for mucky books. I had already located *Lady Chatterley's Lover* in the school library knowing it had been banned until recently. But I was buggered if I could figure out what act Mellors had performed in the potting shed. James Joyce's *Ulysses* was frankly too little reward in titillation for too many pages of reading. There was more violence in A Clockwork Orange than I could stomach for very long, so no luck there.

Then, bingo, I located a book with a twisted woman's torso on the cover! Headless, legless and armless. Brilliant. Probably a ghoulish murder mystery, I thought. I began reading the chapter entitled 'Sex' and encountered my first clitoris, (albeit in writing). Thrilling. As I read on, the 'See You Next Tuesday' word was used! Shocking. Then I was advised to revolt against male-dominated systems. Had the author, physically or metaphorically, been on the same school bus as me, perhaps?

The book I had discovered was *The Female Eunuch* published in 1970 by Australian feminist author Germaine Greer. The book was so topical because in Britain the Sex Discrimination Act would follow five years later. Getting a mortgage as a single woman usually meant getting your father's permission. Married women usually had to get their husband's permission to obtain birth control. In her many years since 1970, Greer has become something of an outlier to the feminist canon, but this library find was pretty revolutionary stuff for a 14-year-old in rural Leicestershire. It may seem like a joke—in search of a mucky book I found feminism, but language was key to what is now called 'the second wave of the women's movement', and Greer epitomised that demystifying impulse.

And the bus journeys? I was literally saved by the patriarchy in the shape of my dear pater. One day, after about a year of this, my Dad, to my immense surprise and good cheer, boarded the bus after flagging down the driver outside our house. Dad had some very choice words for the driver, Big Kev and Jeffrey. Hero. Big Kev and Jeffrey were instructed to pick up my stuff. Dad told the driver that, as an adult he should know better and that he had a duty of care to the children on the bus. This had never occurred to me, moderate violence and verbal abuse being so much part of our daily lives at school. I have never allowed myself to be bullied again. The last I heard, Jeffrey had become a 'holier than thou' minister of the cloth in some obscure Christian enclave, and Big Kev was cleaning chemical toilets on building sites. Nearer my God to thee, indeed.

Having survived all this to obtain five O levels, in the Sixth Form my subjects narrowed to A Level English (by far my favourite), Sociology (it was new), and very reluctantly History (my teachers managed to make both Catherine and Peter the Great seem distinctly mediocre). Sociology was taught by a vibrant, committed young woman, and an older female teacher borrowed from Business Studies who, given her surname, we predictably nicknamed Granny Smith. I made some remark about gender to the younger teacher, and she suggested that she and I organise an event for International Women's Day, which I hadn't heard of before. I had however been to Young Farmers' Annual Harvest Festival and had carved a pineapple into an owl with maraschino cherries for eyes in the 'I Made it Myself Competition' to win third prize.

PROLOGUE

Why not give it a go, I thought?

My expectations were that we would do some things at which men were naturally good. A game of darts perhaps? Woodwork? And some basic car maintenance? You can imagine how much my consciousness was raised when I arrived to find women breastfeeding in public, wearing Lesbian Mothers Against the Bomb t-shirts.

This was in the 1979-80 school year, when various women's groups were becoming more militant. Often generalised under the term 'Second Wave Feminism', this would culminate in the UK with events at Greenham Common in September 1981, when 36 women chained themselves to the base fence in protest at nuclear weapons. In 1982, 30,000 women linked hands around Greenham in the 'Embrace the Base' protest, and in 1983 this more than doubled to 70,000. One Greenham protest saw 200 women dressed as teddy bears breaking through the fence.

Greenham was a reminder of how bitterly contested gender relations were just as Britain was about to endure its first female Prime Minister, Margaret Thatcher, who came to power in 1979. A woman who hated miners, teachers, and football crowds—in fact any kind of collective action, Thatcher would preach individualism. She envisaged a nuclear family, owning its own home, with a few entrepreneurial shares on the side. Shame that when she sold off many of the publicly owned utilities in a process called privatisation, they were bought by multinational businesses, rather than the little gal and guy. This happened particularly in the energy and utilities sectors. In the UK we are living with the consequences of privatisation of our natural resources still today, with water pollution levels rising unsustainably and a cost of living crisis. Generally, Thatcher blamed feckless youth rather than the global geopolitical situation, rising inflation and industrial unrest. I would not see such wilful insularity and ignorance again until the Brexit referendum.

Punk rock was the do-it-yourself response to the dire economic situation in the 1970s, both in fashion and music, and I was drawn to its powerful rejection of tradition. You could just literally make stuff up! Put a safety pin through your ear. Make a dustbin bag into a dress. Dye your hair with fabric tints. Whatever. There were also important precursors to the football fanzine movement linked to Oxbridge student satirical writing, such as *Foul*. Punk was a very creative response to a lack of hope widely felt by young people. I thought Vivienne Westwood was amazing, and dyed my hair pink like Zandra Rhodes.

About this time, I met a very handsome 19-year-old biker who told me he was in a punk band called The Screaming Knees, and reader, I married him. Given how often Simon was involved in accidents, I came to understand why his knees might scream. Simon's motor sport heroes either won or crashed, preferably both. My future husband was much the same. On one occasion, I knew he had been in a collision because he was half an hour late. Simon is always 15 minutes early. He later told me he slid on his knees down the road to avoid a worse collision, only to smash out the car's rear lights with his head. I've learned a lot about resilience from Simon. He wasn't actually registered as a student at Loughborough University but was there so regularly while I studied English that everyone assumed he was. He often fixed the motorbikes of the Engineering students for whom practical work was perplexing. After university, with a decent 2.1 in English I asked my tutor about doing an MA, but he explained kindly that Masters degrees were really meant for people who had obtained a First, of whom there were only two in our cohort of English graduates. I began packing Care Bears, Ken dolls and Barbies at Mattel Toys soon after.

After university Simon and I married on FA Cup Final day 1986 at Hinckley Registry Office at 11am. A few photos, a nice lunch, some speeches, then back to Mum and Dad's to watch the match as it was a 3pm kick-off at a capacity-packed Wembley. A Merseyside derby between Liverpool and Everton, the match saw Gary Lineker score the only goal for the Blues in the first half, before the Reds came back, courtesy of two goals from Ian Rush and one from Craig Johnston in the second. Dramatic for a big game, the FA Cup completed the double for player-manager Kenny Dalgleish as Liverpool had already won the league.

Some of Simon's more refined relatives had assumed we had married in a Registry Office because of their Jehovah's Witness beliefs. They chose to remain in the dining room drinking tea and eating cake, while my family were just relieved not to miss the football. We resumed festivities dancing to the Shalako disco at 6pm, and honeymooned in York for four days. The Railway Museum was thankfully free to enter because we had a 101% mortgage, and could not afford the fees to purchase the house, let alone nice things like meals and days out. This was the Eighties, remember, and greed was good, so you could borrow more on a mortgage than your house was worth. What a great idea that turned out to be. Within two years we were paying 15% interest on our borrowing for the mortgage.

There followed a period of mutual adjustment, as I was only 22 and Simon was 26 when we married. Going to a supermarket on our return from honeymoon, I invited Simon to get whatever he fancied, meaning quite clearly to pick something he wanted to eat for the evening meal. He returned with a £20 trolley-jack for the car, and enquired as to what we were going to have for dinner. Dull it was not!

After a brief stint as a shoe buyer's assistant, and other desultory work, I trained as a teacher of English and taught in a Sixth Form College in Leicester, one of the most diverse cities in the UK. The Iron Lady would be deposed in 1990, largely thanks to her antipathy to Europe, which even Home Secretary Sir Geoffrey Howe could not disguise.

My students in the Sixth Form College taught me more than I was able to educate them. I kept telling anyone who would listen that Toni Morrison was our greatest living writer. But while I waffled on about Carol Ann Duffy, the use of irony in Shakespeare,

PROLOGUE

and Caryl Churchill, they told me about their lives. The quiet pale girl at the back who rarely said anything but exploded in class the week of the Grand National because she hated gambling since her father was an addict. I was known in my pastoral role for also welcoming the goths, who would arrive in basques (Victorian-era closely fitted bodices), fishnet stockings, and thigh-high boots but who were intensely shy. A young Chinese woman in my tutor group had to do extra work in the takeaway to come to class, with hopes of getting her A levels, going to university, and never having to listen to the levels of casual racism that her parents endured in the course of their work. I tutored students who were becoming aware of their sexuality, and negotiating the consequences of what that would mean for parental expectations.

This was a big deal in education for over two decades. In 1988, Margaret Thatcher's Conservative government enacted Section 28 (sometimes referred to as Clause 28) to 'prohibit the promotion of homosexuality by local authorities' including schools. Shockingly, it would remain law until 2003. I remain very proud of my work with the sixth form students, ignoring Section 28 by showing films like Hanif Kureishi's 1985 romantic comedy *My Beautiful Launderette* in film club, and teaching books like Jeanette Winterson's *Oranges Are Not The Only Fruit* in the curriculum. Education should be about helping the individual to reach their full potential. If they can't talk about who they are, how can we expect to help?

All my students were trying to use education to improve their lives in both small and large ways. There wasn't much career progression available then for young women, especially as head of department. But I was influenced by a colleague to have another tilt at an MA, this time a part-time mode of learning, in Modern Literary Theory and Practice. It was tough to study part-time and teach full-time. A technician employed to assist the students helped me in her breaks to learn to type and use a computer. My MA thesis was on Toni Morrison. The day it was due, during the school holidays, the floppy disk (look it up) on the computer I was using got full and I lost about half my work. I had to get an extension and re-type it, crying with tiredness and frustration.

When I had completed university as an undergraduate only five years earlier, and my teaching qualification, the PGCE a year earlier, all our essays were hand-written. The whole thing was a steep learning curve. I won't pretend the thesis was terribly original—or well done, but the fact that it was done at all when holding down a full-time job showed me how much I loved research and academic writing.

A few years later, in 1994 the owner of a wine bar and bistro that Simon and I frequented early doors most Sundays, offered us the licence. Having bought it, we couldn't even use the till at the opening night and had to give the drinks away for free. My Mum was a superb cook, as I have mentioned. Her three-course Christmas day lunch on the farm was often for at least 20 people, including some waifs and strays, sitting on odd chairs that I only saw once a year. Eat turkey while sitting in a deckchair indoors? Everyone welcome! Through her tutoring, I did most of the catering in the bar, and we made a go of the new business. In order to juggle two jobs I went part-time at the Sixth Form College Monday to Wednesday lunchtime, then did all the cooking and food prep from Wednesday evenings to Sunday.

Exhausted, the chance to take voluntary redundancy from teaching came in 1997, and I took it, spending half the money on a week at the Hacienda in Ibiza, and half on my first personal computer. Regrets, I have a few. Had I the chance again I'd have spent two weeks at the Hacienda where I hung out in the pool each morning with a Russian escort who had cheek bones sharper than my grandmother's tongue and seemed about eight feet tall even when she was reclining in the water. While her impressive frame was bedecked in a seemingly endless succession of designer swimwear, I had splashed out £25 of my redundancy on a Marks and Spencer leopard print bikini for the week. The Hacienda was the first high end hotel where I'd seen a pool in the brochure and decided to stay there 75% motivated by swimming. I'd go on to 'collect' other such experiences over the years. With its cliff-top position, the scintillation of the light on water was stunning by day, and even more atmospheric at night due to the low levels of light pollution - like swimming in a galaxy of endless stars.

I had been told at school I had working class legs, which meant that the length of my shin was shorter than the thigh bone, whereas apparently posh people can afford to have similarly long femur and tibia. Trust me, there are serious medical articles that deduce 'Leg length and proportion are important in the perception of human beauty, which is often considered a sign of health and fertility.' My Russian friend had definitely got the aristocratic equally proportioned long-legged memo, whereas my disappointing evolutionary stumps were showcased in high street leopard print. I could make her laugh though, sometimes intentionally, and I think did win bonus points for being a game chicken. Having said all that, two weeks at the Hacienda would possibly have made future employment a moot point. So buying a home computer definitely prolonged my life, even if it didn't necessarily make it more interesting.

At the same time, I obtained a 0.7 job (three and a half days a week) at De Montfort University. This was as a Professional Skills Tutor for a Combined Honours degree. Those students who did not have quite good enough grades to get onto a Joint Honours degree of two subjects, took three subjects in their first year and Professional Skills Training. Hence Combined Studies. Then, they would choose a conventional Joint Honours combination of two subjects for the remaining two years. It was a huge success! We recruited upwards of 450 students per year and many students who couldn't have made it into higher education became the first people in their family to complete a degree.

This meant that Combined Studies as a unit was very well off financially, and this in turn meant that Deans of Faculties were jealous that they had not thought of the idea.

PROLOGUE

It also meant that when I was told that to work at a University I would need to study for a PhD, I was able to do so, because my part-time fees were paid by my employer for the first two years. And when I asked the Combined Studies course leader to use my entire continuing professional development budget to go to the Second World Women in Sport Conference in Namibia in 1998, he was very supportive, having studied for some time in Africa himself.

A brilliant negotiator with the Senior Management team, he even supported my staying in the best possible accommodation, which is why I was in the only 4* hotel in Windhoek in May 1998. Working three and a half days a week at the university, owning and cooking for the bistro, I was by now collecting data for my PhD in my free time, when not actually playing football, I was serving on the East Midlands Women's Football League committee, starting my coaching journey, and attending women in sport conferences.

I had thought I was going to be a Toni Morrison scholar but I didn't find the English department at De Montfort particularly welcoming. There had been a new specialist research centre set up in the history of sport in the 1996/7 academic year, and I had thought to combine the literature and history of football there. So, one day I wandered into Professor Wray Vamplew's office and muttered something about wanting to do a PhD. Wray had lots of mugs with sporting themes on his shelves. He'd recently returned from Australia having been a Pro Vice Chancellor at Flinders University and had begun to work at De Montfort in 1993, later establishing the International Centre in Sports History and Culture as a way of developing the research culture of what had been Leicester Polytechnic, and so more used to vocational education. He was friendly, open to ideas, and kind. We agreed I'd fill in the paperwork. Then in 1998 we refined the PhD proposal to be about the history of women's football.

My parents were puzzled that anyone could do such a thing, although very supportive of this as in everything else. As the first person in my family to go to university, I had not a clue how to go about doing a PhD. I did have the additional superpower of Simon though. In spite of having two jobs, he would drive me up and down the country on Saturday afternoons to interview women with collections of women's football memorabilia, with my first giant, 2 kilo laptop computer I owned, and a scanning machine we plugged into it to copy materials, photographs and scrapbook images.

This joint venture, like many of our other collaborations, would take us both to many new and unforeseen places. Everyone should have a Simon.

CHAPTER I
THE BARBIE WORLD CUP, 1999
Introduction: Thriller in Windhoek

I was excited and nervous leaving the hotel room in Windhoek, Namibia in May 1998, on my way to give my first academic paper at an international conference, only to be confronted by a human rhomboid filling the entire doorframe. Surveying the blockage, I spied an expensive black suit jacket, several ripples of neck fat above a white shirt collar, and what I deduced to be an earpiece on a little corkscrew of white wire. The actual earpiece, like my view, was obscured completely. A voice said, 'Please step back inside Ma'am and close the door.' It took a few seconds to figure out the diamond-shaped gentleman was addressing me.

'Get out of my way please,' I remonstrated, 'I am giving a paper at a women and sport conference in about 10 minutes downstairs. I cannot be late.' In the same even voice identical instructions were repeated to me, like a call and response in an old song. How dare a human lozenge invade my personal space with his considerable rear! I'd flown out specially. Our voices became raised whispers (although I have no idea why we were *sotto voce*), and eventually became hisses. I ain't going nowhere, but I'm not going anywhere any time soon, I sense.

Finally, there's a kerfuffle to the right of me which distracts us both. A whoosh of air, lots of people talking all at once, and an atmosphere of organised chaos, or perhaps choreographed panic, making its way towards us. My adversary's final instruction is emphatic, 'Ma'am, please close the door and do not come out, Michael is walking the corridor.' But the directive was too late. Michael *is* walking the corridor. As I peep on tiptoes under the bodyguard's armpit, I can see lots of hangers on, all dressed in black doing stuff in a fairly frantic but precise way to the main man. A grasping woman primps his hair, although he is wearing a hat; an anguished-looking man reads out a schedule for the next hour; there is lighting, a sound recordist, lots of security detail.

As he passes my door at some speed Michael Jackson looks into my eyes, as if surprised that one of his bodyguards should have a woman's head peering from underneath his arm. He is frightened. I was oddly reminded of the scene in the 1942 Disney movie Bambi, where the anthropomorphised rabbit helps the baby fawn to learn to ice skate before declaring 'Kinda wobbly, aren'tcha?' When I almost met Michael Jackson, in that fraction of a second, he was distinctly off-kilter.

I later learned that MJ was in Windhoek in 1998 to launch a new Neverland ranch theme park to aid tourism to Namibia. Well-meaning but ill-advised. After conflict and struggle for independence from German, British and then South African control throughout the 20th century, at that time Namibia was politically, economically and socially the youngest African country. Whether the idea of a Neverland ranch was intended to bring in international tourists, or even if there was a coherent strategy remains unclear, as the accusations against Jackson for child abuse, financial difficulties and increasingly erratic behaviour eventually ended his career, and influence. His life would come to a drugged end, ruled a doctor-led homicide, in 2009, aged only 50. A rather unusual opening to the Second International Conference on Women and Sport, nevertheless.

Of course, the first person I rang was Simon with a, 'You'll never guess what just happened' call, and the second was to my Mum. We called these my, 'Ma, I got off the farm' calls. Didn't matter if I was in the next village, or in another country I would phone her, often from a call box. 'Mum, you'll never guess where I am', pause, 'Hello Jean, where are you today?' half a beat for dramatic effect, 'Mum, today I am...' She patiently enjoyed my enjoyment. Mum was the best.

I recorded groups of young people and children making footballs out of discarded plastic bags and playing barefoot in my field research in Namibia. There wasn't the same recycling of boots and shirts to Africa then that there is now, and making do didn't involve any big brands. The plastic-bag footballs bounced really well, and had just the right weight for great crossing.

A proposed Neverland theme park was a ridiculous response to pressing post-conflict and post-colonial deprivation. Most of the two million souls living in Namibia would be born into poverty, especially after the recent civil war which had seen many young men killed, so most households were often headed by young women, barely out of school themselves. Access to education was by no means a given. Women's groups with whom I conversed explained that finding food and water was such an important part of daily life, taking most of their time; so the idea of a game of football was an exhausting luxury.

The National Football Association of Namibia had been founded in 1990, shortly after independence from South Africa, and affiliated to FIFA in 1992. A women's football section tried to promote the sport among female adults and girls, though it received little support from the national association. The Namibian National Sports Commission supported and tracked the development of female players in 1997. Volunteers like Julien

Garises and others were leading the way, often funded by charities rather than the football bodies. I had connected with one such charity, Voluntary Service Overseas (VSO). Before returning to discuss the conference in Namibia, here is a little more on how I connected with Pauline Yemm, to understand what good fortune this was.

In 1997 Pauline had just returned to the UK after spending two years within the VSO scheme in Namibia. Established in 1958, the VSO had traditionally provided a gap year experience for public schoolboys (in the UK this means privately educated elite young men) before they went up to university. After broadening its remit to include sport for development and peace, the organization is now one option among many ventures that together constitute the panoply of charitable, voluntary and commercial programmes involved with gap years and internships.

I had met Pauline at an information gathering event organised by a funded researcher working with the FA, who was studying for a sociological PhD on the status of women's football in England, the USA and Germany. The problem was, I was not funded by the FA, a distinction I later found to be important to the governing body, who wanted to control the narrative. While the funded FA researcher was able to advertise a number of roadshow-style events across the country to obtain data, I was not allowed inside as my research was unofficial.

I duly turned up anyway, since the events were advertised ahead of time in the public domain, and stood on the doorstep outside with my questionnaires. When players asked why I wasn't allowed inside, and I responded that my research was considered unofficial, they were very enthusiastic about filling in the forms. Most followed up with phone calls, documents, memorabilia and photographs. The academic term for this is 'snowball sampling', and my subsequent career has the generosity of women football players as its foundation, for which I remain so grateful 25 years on. I met a young woman only a few months ago at an elite coach event who remembered playing against my team in a bitterly fought match—and then me politely knocking on the dressing room door to ask the opposition to fill in my questionnaires.

The players who helped me also enjoyed confounding anything the FA ruled in relation to women's football. So many women who had carried women's football in very difficult times left the game when the FA took over in 1993, and rebranded the Women's Football Association (WFA) with FA marketing. No one in women's football that I had met so far liked the FA, except the very few females who worked at the governing body. I later learned it was a part of the broader anti-intellectualism of the organisation. A lot of people who are more compliant than bright work for the FA and women who had just started to be employed there wanted to fit in with that occupational culture. Thankfully now, increasing numbers are disrupting old patterns of working in the governing body, and I've been fortunate to work with more of these innovators recently.

Back in 1997, Pauline Yemm was one of the people who came along to the roadshows, and hearing I was already planning to go to the Namibia conference in May 1998, provided important background information on African women's sport for development and peace. She also provided networked links for field study. In our conversations, it quickly became clear that the challenges for the female population in Namibia were immense, and my Western notions of sport, leisure and health needed considerable revision. So, I combined field research with attendance at the Windhoek conference, and was able to attend a number of impromptu meetings such as a gathering of women's football administrators from Angola, Botswana, Malawi, Zambia, Zimbabwe, Namibia, Congo, Lesotho, Mozambique, Swaziland, South Africa and Mexico.

It was not just football. There were many stories of women in Africa engaging in sport because of the need for life skills for survival, such as being able to swim, or wade across, a river on the way to school, or college. The development for peace agenda was also a topic of academic study, but several of us had reservations, wondering why it was acceptable to parachute into a given social context, raise aspirations of assertive young women, only to leave after 12 weeks, or however long the project lasted. So there were a lot of discussions at the time about the ethical aspects of Western scholars doing academic work in Africa.

At this time, the academic literature on men's football in Africa was not that extensive, although this would change in the next 10 years with a particular focus on migration. But the literature on women's football was very thin, Eurocentric, and the problems that the administrators above discussed, such as national associations not funding flights to women's international qualifying matches, were hardly known. No matter how little (or much) money a national association had, qualifying for a Men's World Cup was a priority, because of the economic realities of there being no money in women's football. Financial encouragement for women and girls was often presented as an economic luxury.

The Windhoek conference was associated with some stellar names in the world of women in sport, cemented in the popular imagination four years earlier by the inaugural Brighton conference entitled, 'Women, Sport and the Challenge of Change'. The Brighton Declaration was one outcome of the 1994 meeting, attempting to obtain an undertaking from sports organisations, governments and non-governmental bodies to commit more resources to women's and girls' activities.

In what was essentially an attempt at cultural change, the International Women and Sport Strategy 1994–1998 aimed to co-ordinate many disparate efforts internationally. For this, a Working Group on Women and Sport was established to oversee change. The original target of 100 organisations was quickly overtaken and eventually doubled in those four years. Football was one sport of many to be involved. In early 1998 I was at another conference in Brighton where Hope Powell was announced as the new England women's full time head coach, taking over from Ted Copeland.

So, by the time of the Namibia conference in May 1998, the International Women and Sport movement had grown to over 400 delegates from 74 countries. Windhoek responded to Brighton by a call to action, and a greater awareness of the need for connectivity with the UN, and other global actors who were advocating for greater gender equity.

However, coherent collective action proved difficult internationally. FIFA, the world governing body of football has had just nine Presidents since 1904, all male. Even the acting Presidents who filled in were male. Male-led governing bodies were not going to give up power voluntarily. There were too many first-class plane tickets, a surfeit of grand lunches, and the chance of being treated like royalty by global social elites. Who would trade that for something as nebulous as equality, diversity and inclusion?

Instead, Sepp Blatter, the incumbent FIFA President in 1998 was becoming popular amongst the African countries by establishing permanent national facilities. FIFA's Financial Assistance Programme (FAP) was launched in 1998. In 2002, FIFA's FAP contribution to Namibia was $198,000. This was in addition to the Namibia Goal programme, sponsored by FIFA, which provided $400,000 to fund the construction of a permanent administrative base. Through the FIFA Goal initiative, the national facility added a floodlit pitch with artificial turf in 2003. In 2004, FAP introduced a requirement for FIFA associations and confederations to invest at least 4% of their FAP funding into women's football. This threshold was increased to 10% in 2005.

Without wanting to distract attention from the main focus here, those interested in the case study might like to follow up on my paper with Megan Chawansky, *Namibia's Brave Gladiators: gendering the sport and development nexus.* There is also excellent work by the Berkeley-based Africanist Martha Saavedra *Football Feminine: Development of the African Game: Senegal, Nigeria and South Africa* in *Soccer & Society* 41: 3 (2003) 371–92.

In comparison, in the UK the real difference for women's sport generally was National Lottery funding, introduced in 1995, which signalled greater governmental commitment to elite achievement and grassroots participation. Helpfully, Olympic sports are not divided into women's medals, and men's medals, just a national medal table. In the midst of Cool Britannia, the UK was using sport as a tool of soft diplomacy.

Investing in women's sport had historically been seen in the UK as bad form, but after World War Two, Cold War rivalry had meant that countries like East Germany, the USSR, Hungary and Finland had been able to win medals at an economical rate by funding female athletes in relatively neglected disciplines across gymnastics, track and field athletics, swimming and Winter sport. The British were famously slow to follow, most notably winning just one gold, eight silver, and six bronze medals for the 300 athletes sent to the Summer Atlanta Games in 1996. This left Team GB, 36th nationally overall, and was also highly gendered as Britain sent 184 men and just 116 women. All of the 1996 medals were won by men, apart from Denise Lewis' bronze in the heptathlon. This was not for lack of world class talent. Kelly Holmes finished fourth in the 800 metres, Paula Radcliffe finished fifth in the 5000 metres, and Liz McColgan finished a distant 16th in the marathon.

By now the Sports Council had become devolved and in September 1996 the English Sports Council (ESC) had £593 million to distribute. By 1997 it would become rebranded as Sport England. Those interested further can access the archives at the Cadbury Research Library, at the University of Birmingham.

The unification of the Olympic sports under the banner Team GB, saw a rapid change in culture so that at the 2000 Sydney Olympic Games, in spite of only 129 women compared with 181 men in the British contingent, 11 gold medals were returned, of which Denise Lewis (heptathlon), Shirley Robinson (sailing), and Stephanie Cook (modern pentathlon) were included. A total of 10 silver medals saw rowers Guin Batten, Miriam Batten, Katherine Grainger and Gillian Lindsay rewarded as a team, alongside Judoka Kate Howey as an individual, and equestrians Jeanette Brakewell and Pippa Funnell as part of a mixed team.

Kate Allenby won a bronze in the modern pentathlon, as did Kelly Holmes and Katherine Merry in the track and field athletics, and Yvonne McGregor in the cycling. Therefore, four of the Team GB seven bronze medals were won by women in Sydney. The total of 28 medals in all raised Team GB to 10th in the international table. Britain had belatedly learned that funding elite female athletes was good for national morale. But women's football had only just become an Olympic sport in 1996, and the problem of the Team GB representation, rather than the home nations, meant that this sport would not become significant for elite female players until 2012.

The lottery funding was not just good news for Olympic and Paralympic sports. When organisations such as the Marylebone Cricket Club (MCC), which had been for many years a de facto world governing body of the sport since 1787, were turned down for lottery funding because they refused to admit women, they changed their rules to admit 10 honorary female members. That concession to so few females invited to join masked the 18,000 male members, but nevertheless released lottery funding opportunities to an already wealthy and culturally conservative institution.

In the midst of all this change in relation to the status of women's sport internationally, I was in Namibia trying to find my academic voice for the first time. For those of you who are reading this at the beginning of your Doctoral journey, maybe a bit concerned about your knowledge-base, and suffering from the dreaded Imposter Syndrome, my advice would be to get over yourself. Honestly? Such naval-gazing is a displacement activity. Get on with it. You will find your tribe. My first presentation went OK, but was comparable to early Doctoral work. Promising, but not the finished package.

People were supportive. Onwards.

I knew that the international collective action of the Second World Conference on Women's Sport was inspirational, but it was also reliant for funding and recognition on organisations which had obtained their historic authority through the exclusion of women. Often explicitly so. Fabled 'progress' was a myth of women playing catch-up to a future as yet unarticulated.

Like many conferences I would attend on women's sport over the next 25 years, it was also preaching to the already converted. Olympic conferences, FIFA conferences, UEFA conferences, general women in sport conferences—the same tone of progress over and over. While there was strength in finding others doing this work, it also made me aware of who was not present. That is, not everyone could afford to get on a plane to discuss such issues. The vast majority of community champions were volunteers, and they were thin on the ground as conference delegates. So, I would become increasingly uneasy of those like myself in relatively privileged positions of power, who could be funded to such events, compared with those who made a practical difference.

Quite aware that this consciousness was a luxury in itself, it motivated me to give a platform to the voiceless whenever I could. After all, at this time I was playing football for my local team and running it as a volunteer, serving as a volunteer on the East Midlands women's football committee, working through my FA coaching badges and doing research into women's football.

An average football player for my local side, I was intelligent enough to know I was ordinary at best. So, as an attacking midfielder, I obtained the ball, and passed to the good players. It was a simple plan. I could read a game and anticipate where people would put the ball and how they would react. In spite of my limited talent, I fancied myself playing in the style of David Ginola, the French midfielder who had signed for Newcastle United in 1995 and so became Jeanola. Well, everyone in women's football had a nickname, as Alyson Rudd remarked somewhat sarcastically in *Astroturf Blonde* (1999), so it sort of stuck.

I watched my Premiership doppelganger from the 'Cow Shed', better known as the East Stand at Filbert Street, home of Leicester City FC. What the corrugated-iron roofed Cow Shed lacked in comfort, warmth and any concession to the spectator experience, was more than made up for by having front row seats just below pitch height. As we sat, (in the late 90s often waiting to see what haircut Beckham would reveal from under his hat/cap/ beanie), our eyeline was at the same level as the pitch. This gave a real sense of the player's speed as they sped down the wing. It was pure adrenaline for a £25 ticket.

Like Becks, Ravanelli, and Vialli, Ginola was one of the players who revelled in being so close to fans and putting on a show. If I lacked any of his skills, at least I did have good hair and plenty of attitude, if not altitude. Transferring from ES Barwell to

THE BARBIE WORLD CUP, 1999

Loughborough Dynamo in the 1999/2000 season, the programme described me as an experienced tough tackling midfielder, which is football shorthand for saying my knees (and the rest of me) were 36, and I'd not a lot of elegance on the ball. By 2003/4 Dynamo asked me to be player-manager, a polite way of asking me to bow out as a player, and soon! So being embedded in the women's football community, I got to meet unpaid volunteers daily, whereas a conference was a one-off event, and a plush one at that.

To round off the day of my presentation in Windhoek we had a conference dinner. A local man joined us, and began, over dessert, to tell me that he would like me for a wife as I had a pretty face. His mother, he continued, would like me because I had hard-working hands. Declining his charming invitation of marriage, I managed to slip away from proceedings early back to my room. I anticipated the rest of the conference would be relaxing and a chance to decompress.

I was wrong.

On the second day I was approached in a coffee break by two very glamorous blonde women in understated business suits. One I could tell was an athlete, complete with firm handshake and an unwavering gaze. She had the posture of someone used to commanding a room. She introduced herself as Donna de Varona, Chair of the Organising Committee of the 1999 Los Angeles Women's World Cup. Wow. Also known by her married name Donna de Varona Pinto, she was not just an athlete. She had retired from Olympic swimming after representing the US in 1960, and winning two gold medals in 1964. One gold was in the inaugural women's 400-meter individual medley, and the second was a member of the 4×100-meter freestyle relay, both world record performances. An activist and pioneer of women in sports broadcasting, in the mid-1970s, de Varona joined Billie Jean King in establishing the Women's Sports Foundation (WSF), serving as the first President from 1979 to 1984. Helping to raise millions of dollars for the WSF, de Varona was also regularly consulted by governments, the Olympic movement, anti-doping agencies and those applying Title IX in the US, as well as for her broadcasting work, advice on gender equity issues and grass roots provision.

You get the idea.

The second woman introduced herself as Doris Valasek. Also known by her married name Doris Valasek-Dobsa, she headed up the FIFA General Secretary's Office, in which the incumbent at that time was Michel Zen-Ruffinen who was new to the post in 1998, having moved up from being head of legal, and would serve until 2002.

The two women explained they were in Namibia to understand what was happening globally in women's sports, and wanted to make the Los Angeles Women's World Cup 1999 a historical landmark in popular reach. They had no idea that anyone was studying women's football as an academic specialism. We carried on the discussion over lunch, dinner and breakfast meetings. I was asked about the history of football, specifically men's football, Olympic history and what the Women's World Cup might learn from previous tournaments. Below is a summary of my answer in a few paragraphs.

The US Men's World Cup in 1994 had both been a breakthrough event in America, and was in some senses the first modern World Cup. Italia 90 had already forged cultural innovations in the way that football was sold. In Italy, Lucciano Pavarotti had added his classical endorsement, but there were no fan parks; instead, local bars and trattorias sold local food at only slightly inflated prices. In Italy, tickets for group games passed hands for face value or skimmed a little more, and an alcohol ban was easily circumvented. West Germany won in 1990 over Argentina 1–0 in the final, managed by Franz Beckenbauer.

Compared with this, USA 1994 represented a trajectory of hosting Men's World Cups in new territories that is still with us today. Having fizzled out in 1984, the US professional male league was revived with Major League Soccer and a new series of male home-grown stars. Revolutionising the way World Cups were televised, the format would be expanded to 32 teams afterwards expanding global media reach. But the financial success of 1994 came at the cost of socially and economically excluding millions of US citizens, especially youths who actually played the game.

It would not be hard in 1999 to outdo the previous two Women's World Cups which had been held in China in 1991, and Sweden in 1995. FIFA viewed the women's game as a financial liability—not an asset. The inaugural PR China event in 1991 was actually called the '1st FIFA World Championship for Women's Football for the M&Ms Cup.' Brazil, PR China as hosts, Denmark, Germany, Italy, Japan, Nigeria, Norway, New Zealand, Sweden, Chinese Taipei, and the United States comprised the finalists. The USA won 2–1 over Norway, with Michelle Akers-Stahl the standout player and Golden Boot winner. It was said 510,000 spectators attended in total across all the matches but this number should be treated with caution. Large crowds had been guaranteed—not by a big football fan culture in China, but by very cheap tickets, often given away to factory workers, students, and children.

Four years later in 1995, the Swedish organisers were not convinced a women's football tournament would draw large enough crowds, albeit Finals now had a World Cup title. The twelve team tournament was played in midsummer, a traditional time for Swedish civic festivals, alongside an athletics meeting, and hosted in provincial towns. Australia, Canada, and England made their debuts. Brazil, Nigeria, Japan and Denmark were represented again. A notorious time-out rule allowed two-minute breaks to be called at any time, for reasons that were never fully explained. Once Norway won, beating Germany 2–0 in the final match, the team celebrated with 'the snake' which involved the team crawling on all fours behind one another to twist and turn across the pitch in a serpent-like form. It was rumoured to be the idea of the Golden Ball winner, midfielder Hege Riise. The USA came third and PR China fourth.

THE BARBIE WORLD CUP, 1999

Atlanta hosted the inaugural Olympic Games women's football competition in 1996. it provided a boon to the host nation, and was an ideal bridge between the 1994 Men's World Cup and plans for Women's World Cup 1999. In Atlanta, the women's football tournament was an eight team competition. Brazil joined the USA, PR China, Japan and four European nations who had finished in the top eight in 1995, namely Norway, Sweden, Denmark and Germany. Importantly, average crowds at matches were 43,000 people, and with the gold medal match, almost 77,000 supporters caused traffic jams to get to Sanford Stadium, revealing for the first time in a FIFA-endorsed event the potential for mass public spectatorship for elite women's football.

There was an informed, articulate, affluent LGBTQI+ community travelling to women's football matches as fans, and I began to connect with many of these supporters on the world wide web, which universities had access to early on for research. This multiplicity of support had also been overlooked in favour of a narrative of women's football being 'family friendly.' It depends how one interprets the 'family' unit. But there were also feminist fathers, whom I wrote about in my research, concerned to empower their daughters, and all kinds of friendship groups represented. The LGBTQI+ community remains one of the most powerful forces for the growth of women's football, but still neglected and under-represented at the highest levels of governance and in fan provision still today.

All of these factors would contribute to the landmark event that the 1999 Women's World Cup would become. LA was a combination of large metropolitan areas, the epicentre of the world entertainment industries, and a very pleasant place to be in July, during the school holidays. There were lots of opportunities for sightseeing fans, and transport systems were well established. For the first time the Women's World Cup finals were a 16-team tournament with PR China, Japan and the People's Republic of Korea representing the Asian confederation.

Nigeria and Ghana qualified from Africa; Brazil, Canada and Mexico for the Americas; and in a heavily Eurocentric tournament Denmark, Germany, Italy, Norway, Russia and Sweden took six berths. Australia was the sole Oceania team. The US qualified as hosts. LA was ethnically and racially diverse, a place where diaspora populations could support their 'home' team, or regional representatives.

Five of the eight stadiums used in 1994 were used again. When planning began in 1996, there were expectations of smaller stadiums being used, but larger American football sites were eventually hosts to cater to demand. The huge potential was obvious. What was different than previous mega events like the Olympic Games, was that WWC '99 would be entirely about female athletes, and elite football players. The personal stories were compelling.

So, when I said all this to Doris and Donna in Namibia 1998, effectively 'build it, and they will come,' it chimed with plans already set in motion two years before.

By the end of the four-day conference in Namibia I had a much clearer idea of the scale of the ambition for Los Angeles. Donna and Doris explained that by selling the tickets in a long-term strategy, at affordable multi-price points, they intended to fill major stadia, like the Rose Bowl which held over 90,000 people, for the Women's World Cup final.

Soccer Moms, a US phenomenon, who drove their kids miles to practice and to play, were heavily invested emotionally in the wellbeing of their offspring. If you read the autobiographies of stars like Megan Rapinoe, the stories make clear that this was a whole family commitment of hours and hours of travel, training and sacrifice. So, selling at grassroots to clubs, leagues and regional talent centres meant that families could plan their summer break around the World Cup schedule, and also encouraged a community feel as whole teams bought tickets together.

For those in the US who had been priced out of Men's World Cup in 1994, now was a chance to watch elite women's football in a sport where the US women's national team was leading the world as Olympic champions. Michelle Akers, the standout star of the US women's national team at the women's world championship in China 1991 had become so popular as to adorn breakfast cereal boxes, thereby branded The Food of Champions. Kristine Lilly already had over 100 caps, rare in global women's football. In spite of being beaten in the semi-finals in the 1995 Women's World Cup by the eventual winners Norway, the US remained the glamour team of women's football, winning the inaugural Olympic gold medal as hosts in Atlanta 1996. Even with the 1994 Men's World Cup a success, an Olympic gold medal probably meant more to most Americans, than winning a soccer tournament. But now the women could do both on home soil, a feat that the men couldn't match. So, the plans for 1999 had considerable traction from a domestic fan base.

As the conference wound up, Doris and Donna asked, was I interested in consulting for FIFA? First, in providing a presentation on what lessons 1999 might learn from previous (men's and women's) World Cups and Olympic history? Second, could I summarise the new academic work on women's football? Thirdly, they were looking to draft and then refine the FIFA Los Angeles Declaration for women's football, using the Brighton Declaration on women's sport in 1994 as template—could I help with that too?

'Sure' I said, 'yes. Fine. Why not?'

Returning home, I made my PhD supervisory team aware of the industry connections I had made, but colleagues were underwhelmed. At least one De Montfort-based historian dismissed studying women's sport as a viable academic career strategy. But at that time there was no woman working full time in the History department, mainly young men likely to kick a football about in the office. So, it was a lukewarm welcome back. Ho hum.

However, FIFA, via its university arm at the International Centre for the Study of Sport (CIES), at the University of Neuchâtel, had made connections with De Montfort staff to validate a Master's degree in the Humanities, Business and Law of Sport. Before joining UEFA's legal department in August 2000, Gianni Infantino worked as the Secretary General of the CIES at Neuchâtel. The move sought to position FIFA as a serious force in education, to raise its credibility as an organisation. Partner institutions in developing the MA were SDA Bocconi Business School in Milan, and the University of Neuchâtel (UniNE). The course was validated across discussions in 1998/1999 to be launched in academic year 2000/2001.

The FIFA MA validation required a lot of paperwork. I was listed on the teaching team as a Senior Lecturer position in the Humanities Faculty writing on women's football, both of which helped the gender equity aspects of the proposal, which was slight. As I had previous validation expertise, as part of the teaching team we discussed a lot about the process of bringing the course to life. Each intake of the FIFA Master's had at least 30 of various nationalities, and still runs today, with a lively alumni community. It's always great to connect once again with those whom I taught. Past students and I often laugh that in the early days of the whole Leicester FIFA Master's module, I was given one afternoon per year to teach about the whole of women's football. I supervised final projects, marked across modules and graded Final presentations. For 16 editions I did what I could in terms of raising the level of engagement with gender studies but my it was a slog. It's really lovely to go to international events, meet alumni and hear how they've changed world sport.

At the same time, I was part of an institution-wide £1.8 million project to embed key skills across every module in the curriculum at undergraduate, Master's and postgraduate study. Large scale validation such as this included writing learning outcomes, and navigating the various De Montfort committees. BA Education Studies was also being validated as an undergraduate degree at the same time, mainly for students who wanted to become teachers before they could go on to study for a Postgraduate Certificate in Education (PGCE) in order to qualify. Hours of committee work then.

I was also progressing my coaching career, having passed the first level of the FA qualifications at an all-female course led by Jim Kelman in Berkshire, and having registered for the UEFA B Licence Parts One and Two, mentored by Jim. Part Two was an all-male course, apart from myself and another woman. It was a totally different experience to the all-female course. I was literally running out of hours in the day, juggling a career and study in academia, running my own business with Simon, and coaching on top of my playing and regional league commitments.

Simon and I made the decision to sell our business in 1998 and that made life simpler. We sold the bar and moved to a new house in February 1999. In the meantime,

I found I would be going to the Los Angeles Women's World Cup in person, and better still, Simon would be joining me!

It was beyond my wildest dreams. And I manifest starry-eyed.

Jeanola and Simone in LA

As I levitated into the First Class cabin of the BA flight to LA, less than two years after beginning a part-time PhD, I swear my feet did not touch the floor on the way to my seat. First Class is tiny, maybe 16 people. There were what looked like the remnants of Mötley Crüe scattered about, though Tommy Lee had gone AWOL. There was a tall recumbent man in a leather top hat and sunglasses who may, or may not, have been conscious. Slash? It was difficult to be sure as the men in black all took sleeping pills with their champagne in the first half an hour of boarding.

Thankfully Run DMC were not inclined to sleep and were sitting at the bar. I had been a big fan since the 1986 song 'My Adidas'. In my teens my dad's friend, David Luck, had a sporting goods shop in our village which was so unusual given how tiny the population was that he may as well have been selling unicorn triplets! My friend Bev had size eight feet as a girl. I had size two. We cried a lot on shoe shopping trips and didn't buy much. But in the 1970s Adidas paid their trainees half wages to learn on children's shoes which they then sold at 50% of the adult price. This did not solve Bev's woes, but it rescued me from sensible Clark's brown sandals. A lifelong obsession with sportswear followed. I got a job in a printing factory aged fourteen just to buy Adidas and became one of David Luck's best customers.

I was also into the Italian brand FILA and had a white tennis jacket with a zip pocket near the wrist only large enough in which to put coins or a locker key. I didn't own a locker, and due to my sportswear habit didn't have spare change. On a farm my white FILA tennis jacket was impractical, I grant you that. After I went skiing with school I returned with a pair of Moon Boots to pair with the jacket. Which even the cows considered eccentric. With its white fleece body, embellished by a blue and red FILA logo, I wore the tennis jacket until it disintegrated as a somewhat greying testament to youthful enthusiasms. I've no idea what happened to the Moon Boots.

Back on the plane, Run DMC were very jolly and welcoming on the flight as I told them my Adidas story, though I assume they'd heard hundreds of similar versions. However, glass of champagne in hand, I knew I had to work as soon as I landed, so it was a lovely hour before I noticed those guys getting seriously comfy on their barstools. Time for some shuteye. I was attending meetings as soon as we landed. Better be professional. Regrets, I have a few…

THE BARBIE WORLD CUP, 1999

The only dent in my day was that poor old Simon, my bagman, was back in economy as we had failed spectacularly to get him upgraded in spite of our considerable powers of persuasion. FIFA had paid £5000 for my flight I later learned when someone mistakenly shared the manifest with me, thinking I worked for the world governing body full time. Simon's flight cost us £500.

After my lunch, eaten with fancy cutlery and sipping the finest wines from etched crystal glasses, I took Simon my chocolates as a vote of sympathy. I briefly heard the vestiges of Mötley Crüe stir about an hour before we landed as I passed on the way to the First Class bathroom. Someone asked who that was, as I passed. Was it Sporty Spice? Given that Melanie Chisholm is ten years my junior, could actually sing, and was 1.67m to my 1.52m, I can only assume the sleeping pill and champagne cocktail was a doozy. Quite honestly, you'd have had to take elephantine quantities of tranquiliser to mix me up with Sporty Spice, but we all thought we saw rockstars on the plane that day, so who am I to judge?

More seductive even than flying First Class to LAX, was being whisked through security, a cliché but also an apt description, into a limousine with blacked out windows and two signs on the windscreen. One bore the initials VIP, and the other my name. There really are VIPs and VVIPs at major sporting events, and I didn't qualify for the second V. But, you know, I'll take a limo at my discretion, with one V any day of the week.

Simon of course accompanied me in the limo, much more cheerful now than he had been in economy, and a while later we were deposited at the LA Century Plaza and Towers hotel where the FIFA party had booked entire sections and floors. There were door security staff in Beefeater costumes at the Tower where we were staying, almost like fancy dress, complete with decorative pikes and white starched ruffs.

It was over 34 degrees in Los Angeles. But the Beefeater allusion to the Tower of London symbolised LA's version of the historical importance of the hotel, built when 20th Century Fox sold off some of its backlot due to the catastrophic financial losses of the film Cleopatra, starring Liz Taylor. Simon and I settled in, got told off for wearing jeans to a FIFA ExCo rehearsal event and were instructed to wear smart clothes at all times. Appearance was key.

My mobile phone at the time was a tiny blue Nokia which fitted into the back pocket of my jeans, where it lived most of the time. There were no phones that took pictures as such back then. There was no airtime plan with which to call home, just payphones or the hotel room handsets. I didn't get my first iPhone until November 2007 when it was released in the UK. So, all the images I have of the trip to LA are Simon's snapshots taken with a proper camera. This includes the cover image of this book. That funny expression I have is me looking at Simon, as if to say, what the hell am I doing, shaking hands with Sepp?

I rang my Mum and Dad from the hotel. 'Mum, you'll never guess where I am today', pause, 'How's LA Jean?' I confessed to being a bit nervous. 'You're as good as anyone else,' said Mum, 'just do your best.' 'Greet Blatter as one football genius to another,' said Dad. Sterling, if costly, advice. That week, two 10-minute phone calls cost $99. The Century Plaza and Tower was pricey. I would later learn that FIFA has minimum standards of the five-star hotels that they use, and a whole advance logistical crew had planned the comfort and well-being of guests.

My main purpose, beside attending the launch of the Los Angeles Declaration on Women's Football, was to deliver an academic research paper at the women's football symposium, just before the fourth Extraordinary Congress in FIFA's history. Previous Extraordinary Congresses had taken place in 1908 (Brussels), 1953 (Paris), and 1961 (London). While ordinary congresses were usually held bi-annually until 1998, an Extraordinary Congress, or ExCo, had to be voted by the FIFA Council with the support of one fifth membership. An ExCo was necessary because the 1998 FIFA Presidential election had been particularly controversial, with the exit of João Havelange, who had been president for 24 years. His successor Sepp Blatter wanted to steady the ship.

The febrile atmosphere was noticeable as soon as we landed. We reported to a FIFA welcome desk installed at the Regent Beverly Wilshire Hotel (Burgundy Room) which ran from 8am on 3rd July to 10pm on the 11th July, the day after the Final. Women's World Cup 1999 was hailed as an historically groundbreaking event at the time, and it was in many respects. But being there, it quickly dawned that women's football was for the majority the sideshow to the ExCo and its politics—not the main event. Even so, the welcome brochure to the FIFA ExCo in 1999 in the name of Dr Bob Contiguglia, the President of US Soccer, and Sepp Blatter, called the World Cup 'one of the greatest shows on earth' and therefore right at home in the movie capital of the world.

As soon as I was issued my lanyard on the way to another rehearsal a few hours later, I realised how misogynistic the atmosphere would be for the remainder of the trip. The polite FIFA official who handed me my accreditation looked bemused, raising an eyebrow. She looked even more quizzical when gifting Simon his identification, and muttered in French to her colleague. The penny dropped. My lanyard announced 'Professor Jean Williams'. Which I was, but wasn't, on a number of levels, having only just started my PhD study. FIFA had also assumed I was a male football expert of French-Welsh heritage, Jean Williams.

My husband was handed a lanyard marked 'Simone Williams'. Since I was a French-Welsh male professor, FIFA had assumed I had misspelt the name of my female partner. Excited by the exoticism of the extra 'e' on his name, Simone found out that he was to be invited to the Ladies Programme. This had been organised on the basis that no woman would want to go to a FIFA Extraordinary Congress to talk about something so dull as football.

THE BARBIE WORLD CUP, 1999

Simone had some tempting offers in LA. For instance, the Journée des Dames for the 9th July departed the hotel at 10.30am, for an-invitation only guided tour of the Getty Centre, 1200 Getty Center Drive, followed by lunch at The Grove, and return to the hotel at 15.00 hours after which there was private time to shop. Simone was invited on shopping and spa days on Rodeo Drive, to the Guggenheim for a guided tour, then a girly lunch at the Ivy—and anything else that LA could offer… except football. I later learned that FIFA had insisted that each national association send a man and a woman as delegates. However, not all of the women that accompanied the men were employees of the national football association. Nor were they necessarily current wives or partners of the male delegates. Quite a few appeared to be somewhat recent LA-based acquaintances.

So, the social programme for the whole event assumed that men would be at the business end of the football, and the women would be off doing something, anything, else. Simone was endlessly entertained by this. Sadly, I found my French was not improved. Simone still has the pastel silk head scarf, and pocket powder compact that was gifted, while I have my silk FIFA tie, and a rather lethal-looking letter opener. All unused of course. In fact, we were inundated with FIFA-branded trinkets and mementoes to mark the occasion, such as pin badges, pennants, notepads and so on. I've even got a Limited Edition Swiss watch, number 18 of 50, for those who presented, among other mementoes.

However big Los Angeles was for women's football, and it was incredible, it was very much not the main point of their visit in 1999 for most FIFA delegates. Thank goodness for the legendary Swedish striker turned coach Pia Sundhage who was invited to speak and brought along her guitar, singing 'Raindrops Keep Falling on my Head'. Being so short, I was obliged to use the box on which Blatter usually stood to address delegates when it was my own turn to speak, because the microphone would not bend any lower on its stalk. It was, I was told, the Presidential box. As such, an honour.

I was on a panel with current senior vice president of the Asian Football Confederation Zhang Jilong of the PR China, Marie George Buffet France's Minister of Youth Affairs and Sports, and Anita De Frantz the first female vice-president of the IOC executive committee. I was so far out of my depth as to not be able to see land. But Sheila Begbie and her compatriots from Scotland were very warm and friendly after I had spoken, as was Tom Sermanni, previously Australia women's national team coach. Referee Sonia Denoncourt was kind, great fun, and courteous.

FIFA hospitality events were not so much generous as astounding. There was such a disconnect between the fan experience of those who had bought tickets, and entertaining FIFA delegates. The entitlement was glittering. There was bountiful razzamatazz, and copious amounts of the old razzle-dazzle. I couldn't help but think how did any of that actually develop grassroots football? But of course, most of the hospitality was aimed at winning FIFA hearts and minds for Blatter, not destined for the wider football community.

The women's football symposium had its own dinner on Wednesday 7 July at the Bel Air Bay Club, 16081 Pacific Coast Highway, Pacific Palisades. Coaches departed the hotels at 18.30 hours, for a 19.15 reception where a fantastic acapella trio sang while we had 'clinky-drinks' and canapes while taking in the expensive and exclusive ocean views. Then a band played, dinner was served and more hospitality until the coaches returned at 22.30 hours for the journey back to the hotel. Talks continued the next day at the women's football symposium.

But I just couldn't connect my experience of trying to get monthly subscriptions from players and clubs affiliated to the women's East Midlands' League, in our volunteer meetings in a pub in Nottingham on a Monday evening, with the scope and scale of how money was being spent on FIFA hospitality. I knew I was being naïve, but I had only to look into the eyes of the women who had been at the Second Women in Sport conference in Namibia, like Julien Garises, to see that they were beyond shocked too. It took a while not to be hypnotised. To understand that what was overpowering for me, was unimpressive to others. Because they were used to so much more.

The party of Thursday 8 July to celebrate the ExCo cost US $1.5 million. In 1999. Paramount Studios boasted a 65-acre lot 'for performers, elephants, ice rinks, lakes, explosions, and up to 5,000 of your closest friends.' Even so, this did not meet with the expectations of seasoned FIFA representatives. Simone and I were accompanied into the entrance of Paramount by various FIFA guests who could be heard complaining that the Laurel and Hardy, Marilyn, Charlie Chaplin and Fred Astaire tribute actors greeting us were not real Hollywood stars. Reception drinks, speeches of welcome, mingling, canapés and nibbles, chatting, back-pats. Stilt-walkers, jugglers and fire-eaters accompanied us from reception drinks to Paramount main street where our meal would be served, after more toasts and clinky-drinks. Professional dancers were on hand to waltz, salsa, mambo or tango with guests depending upon personal taste and sprightliness. There were live singers fronting a swing band, at some point fireworks, never-ending wine, and behind it all an elaborate choreography of politics. Back-slapping, hand-shaking, wordless agreements and a kaleidoscopic panorama of who was talking to whom at any one point.

I saw my husband as I had never seen him before in nearly 20 years, cutting a rug on the dance floor with a Princess from Malaysia. He later reported that dancing was a good excuse to enquire about the possibility of an invitation to the Malaysian Grand Prix. I do not know whether it was his chat up lines or his dance moves, but the invitation to the Grand Prix never arrived. Perhaps Simone should have taken the coach to the Guggenheim after all? After farewell pyrotechnics, we were escorted from the main lot at Paramount by firewalkers, clowns and celebrity tributes to our coaches at 10.30pm

THE BARBIE WORLD CUP, 1999

for the return to the hotel, and on to the main event the next day—the ExCo proper. Sadly, there was no ice skating, or actual elephants, nor were there ice skating elephants.

Next morning Sepp Blatter delivered his now famous 'house of FIFA' ExCo speech. We have two numbered bricks from Sepp's house. An accompanying document outlined 'The House of FIFA, Vision and Aspirations for the Future' urging the associations to join the President in building his solid house for all the FIFA family for the future. The Blatter building metaphor had trust as its solid foundation, democracy and solidarity forming its walls. Quality and universality comprised its ceiling and roof. Given that there had been a walkout by Asian national representatives over the lack of places for Asian Football Confederation (AFC) teams in the 2002 Men's World Cup, this was perhaps at best overly optimistic.

The housing metaphor was a front for insecurity. In 1999 Blatter was not in as strong a position as he later came to be, mostly with the support of the African nations. But the building trope had particular resonance when many of the headquarters of member national associations were still based in temporary accommodation. In Namibia in 1998 this had been in a re-purposed wooden church building which needed considerable renovation. So no wonder building permanent facilities bought a degree of loyalty. Accruing support in Los Angeles hotel lobbies, Blatter wandered around like a suave, but vaguely sinister, penguin enthusiastically shaking a flipper with anyone who would exchange pleasantries.

If Blatter was smooth, his progress was not. Blatter's rival for the FIFA Presidency in 1998, Nils Lennart Johansson, had the look of a big old barn at risk of disintegrating in an earth quake. He was a vast guy, visibly reverberating with rage. Johansson was the antithesis physically of Blatter. Large, friendly in a vague kind of way, and solidly dependable if not especially mobile. He was apoplectically furious. All the time. Blatter was at this stage a bit like a Teflon Dorian Grey, silver-tongued and slick. Nothing had stuck to his reputation, yet. Johansson was the alter ego painting that had come down from the attic to haunt Blatter, having aged immeasurably. The Swedish administrator wore the sign of every negotiation, compromise and weary resignation to football politics on his face: I have never seen another human being look so exhausted—and I have run the London marathon.

Having worked his way up to lead Swedish football, in 1990 Johansson became head of the UEFA confederation and challenged Blatter for the FIFA Presidency in 1998, losing by 80 votes to the latter's 111. Johansson would remain at the helm of UEFA until 2007 when Michel Platini took over. He publicly criticised Blatter for financial mismanagement, alleged bribery over votes, and went so far as to vote for Issa Hayatou of Cameroon in the 2002 FIFA Presidential election, although this was largely gesture politics. Hayatou would lose by 56 votes to 139, in 2002 to Blatter.

Nevertheless, the physical disparity between Blatter and Johansson was an amusing contrast as each shook as many hands as possible, while avoiding one another as much as was humanly conceivable when forced to be in the same room. Per Ravn Omdal, of Norway, who was a big deal in FIFA women's football committees at the time, was at Johansson's right hand throughout. He circulated after Johansson with the attitude of a man who thought that someone had filched his spare change, and would like to check *your* pockets to get it back. Omdal's surveillance from under owl-like brows, made sure each delegate knew of his scepticism both of Blatter, and of themselves. Omdal served as the European member of the FIFA Executive from 1994 until 2002, when a major changing of the guard took place. But for now, at the end of proceedings on 9th July, cocktails and a light buffet were offered by FIFA and Coca Cola in the Los Angeles Ballroom, at Century Plaza. I half-expected, half-hoped for a proper bunfight.

There was also another layer of politics, particularly for historians of World Cups. I mention it here because later, when England failed to secure the Men's World Cup of 2018 or 2022, which we know went to Russia and Qatar respectively, the FA presented themselves as wounded victims of an upsetting, unfair process. For a £15 million bid in 2018 England were eliminated in the first round after infighting, controversy, and false hope securing only two votes, one of whom was provided by an Englishman, Geoff Thomson, on the FIFA Executive Committee. Japan provided the other. But the FA had a longer history of bid problems.

Out in LA in 1999, I was reminded that in its dealings with European nations in the 18th century, England, and more largely Britain, had become known as 'perfidious Albion', meaning deceitful, and untrustworthy in international relations. While the old name for England, 'Albion' means white land, probably from the cliffs of Dover, 'perfidious' implies outright treachery. By the time the FA landed to try and make friends and influence people in LA in 1999, the offence had been caused by English duplicity, they were not the wronged party.

Back in 1993 the FA Chair Bert Millichip had entered into a 'gentleman's agreement' that England would support Germany for the 2006 Men's World Cup, in return for their endorsement for the 1996 men's Euros. Having hosted the Euros in 1996, the FA changed its mind and began to bid for the 2006 Men's World Cup as a rival to Germany, Brazil, South Africa and Morocco. It was not a smart move. Lennart Johansson had withdrawn his support for England's 2006 bid as a result, supporting Germany more vigorously. In return the FA had supported Blatter for the 1998 FIFA Presidency, although he had already said he'd like South Africa to host in 2006. UEFA President Johansson had several reasons to be livid in LA, one of which was the Mr Bean-esque presence of the perfidious FA bid committee.

The FA's 2006 world cup bid committee was led by bland men in beige suits. In spite of the considerable glamour of Sir Bobby Charlton, and Sir Geoff Hurst, who were both undoubtedly patriotically devoted to their duty, the biggest highlights were the

THE BARBIE WORLD CUP, 1999

electric blue loafers of the MP for Sport, Tony Banks, as they criss-crossed various hotel lobbies in LA. Banks would later become the special envoy in charge of winning the 2006 World Cup, but looked more like he should be hosting *Dancing with the Stars*. Inspired by his love of Chelsea FC, Tony sashayed, quick stepped and jived across vestibule after atria relentlessly in search of a world cup vote, while Simon and I hummed in unison 'Blue is the colour, football is the game, we're all together, and winning is our aim.'

The 2006 England bid, built upon jilting Germany, and knocking down historic Wembley stadium, only to rebuild it with someone else's money, was always a false hope. A clear strategy was notably absent, as was humility. The campaign involved an alleged improper loan to the FA of Wales for an estimated £3 million plus, parties for Chuck Blazer and his acolytes, and the alienation of key international football partners because of the broken gentleman's agreement. As dramatic ironies go, onlookers in Los Angeles could see that the main actors at the FA were at the mercy of events, even while they were sure that they were shaping them. For further details, I recommend a strong cup of tea, and the official version of events available at the Department of Culture Media and Sport website.

That said, I am not for one second defending the award of Men's or Women's World Cups as in any way a transparent or robust process. Just that whatever the perceived and actual nature of the exercise, the English did not excel at either. This has to be balanced. The great Uli Hesse writing in The *Three Lives of the Kaiser, a Biography of Franz Beckenbauer*, suggests that Germany's 2006 bid had only five key staff until October 1998 when Fedor Radmann joined as 'chief co-ordinator.' So Beckenbauer, Radmann, Wolfgang Niersbach, Horst Schmidt, Wilfried Straub and Egidius Braun lined up against the England bid.

Radmann, who had prior experience of organising ice hockey World Championships in Germany, and Olympic connections, personally knew about half of the men who would vote on the 2006 World Cup. Beckenbauer had influence both in the US, and in Europe, and of course worldwide fame as a player, coach and as Vice President of the German Football Association. He had won the Men's World Cup as a player and coach and now headed Germany's bid. With Morocco and Brazil peripheral in the process, Blatter let it be known that he favoured the campaign led by Nelson Mandela for South Africa, which had already hosted the Rugby World Cup in 1995, and the African Nations Cup in 1996. A vote for South Africa was an endorsement for Africa which had never hosted the football World Cup tournament before. Beckenbauer and Radmann were in Los Angeles, but I did not recognise anyone from the South Africa bid.

When FIFA finally decided who would host 2006, England won five votes to South Africa's six and Germany's 10 in the first round. Morocco was eliminated. In the second round, South Africa matched Germany on 11 backers, and England were eliminated with just two votes. Then, decisively but narrowly, Germany won hosting rights by 12 votes to 11 against South Africa, with Scottish-born Charles Dempsey of the New Zealand Football Association abstaining and then swiftly departing the vote to return to New Zealand. Dempsey said that he was placed in an impossible quandary. The exact nature of his discomfort remains elusive to this day. Enough of the history lesson, back to the football.

In a good value scheduling choice for those in the stadium, both the third-place playoff and the final of the Women's World Cup 1999 were to be played on the same day on Saturday 10th July, presumably to ensure a full stadium for the television audiences and to report record numbers for both matches, all of which were accomplished. But we would sit through over five hours of football and ceremony. The first departures to the Rose Bowl from our hotel were at 9am for a 10.30 kick-off. We had our pick of seats. The second coach parade for the Rose Bowl from FIFA hotels was 11am for the opening ceremony at 12.50. It would be between 34 and 40 degrees at various points in the day. Apart from the semi-finals, the tournament had used double-headers, particularly when advertising its advance discounted ticket sales as an opportunity for fans to see the world's best on home soil.

Conclusion:
The Football Mothership Calling me Home

Back in LA, I had first alarmed Sir Bobby Charlton in a hotel coffee shop, just as the unsuspecting demi-god was ordering a cup of tea, thinking no one knew He who walked amongst us. Had Jesus been ordering a chai latte I could not have been more graced. Given that I had been taught by my Dad to perform 'we are not worthy' prostrations in front of the telly every time the England and Manchester United star appeared, Sir Bobby perhaps got away lightly. But he wasn't to know that. There is a brilliant essay, in a wonderful but flawed book, *The Football Man* by Arthur Hopcraft when the author writes about what it must have been like for George Best and other stars to continually meet people made daft with giddiness when encountering their football hero. A giddy kipper as the English say, although I have never met a fish quite so delighted as I was that day in the hotel coffee shop.

Poor Sir Bobby reacted like he thought it might be an assassination attempt. I was entirely overawed. Even meeting Pelé in Harrods hadn't been the same. I did manage to calm down enough that when we met at the social events listed above Sir Bobby was very generous with his time, and Simon, always relaxed, was able to have some lively conversations with Norma. Simon and I sat in section 19, row 38 seats 7 and 8, just behind the legend and his wife at the final, and I was struck by them watching all of the football for both matches, as the sun was relentless. Sir Bobby wore his 2006 World Cup bid cap; Norma sensibly opted for a straw boater. I was going to watch a World Cup final with Simon, in proximity to Sir Bobby and, of course, Norma. It was not so much of a dream come true (because I had never had that much imagination), but more like the football mothership calling me home. Excuse me while I kiss the sky!

Not everyone shared my level of excitement. The majority of FIFA delegates were not particularly interested in the matches, especially as it was women's football. But on the day of the final, there was palpable disdain for punters who had actually paid for tickets to sit in a hot stadium, when there was a running high-end buffet in air-conditioned hospitality. Not even Sissi could distract them from the AC. Lawyer Michel Zen-Ruffinen's children had a high old time, including going off with Simon's 1999 souvenir cap to mark the occasion. We had to obtain alternative headgear since the sun blazed all afternoon. Doris Valasek and Donna de Varona must have been delighted by the spectacle of the full stands. The bidding scandals over rumours of brown paper bags full of incentives passed over in hotel rooms was just beginning to foment, and Zen-Ruffinen and Valasek would be key to the public awareness of those events. But that was in the future.

Many people staying in FIFA hotels just went shopping or to lunch instead. There were a lot of empty seats in the Rose Bowl stadium, especially in hospitality, although the often-reported total is 90, 185 tickets sold. The elaborate sunflower flower arrangements which needlessly decorated the VIP areas wilted unadmired in the heat.

US Soccer had been building to this day since 31 May 1996, when the Women's World Cup was announced for Los Angeles, on the same day that Japan and South Korea were awarded the 2002 Men's World Cup. Regardless of what was going on in hospitality, it takes nothing away from the huge, ground-breaking public interest in the Rose Bowl on final day. Ticket sales were like nothing else for a women's tournament, and I would not witness the like again until Australia 2023 when the fan base exceeded what I saw in LA. Comparably, the overall number of spectators in 1999 far surpassed any previous tournaments. Even by conservative estimates, there were around 1 million spectators in 1999 in 32 matches, across 17 events, because of the way the double-header matches were organised in the same stadium, apart from the semi-finals.

Most official FIFA sources claim 1.4 to 1.5 million spectators in 1999, a figure unrivalled until the 2015 Women's World Cup in Canada. The organising committee viewed each double-header as one event, meaning economies of scale in hospitality, television rights and sponsorship deals. But it also allowed the organisers to count 90, 185 for the third-place playoff game, which probably would not have happened, had it not been a double-header. So, there were PR benefits as well as logistical reasons to host two matches per venue. Not least, the $30 million budget, a 10th of what was spent on the 1994 Men's World Cup, returned an impressive profit of $4 million, and easily repaid the $2.5 million loan from US Soccer from the profits of the 1994 Men's World Cup.

The spectacle of a World Cup final was also changing culturally, and this resonated with many diaspora communities in the USA, as well as globally on television. The 1996 Olympic finals had featured hosts USA versus PR China, and been overseen by female officials, led by Norwegian referee Bente Skogvang, Nelly Viennot of France had run the line, along with Maria Rodriguez of Mexico. Bente has become an admired academic with whom I have had the privilege to work on a number of occasions, and along with Sonia Denoncourt of Canada, pushed through important reforms at FIFA to raise the profile of female officials. Im Eun-ju of South Korea, Tammy Ogston of Australia and Hisae Yoshizawa of Japan also initiated important regional developments in both officiating and leadership roles.

Encouraged, Blatter had approved a move to use only female officials in 1999. There remained a Eurocentric bias. Three of the four officials in the 1999 final were from Europe; Referee Nicole Petignat is Swiss; assistants Ghislaine Labbe, French, while Ana Perez is from Peru, and fourth official Katriina Elovirta, Finnish. The third-place match had been officiated by Im Eun-ju, Hisae Yoshizawa, Maria Rodriguez and Virginia Tovar of Mexico.

Again, the USA met China in the final game in 1999. Striker Sun Wen was at the height of her skills, taking home the Golden Ball, and sharing the Golden Boot with Brazil's Sissi, both with seven goals and three assists. For me, left-footed Sisleide do Amor Lima, Sissi, was the most exciting player of the tournament—even with US centurion Mia Hamm on imperious form. Her story is the stuff of women's football legend. Having gone to the 1988 invitational tournament in Guangdong Sissi was not released by her club team to go to the first Women's World Cup in 1991 with Brazil. In 1999 Sissi scored sophisticated goals at crucial times, including a dramatic golden goal in the game against Nigeria on 1 July to set up the semi-final on 4 July with the USA, which the hosts eventually won 2–0. Sissi won a bronze medal, the Silver Ball and the Golden Boot in 1999. It would be her only World Cup. She was not selected in 2003 due to her age, and alleged disciplinary issues. Honestly, watch the goals again and the documentary about her life and its impossible not to feel we were deprived of a great talent in both in 1991 and 2003.

Culturally, the merchandise of the tournament placed women's football in the mainstream. I personally had never seen Soccer Barbies before, and they came in diverse skin tones, with a range of first names, hair-styles and wearing shirts from different player positions. Men, whom I would later call 'feminist fathers', would walk into LA restaurants wearing a Mia Hamm shirt, in honour of their daughter's hero. Dad and daughter shirts; Mum and son shirts; the merchandising of the tournament was reflective of the cultural changes that organisers had hoped to encourage.

The television audience was a huge 40 million people. A post-impeachment Bill Clinton was booed for sitting in the press box, while Hilary and Chelsea were cheered. After engaging in an affair with intern Monica Lewinsky, Clinton had subsequently been acquitted, but had not won back public favour. The fabled family audience for women's football was not impressed.

There was an atmosphere of a teen concert, so many under 21s were in the stadium. At the closing ceremony, British teen star Billie, later to be known by her adult full name as musician and actress Billie Piper, sang 'Because We Want To' which was the tournament's official song and her debut single. Hanson, a US trio of brothers whose 1997 hit single 'MmmBop' had projected them to global fame, sang the national anthem acapella, while fighter jets flew overhead. The seemingly ageless Jennifer Lopez performed 'Let's Get Loud' as if her very life depended upon it, well before she was Jenny from the Block.

It was difficult to reconcile the palpable excitement of the crowd and the indifference of those benefitting from the FIFA hospitality. This was how the business of sports worked, and it was very much exchange as usual. For sponsors, administrators, guests, and others who were enjoying the freebies, the behind-the-scenes action was where the deals were being done. Nothing personal, this is commerce. It wasn't until I attended several such events and researched the mechanics of the industry that I better understood the mix. Of course, I was enjoying the benefits too, and that could not be ignored.

The week of the final in LA was my Wizard of Oz moment with the football industry. In the movie the protagonist Dorothy has gone to the palace of the Great Wizard of Oz to ask that she return home, as he had promised. But Dorothy's request is declined and she is told to return the next day. During the exchange, Dorothy's dog, Toto pulls away a green curtain in the hallway to reveal the Wizard, not an inspiring divinity, but a frightened, insecure old man. I had looked behind the FIFA curtain and found the people at the head of world football, particularly in the form of Blatter, to be rather ordinary with failings, and frailties just like everyone else. There were no omnipotent football gods (apart from Sir Bobby and Sissi), just people who wanted power and influence, and would use resource to amplify their personal aura.

It would be too strong to say I was disappointed, because crikey, how could I possibly feel let down? On that July day, all I could see were the empty seats and think about people back home who I played against who would have given anything to be here. It was just work for the FIFA administrators who had selected the five-star hotels, arranged the luxury coaches, and booked the budget busting entertainment. There was no magic. The matches were merely the shop window for a much bigger retail operation that got the goods to the storefront. Chastening knowledge and a loss of innocence for me to comprehend that football, something in which I had always found pure joy, was also a series of interlocked industrial complexes, each with its own form of logic in how the money was made. A lot of what I believed in was an elaborate fabrication, largely of my own making. I had to take ownership of my own collusion and to engage more critically with the many faceted realities of how large events came to town.

From my photos I can see how unrehearsed the teams were in the pre match formalities. For the third-place game, won eventually by Brazil over Norway 5-4 after 120 minutes of play, the teams held hands as they first wandered onto the pitch. No traditions, no rehearsal of pleasantries, no set expectations. There were just not the formalities and pre-match choreography we would expect today. Remember, this was a world cup even before Sincy (Christine Sinclair) even played for Canada seniors. It was also a world Cup before Marta, although in this case Brazil won third place thanks to the legendary penalty conversion of the ageless Formiga. It may have been proximity to Sir Bobby, sunstroke, or Formiga's joy that made me delirious, and the final hadn't kicked off yet!

After a goalless draw, and penalty shootout for third place already overrunning, the final itself moved inexorably to the same brutal result. The USA and PR China also finished 0-0 after added extra time and golden goal rules. Tony DiCicco managed the US squad to the penalty kicks, as did Ma Yuanan for PR China. Briana Scurry, the Black goalkeeper for the US was noticeably on form, having allowed in only three goals when the US won their Olympic gold medal in 1996, and replicating this feat in 1999. Her save of Chinese number 13, Liu Ying's penalty, arguably won the World Cup for the US as much as Brandi Chastain's conversion of her penalty, for the 5-4 scoreline. However, Scurry's stellar career, and the lack of diversity in the 1999 squad was by and large overlooked by the media, as much as Chastain's eye-catching moment of individual celebration took the headlines. Until that moment a metaphor of family and togetherness had united the '99ers', as they came to be known.

But no goal in four hours of open play on the 10th July was not the final that the organisers were hoping for. Thank goodness then, for the hosts taking home the title. There is no doubt that this conferred a gloss on football for women as only Californication can, and it was to be a global story. It was a great occasion with which to be involved, but the football was a bit of a grind, as many world cup finals can be. All four teams wanted more not to lose on 10th July 1999, than to *win*.

Then of course, the huge comedown after a major tournament. It had been exciting, thrilling almost psychedelic. Intense, tightly choreographed, and awash with cash. But I had become queasily uneasy. As I said goodbye to friends from Africa that I had met in 1998, and saw again in 1999, I could not reconcile the level of luxury we had experienced in America with what they were returning to in their efforts to engage youth in positive behaviours. Nor could I resolve my own relatively privileged experience of working with women's and girls' village teams in the East Midlands, and the financial problems that were part and parcel of that experience with the waste that was integral to a major tournament.

I was helped, a consolation for such loss of innocence, by the writing of the late Grant Wahl, Jen Doyle, and others who began critiquing women's soccer at about this time and with whom I began to connect via the internet, in the days before social media. Later writers like Shireen Ahmed, Brenda Elsey, Laurent Dubois, Gwendolyn Oxenham, Josh Nadel, Lindsay Sarah Krasnoff, Martha Saavedra, and other writers would develop the critical engagement while the mainstream media often ignored the stories, other than at major events.

There was huge cause for optimism. The 20 players of the 99ers would go on to become entrepreneurs, stars of their own professional league, and media darlings, by the time of the next Women's World Cup in 2003, also in the USA. Personally, by the time I got back on the plane, I had been invited to speak at a number of events across world football in Oceania, in South America and in Africa and was looking forwards to telling my family all about it. I had accepted an invitation from Josephine King, the President of the Oceania Football Confederation since 1987, to speak at a women's football symposium in New Zealand in early October. She was the daughter of Charles Dempsey, and, judging by how she was received in LA, the equivalent of what passed for football royalty. We booked flights, planning to stop off in Hong Kong for a few days, a place that I had always wanted to see.

I was shocked to find on my return that Mum did not look at all well. I realised that in my excitement in the build up to the tournament I had not looked in on her as often as I usually did. No excuse really, but because of work, the trip, a new house, doing the PhD, and my coaching badges, plus the actual football, I had neglected to visit as often as I might. We discussed how she wasn't happy with her NHS doctor, getting some private tests done, and booked them in for the coming weeks.

Just before the new term started that September, I was informed that Combined Studies would have its final student intake that year; the Faculties had decided to disaggregate the programme and take it under their control on a discipline by discipline basis. This meant that my 0.7 post would be under review for redundancy, unless I could find redeployment. I now faced the prospect of losing my major source of employment, having taken on the largest mortgage I had held to that point, for an old house that needed complete renovation. We were unlikely to sell it for what we had paid. But there were still 300-odd students to enrol, so on with the new academic year we went.

At the end of September I took my UEFA B Part Two coaching examination and failed on a goalkeeping topic. Never my strongest area. I had planned a weekend away before term started, and I lay on my sunbed in Ibiza infuriatingly able to see the correct phases of play unfold in my head. I had not been sufficiently focussed on the day of the test. The certified legend that is Jim Kelman was enormously encouraging, but I lost a lot of my confidence. John McDermott was not supportive. I didn't know yet about his role in the Vanessa Hardwick case. As I've said quite a bit about that elsewhere, all I will say here, having worked in education for decades, is that the way the courses were led in 1998/99 discriminated against women because the atmosphere was so intimidating. I am glad that Audrey Cooper and others have since joined and are developing more elite women coaches, and coach educators.

Certainly, I had to give it two more gos before I got the UEFA B Part Two award and by then any remaining confidence had evaporated. Had I had a mentor or connections, some of that could have been addressed. But you were either in, or you were out. Since it needed a referral to the A licence there was no progression possible.

I knew I had done the necessary preparation over two years. I could tell you exactly where I was when David Beckham got sent off against Argentina in the 1998 Men's World Cup, after kicking out at Diego Simeone in the round of 16 with the scores tied at 2-2. Ten-man England lost on penalties. I was in a bar in San Marino doing match analysis for my coaching badges. Pierre Lanfranchi suggested I shadow on a Sports Master's programme as insight for the FIFA Master's we were developing at De Montfort. I was the only woman and the only Brit in the bar, as my San Marino hotel room did not have a television and I was doing match analyses across the whole tournament. The Italians, and the San Marino nationals, gestured to me pityingly that Simeone had picked Beckham's pocket. They meant that Simeone had fooled Beckham into the red card with his own previous weak foul, and ruffling the Englishman's hair to provoke him. The Beckham sending off wasn't a red card offence but 'el pibe' (the kid), Simeone, had won this sending off with all the guile of a street-smart rogue.

I'd also spent weeks in 1999 doing live match analyses in preparation at the likes of local clubs like Nuneaton Town and other men's matches at the highest levels I could access. Asked why there are so few elite female coaches, part of the answer is a lack of women in the pipeline, even those who do apply to do their badges tended not to get help as individuals, either practically or personally. If you failed, there was no safety net, and going on courses as the only woman was really tough and isolating, even if armed with a professional background in education. Add to that, in order to progress to the A licence there had to be a personal referral. It was clear that having taken three times to pass, I wasn't going to get the support, even had I found a spare £7000 to pay for the A licence, with no prospect of working in football on the horizon. So, what was the point? It was just one more thing. I did follow up with some work at Notts County and Loughborough Uni second team, funded by an FA mentoring scheme, but it ended abruptly with no explanation and there seemed little prospect of paid employment.

THE BARBIE WORLD CUP, 1999

On Monday 4th October as I went to get my morning coffee on the way to teach, a charmless Human Resources officer, having a cigarette outside the coffee shop, told me in an offhand way that my post had been made redundant effective from the end of next academic year. Since I was part time and had only worked there for two years, he told me, I would be lucky to receive a couple of thousand pounds in redundancy. Simon joked the job description should be called Human Remains.

On the Tuesday night we took Mum for a series of private tests where the doctor told us she had multiple and complex conditions requiring immediate treatment. He booked us in again for more tests Thursday evening. On Wednesday I went to football. On Thursday I had a clear premonition of what was coming as I watched Mum struggle to get onto the couch in the doctor's office. The specialist prescribed tablets for immediate use, and said we must admit her to the NHS urgently, but she asked us to wait until the next day.

On Friday morning at work, I had a phone call to say Mum wouldn't wake up. I raced over.

At 12 noon, pretty much on the dot, she died.

CHAPTER II
THE HANGOVER WORLD CUP, 2003
Introduction: Falling

I was giving it beans, singing along to Britney Spears' *'Baby One More Time'* in the shower in my New York hotel room. 'Oh Babay babay, how wuz I supposed to know that something wasn't right here?' Britney was on MTV, blaring out from the television, when the phone in the bathroom rang. I was thrilled! In drama, Chekhov's gun principle suggests that small details, like the introduction of a pistol, will be important (such as being fired at a key point in a subsequent scene). Knowing this, I cannot tell you how many times I had previously looked both perplexed and expectant over the years, as to why anyone would put a telephone in a hotel bathroom? What on this planet could be so urgent that you would have to answer right away?

And—why did mine never ring?

When I answered it was Simon. 'Are you OK?' Simon sounded frightened. Simon has immaculate manners. It is the first thing you will notice when you meet him. He is terribly, terribly well brought up. But there was no, 'Hello, how are you?' or anything. Odd.

'I'm fine! I had a run up to Central Park, and had a coffee and a pastry on the way back. It's a beautiful morning here. Blue skies. Not a cloud in the sky. Autumnal, crisp and clear.' He could clearly hear Britney in the background. 'Put the news on Jean.' My heart sank at the tone of voice. In 20+ years, Simon had rarely delivered an imperative in my direction. There was anxiety in his voice, and Simon is always calm. 'A bloke at the factory where I am working heard it on the radio. I thought they were winding me up. You know how blokes are in factories with the practical jokes. But it isn't a wind up. There's been an attack. Can you see anything?'

'Err, riiiight' I replied. What he was saying didn't seem remotely relevant to my situation at that moment. Why was the normally unflappable Simon calling to tell me about an attack? I was buzzing from caffeine, the run, Britney and being in New York about to meet some famous entrepreneurs. I couldn't compute.

'The guy in the factory asked me if you were in the US. I told him you were in New

York. He says that they have flown a plane into one of the Twin Towers. He has one of those little hand-held TVs. He has it for the horse racing. He's shown me the plane hitting the building. It's on repeat news here.'

'What?'

'He's shown me on his hand-held TV. It's all over the news here. They've just flown a second plane into the South Tower. Put the news on Jean.'

I changed channels to the news, and suddenly could see the blue New York sky I had enjoyed this morning had a trail of smoke streaming across it on the screen. I looked out of the window in my hotel as I was midtown, facing downtown. Nothing. 'But I can't see anything outside Simon. Is this happening now?'

'Yes, its live and your hotel clearly don't know anything about it either because when I called the front desk they put me through to your room straight away. The receptionist sounded really calm. What will you do?' But Simon knew what my response would be.

'I'm going to my appointment. I am not missing that. I can't.'

He counselled: 'I don't think they'll see you. It's really serious. You maybe shouldn't go out on the street.'

I was adamant, replying. 'I haven't come this far not to make the appointment. I am not giving her the satisfaction.'

'Alright, let me know how you get on. I'll keep watching the news and update you before you leave the hotel if there's anything. Please be careful.'

'I'll be fine.'

As we rang off, I got into business clothing and prepared to make my appointment. Blooms and billows of cloud, fire and ash just kept scrolling over the TV screen against the perfect blue sky. I would have to rely on my wits. I still had my blue Nokia phone but it was SIM only with no international reception, hence having given Simon the number of the hotel reception to contact me if I could not get to a public payphone.

The Twin Towers? I had only been and walked around the area the previous day after arriving in New York, thinking to go to the Top of the World observation attraction later on my trip. It had been a pure azure day also, and having already done the Empire State Building observation deck on a previous occasion, I had thought how amazing it would be to see south Manhattan.

On the way to my appointment, I will never forget the quiet on the street. On any given day, the traffic in New York catastrophises in modulations of both hushed and high hysteria. Normally New York traffic is an entertaining conversation conveying the intensity of the threat-level at a given junction. Yellow cabs bip, and bark with their horns, 'coming through, coming through.' Ambulances warble and wail in despair, 'someone's hurt, oh help us someone's wounded.' The fire truck horns blare imperatives, hoarse hysterical lookouts startled by imminent attack, 'get out of the way, run for your lives, it's coming!'

But there was a quiet calm from 14th Street upwards that was eerie. We could hear that a calamity was indeed happening, nearby, but elsewhere. The devastation sucked the soundscape out of the rest of the city, as if those not directly involved were surplus to requirements: which we were. There was a very sobering sense of mortality to have the luxury not to need the attention of professional experts just at that moment. What do you do with that? The unspoken code on the pavements was 'Get on with it, be aware, ready to react.'

Once I was out of the hotel, I could only use public phones to call home but I had mapped out a few on a route I had taken the day before, to test my walk from the hotel to my appointment. So, there was a backup plan to call Simon if I was at all concerned. I wouldn't call my Dad, as what could he do? He would only worry. I knew Simon would call him anyway to say he'd spoken to me.

Asking the receptionist about the news on my way out, she clearly hadn't heard what had happened, and looked at me disbelievingly. The doorman was following the news on the television in the window of the bank opposite. He looked grey, well beyond nauseous as if he were aging in an accelerated way, like someone had sped up time. The streets were abuzz with information, and people figuring out what to do. It was very pragmatic. Very New York.

I had two main motivations to get me to my appointment on 11 September 2001 in New York. One was a world-renowned entrepreneurial carrot, and the other was an irritating academic stick. The cane came in the form of the new Head of School of Education at De Montfort University in Bedford. There is a truism in higher education that those who are head-hunted by institutions are often proposed by their existing university to Executive Search firms, in order to solve an immediate problem. This often involves passing their anti-social behaviour on to someone else. This individual was head hunted to De Montfort, heralded by an email instructing us to be in awe. We were not. But the Head of School had saved my job. Credit where credit is due, and I remain thankful for that decision still today.

Having come within a week of being made redundant in July 2000, I had effectively given up on the PhD. Making a salary had to take priority. I applied for a redeployment post, full-time as a Senior Lecturer in Education Studies, with a specialty in English across the curriculum, which was expanding across teacher training and academic routes. Initial Teacher Training Education (ITTE) courses begin before other academic subjects to get the necessary content in before the applied elements in school. Having been interviewed under redeployment circumstances, I was offered the post from 1 August on two conditions. One was that it had to be a full-time post, not a flexible or part time role. The second was that I would be based at the Bedford campus, 80 miles away, and if there was to be a 9am start then I should check in with my line manager by half eight. A 160-mile round trip five times a week, did not make for much else to enjoy.

But it was a job. I should say that education departments were the Cinderella of many ex-Polytechnic universities, because the teaching loads were so high. Essentially, it was a vocational training arm with several contact hours per day.

This would not have been so bad in September 2000 had there not been a petrol shortage. It was a national crisis, albeit a short-lived one. By 12 September, 3,000 petrol stations were dry, with one nearby privately-owned station selling fuel at £11 a gallon. The NHS was put on an emergency footing; schools closed; and the Post Office struggled to fulfil deliveries. The train wasn't practical, as it was a campus-based university outside the town. The hypervigilant Head of School had explicitly asked colleagues at Bedford to check in with me before 9am starts for which I was timetabled most mornings. I found myself queueing at supermarkets during my lunch hoping to get enough fuel to get home, and then queueing again at night. I stuck the situation until Christmas, and then asked HR for my redundancy. But there was a sliver of a glimmer of hope.

In January 2001 there was to be an expansion of Education Studies at De Montfort University, Leicester. I was offered the opportunity to take that post, so long as I acted as Programme Leader for the whole course. Another full-time role. As well as the administration of leading the whole BA course, from recruitment to graduation and postgraduate provision, I taught across nine modules with over 20 hours of contact per week, plus pastoral supervision. It was better than contemplating cycling to Bedford!

But Education Studies was also undergoing an inspection of the quality of teaching. I was to lead the inspection from the internal team, on top of the rest. The Head of School's speciality was leadership, motivation and improvement in education. Rather than wow us with her expertise in leadership, motivation and improvement, she spent the day before the inspection, not reading the 100 folders of documentation we had been required to provide, but dusting the shelves. Mr Sheen and duster in hand, she outlined our curriculum shortcomings, while improving the shine of the furniture. Not a guaranteed strategy of success in an inspection but we passed with respectable gradings.

Amidst all this, there was very little active research in Education Studies at De Montfort but I had won about £6,000 from a rarely available pot of funding in April 2001 to research the newly founded professional women's soccer league, set up in the wake of the 1999 USA victory at the Los Angeles World Cup. Hence why I was in New York, where the league's offices were based.

I only could imagine the public satisfaction of the Head of School in my wasting rare research funding had I travelled to New York but not made the scheduled meeting. It was not an enjoyment I was willing to concede. Obviously when I made that judgment, I had no idea that I was in the middle of a true disaster.

Thankfully the carrot was a career highlight. I was in New York to meet John

Hendricks of the Discovery Channel, and Animal Planet. This was a big deal. Hendricks was behind the Women's United Soccer Association (WUSA), an international professional league for women's football drawing in major talent from across the world. The 20 victorious American national team players from Los Angeles, known as the '99ers, in partnership with entrepreneur Hendricks, formed WUSA, an eight-team league, in February 2000. The 20 founding players were Michelle Akers, Brandi Chastain, Tracy Ducar, Lorrie Fair, Joy Fawcett, Danielle Fotopoulos, Julie Foudy, Mia Hamm, Kristine Lilly, Shannon MacMillan, Tiffeny Milbrett, Carla Overbeck, Cindy Parlow, Christie Pearce, Tiffany Roberts, Briana Scurry, Kate Markgraf, Tisha Venturini, Saskia Webber, and Sara Whalen.

Most of the '99ers were well-known enough to be known by their surname, nickname or first name, and were initially paid $80,000 per season in the WUSA launch. Hamm in particular was doing much better than this, having resonated with Nike who named the largest building at their corporate campus in her honour. With the combined profile of Hendricks and 'the '99ers effect', as the cultural moment around women's empowerment was called, investors, sponsors, and profile followed. The business premise was that by connecting with existing media organisations, such as Time Warner Cable, Cox Enterprises and Comcast, the league would be able to televise games, reaching a much larger audience than the spectators in the stadium. Such seasoned production companies would also know how to package and sell the broadcast rights to a wide consumer audience, when the league expanded its franchise, as it expected to do, to 12 teams.

Having narrowly lost the 2000 Sydney Olympic Games gold medal in extra time to a controversial golden goal scored by Norway's Dagny Mellgren, the US was still the globally dominant team in women's soccer—but not unbeatable. Mellgren's winning Olympic goal was controversial because it hit her arm, to drop perfectly for a strike. Had VAR been around, this would not have gone without further investigation. But it won the Olympic final 3–2 to Norway, the other principal national team, who by 2000 had won Olympic gold, a World Cup and a European championship title—which for a country of 5.5 million people, and with handball a more important sport for women, was a considerable achievement.

The WUSA league played its first season in April 2001, and was the world's first women's soccer league in which all players were paid professionals, although there were pay differentials, and a cap on the number of overseas players. The Boston Breakers, New York Power and Philadelphia Charge were formed in 2000, and Atlanta Beat, Carolina Charge, San Diego Spirit, San Jose Cyber Rays and Washington Freedom were formed in 2001.

A cooperation agreement with Major League Soccer (MLS) promoted cross-league public relations because the MLS wanted to launch its own women's league, or so it said. Tony DiCicco was made commissioner and I had an appointment to discuss the USA win in 1999, and his role in the WUSA venture, on 12 September at their offices in New York.

With Hendricks' contacts, there were initially big prospects for a range of World Cup stars including Sissi of Brazil, Sun Wen and Gao Hong of PR China, and Germany's Steffi Jones and Birgit Prinz. Other well-known players who were from less successful nations also migrated to one of the four slots available for overseas players on each roster. These included individuals who would go on to make names for themselves in club football, like Maribel Dominguez (Mexico), Julie Fleeting (Scotland), Marinette Pichon of France, Cheryl Salisbury (Australia), Homare Sawa (Japan), and Kelly Smith of England. Charmaine Hooper of Canada would be second highest scorer in the inaugural season with 12 goals, behind Tiffeny Milbrett's 16. And Sissi, my idol of the moment, matched the great Kristine Lilly with 10 assists in the first season. I had at this point no idea that Sissi would never grace a World Cup stage again.

Although I was in on the research of the new league early, it was rumoured that most of its founding $40 million was being burned through in maintaining offices in Manhattan, big launch parties, and fan festivals with lots of players flying in. There were also whispers of generous salaries, including that of the CEO, Barbara Allen, after moving into professional sports from selling Quaker Oats. I was scheduled to ask her about this in our interview. Could the corporate sponsorship so evident at Women's World Cup 1999 be translated into the new league? Could long term deals also be struck with those corporate sponsors in what was already a very crowded market for professional sports leagues in the US? What was the similarity between selling breakfast oats and women's professional soccer?

I was also interested in the terms and conditions of the overseas players in particular. Where were they staying? How were they spending their non-playing time? And what support was available to them in their welfare and travels, including sports medicine? Of particular interest, the FA had announced their own plans for a professional league in England with the start anticipated in the 2003/4 season. Given the lack of qualification in 1999, this seemed optimistic. But I had been able to secure key interviews with leading personnel to explore the issues. Another reason to make my appointments in September 2001.

The New York Intercontinental, The Barclay Hotel was on 111 East 48th Street, and the Discovery Offices were closer to the financial district downtown, with its northern edge on 14th street. The World Trade Centre (WTC) complex was located in this financial neighbourhood. I set off on foot to be most in control of the situation if it should change. Unlike every disaster movie I had seen, people were being incredibly practical and multitasking. Not one person panicked. Many were talking on their mobile phones, while also stopping to watch the television screens available in the windows of shops and banks alongside the pavements. By now billowing thick smoke and fire from the top of the buildings was visible in the air and I kept looking up, as I made my way to the meeting.

But I knew instantly that I should not have kept the appointment.

The doorman outside the building had tears in his eyes because some of the staff from businesses in the facility had offices in the WTC buildings. There was an estate of more than seven buildings affected. Explaining I had come all the way from England, I made my way to the reception where again the woman who received me was crying. I very briefly waited in a 39th floor reception room for John Hendricks without any expectation that he would see me.

News came that he was taking phone calls that the South Tower was in an unstable condition. Unimaginably, impossibly, inevitably just as we watched from the large plate glass window looking down to lower Manhattan, South Tower collapsed seconds before 10am. Although this was the second tower to be hit, it had been struck at a lower point in its structure than the first. The meeting was now definitely over.

Speaking briefly again to the doorman, he had heard of plans to try and evacuate Midtown Manhattan, which seemed bizarre because of all the life out on the street as commuters and tourists fled. An hour later, Mayor Rudy Giuliani told New Yorkers: 'If you are south of Canal Street, get out. Walk slowly and carefully. If you can't figure what else to do, just walk north.' Landmarks would be closed in case they were targets. Over a million workers and residents south of Canal Street were evacuated, and police effectively stopped pedestrians from entering Lower Manhattan higher up, as I had experienced.

With subways closed, vehicle traffic restricted, and tunnels blocked, most people fled on foot, many by bridge and ferry to Brooklyn and New Jersey. People were helping those who could not walk very far to access public transport early to get home already. There was a lot of practical support for less mobile and older pedestrians trying to get away from midtown Manhattan too. It was clear that for some this journey would last hours. I was torn. Could I be of any help? I should at least try.

I got down to 14th Street, which was being barricaded off, with both armed forces and rescue services giving very short shrift to well-intentioned volunteers who were more likely to turn into liabilities rather than assets. Since we did not yet know the full scale of the devastation on the day, (and would not for some time), going there was a hopelessly naive impulse on my part which I regretted soon after. In my experience, people going downtown to help was not accident-gawking or rubbernecking. It was a genuine impulse to assist, and again unlike disaster movies where people fall over themselves to run away, I was struck by how many folks on the streets of New York walked towards the area to see if they could help.

However, this was short-lived. Some commentators are now critical of romanticising the degree to which strangers helped one another in those hours, and in the coming days. But my impression was not sentimental so much as pragmatic. There was the real fear of looting, and the army were on the streets by mid-afternoon. It was an immediate response to an urgent situation.

Later first responders would suffer from the effects of asbestos, post-traumatic stress disorder, and other consequences of being on site. So, the emergency services did many people a considerable kindness in turning us away, putting up incident screens, and absorbing the horror themselves. The number of Ground-Zero-related illnesses, years on from the attacks, suffered by those on the front lines—from emergency services to retail and health workers—continue to have a long-lasting legacy on the eventual number of people directly and indirectly killed as a result.

Making my way back to the hotel, I thought it most practical to put an overnight bag together in case the doorman was right, and to get as much information as possible. There were lots of police and military on the streets, putting up roadblocks and cordoning off areas, so walking again seemed most sensible of all. All the cabs were being hailed and buses were visibly at capacity. Half a million evacuees escaped by boat, including free ferries, incongruously full dining boats, and tugs.

There was no way to call Simon, because most of the phone masts had been on the Twin Towers, or on buildings affected by their collapse, after the North Tower went down about half past ten. The fuel from the airplanes had accelerated the fires in the buildings, causing them to burn even more fiercely. I later learned that Simon had put me on the missing person's list because he didn't hear from me for 24 hours. The phone lines in the hotel were completely jammed because lines were down, or calls at capacity, and when I found out that there were no plans to leave Manhattan for those who had accommodation, there would also be an early curfew to prevent disorder on the streets at night.

I had been booked by my university travel agent into the hotel for three nights, so I was OK for tonight and tomorrow. I didn't have a credit card. I hadn't got a workable mobile phone. I had about $100 in cash. I had what was known as Switch, which we now know as a debit card, but banks required users to register to withdraw money abroad before traveling to avoid fraud, and I had only planned to stay three days, so had not called them. There was no chance of calling them now. But I had bed and breakfast for two more nights. After that, I would have to work it out.

I made my way up to Central Park, where people were already holding a vigil for the increasing numbers of casualties we saw on the scrolling news. Minute by minute the numbers rose, and were reported sombrely by the newscasters, who relayed each small detail of information as it became known. As we now know, many of those lost would never be recovered, so it was a crazy jumble of glimpses of possible facts, only for updates to invalidate what we thought we knew. Huddled together in small groups, mourners lit candles, prayed, and quietly sang near the John Lennon 'Imagine' mosaic, in the Strawberry Fields area of the park. It was weird. To be safe and hear singing as so many people died a few miles away.

The worst images after the initial impact were of the people who had been trapped, particularly in the North Tower where the centrality of the placement of the plane caused there to be no way out. What became known as 'The Falling Man,' was played over and over again on television. This was a an oddly blithe euphemism for what it represented. These were men and women in their work-gear, trying to escape or jumping to their certain death, rather than endure what was happening in the building. Later reports said that those close by initially thought the unique thud was caused by falling blocks of concrete before realising the dreadful reality, that the horrific noise was bodies hitting the ground. The sound of the end of choice.

An image taken by Associated Press photo-journalist Richard Drew, symbolised the dreadful decision that some of the trapped people made to escape the smoke, flames and heat by exiting through windows high up in the building. There have been estimates of 200 people either losing their grip while seeking safety, or deliberately falling to their deaths. The Drew image was condemned as insensitive at the time, as were impromptu shots of falling people. They had no choice in their deaths being recorded. But the images have been subsequently viewed as an artistic response to an impossible choice or an unavoidable accident: the people looked especially incongruent given that mortals in their final minutes were captured in their office attire, having presumably gone to work on what they assumed would be an ordinary day.

It was incredibly difficult to comprehend the enormity of what had happened as I walked around Central Park, as other people also tried to cope. There was pragmatism, and a good deal of well-mannered helping of those who were obviously less able. In that sense, assertive New York seemed to have given way to empathetic New York.

How to process? Those like me not directly affected were safe from the immediate impact of the Twin Towers collapse, although the intensity of smoke and heat damage would take several days to clear, and later eight months to clear across the World Trade Centre site. There was no way to act appropriately, but the motivation to do something to help was an overwhelming part of the trauma. How to comprehend the scale of the personal loss, damage, logistical challenge, and carnage? So, there was the luxury of survivor's guilt, and avoiding the immediate security and rescue issues, which were inconceivable. But there was also powerlessness. What was meaningful to do, say or think given the scale of what had happened?

Overnight on the 11th September in New York, we were advised to keep all windows closed because of the smoke and dust. Several of the hotel staff chose to stay overnight in the facility to keep things running, so I was safe and well in considerable comfort. However, the hotel and flight had been booked through the university travel operator.

For now, all planes were grounded. What I *didn't* know was how long it would be before I got home, and how things would change after my first three nights ended.

I decided to rest up, stop watching the television, because there was no other coverage than the rolling news and the dire consequences of the aftermath, and wait to see what September 12 would bring.

That morning, I decided I might go to the Tony DiCicco appointment just in case he had been forced also to stay in New York overnight. Of course, the office door was firmly closed. In shock, denial, and disbelief, trying to use my prepared schedule was a coping mechanism. I had simply not been able to digest how impactful the 9/11 events would be on US attitudes to domestic attack, and on my own reaction to being in the vicinity of such a disaster. I used exercise and fresh air, running up into Central Park again and around the lake.

Wall Street did not open again until 17 September, with the subway opening on 21 September. The 2001 New York City mayoral election was postponed, and curiously Rudy Giuliani, who could not run in these elections because he had served term limits from 1994 to 2001, became the main face of the public news. President George W. Bush was transported to a secure location on Air Force One. Amtrak initially closed, then increased passenger capacity to deal with the loss of flight passenger options.

There were real fears for Muslim individuals, businesses and groups as 'Islamophobia' spread in response to the attacks. It was horrible to see the boarded-up businesses, and irrational violence towards Muslim groups for what had been a targeted and sophisticated operation by a specific terrorist faction. As well as grief, there was huge anger on the New York streets that grew quickly across America.

The Islamophobia was shocking to witness and directly related to a sense of outrage at the scale and ambition of the attacks. There was both a defiance and a callousness to carrying on with everyday life but no one was unaffected. It remains one of those global media moments, like the outbreak of wars, death of great stars and natural disasters where everyone remembers where they were when they first heard the news. Most New Yorkers had thought their safety inalienable. The ferocity of the xenophobia that followed was partly because that certainty had been removed.

Within a couple of days, I was able to call Simon; then my Dad; and then other family members from a payphone in one of the museums that had opened to inspire morale, and offer reflection in response to the situation. In the days that followed, I was able to visit most of the art galleries and museums that provided important spaces for communication and fellowship. Dad sounded relieved, but in a stiff upper lip kind of way, as he had served in, and survived, World War Two. I knew he didn't want me to be frightened, and I wasn't. At no time did I fear for my safety in New York. If anything, my dominant instinct was curiosity.

Simon reported that the factory where he was working was being very good in allowing him to use the fax machine to send money to the hotel, allowing me to stay there for more nights. I never felt I would be displaced. The days passed in a mix of extra slow time, when things began to open up sluggishly and with a sense of torpor, and shock in the miracle of everyday life, and searching for a flight home. We couldn't locate Virgin customer service by phone, either in the UK or US, so Simon sent me their street address and I walked there. The queues tailed around the block. Just over a week after I had arrived, I was able to board a flight, sip my G&T, and come home.

The overall experience of being so close to violence, but not actually in any danger, was oddly dislocating. The trip also had a triggering legacy, as I had personally been shocked by bereavement in both 2000 and 2001. I had attended the funeral of a friend aged just 30 just a few weeks before I flew out to New York. Loved ones seemed to be continually falling like Autumn leaves. Could everyone please stop dying?

The images of the falling people in New York were shown on a loop, over and over again, on the day of the destruction, and for days after played in my mind, long after I wasn't watching television. The long-term legacy of 9/11 for me would be the fear of falling from a great height; not so much being at heights themselves, but the fear of falling. This has become worse and worse with age as my own balance deteriorates and sense of my own mortality accelerates. I have only to watch something, anything, with Tom Cruise in it and I virtually have to lie on the floor to make sure I am alright. There are bits of the Bond film *Skyfall* I still haven't watched because of the vertiginous outdoor stunts. You get the idea.

A revolving restaurant though is not something I am ever going to give up, even when it has a glass elevator, like the Skylon Tower in Niagara Falls. Once I am up, and the height just doesn't seem real, I am fine.

My uncle had left me a very small gift in his will with which I had bought a summerhouse for the garden before I left for New York. Simon's Dad had overseen the concrete base being put in while I was away. There was a little Welcome Home banner over the base when I walked in the house. Everyone was sure I was coming home. And I did.

I had managed to find out absolutely nothing about the Women's United Soccer Association, other than the location of their offices in Manhattan. The Head of School didn't ask about my welfare, well-being or the state of my research. Soon after, she was head-hunted again to another university. Simon took me off the missing person's list, and I returned to teaching in time for induction week. I had not been savvy enough to take up university travel insurance that must have been on offer, so the financial balance of the trip was funded by Simon.

By then De Montfort University's expansionist policies were reversed and it sold off campuses in Lincoln, Bedford and Milton Keynes, so the Education Studies group I was still leading became part of the Faculty of Arts and Humanities at Leicester. This was great from a travel point of view, and for moving into a department of Humanities where research was taken more seriously than in the School of Education.

But it was not all good news. The Senior Management Team at Leicester somehow decided that my PhD first supervisor Pierre Lanfranchi was surplus to requirements. I still don't understand all the details to this day, so this is a bit hazy. His protégé Matt Taylor, on some kind of a fixed term contract at De Montfort, was given notice, and moved briefly to Portsmouth University. Pierre went on a kind of personal industrial action in response, leaving me effectively without a supervisory team for the PhD. A version of academic musical chairs followed, then Professors Pierre Lanfranchi and Mike Cronin found themselves working together. After four years, Mike moved on to become Academic Director of Boston College Ireland in 2005, but remains great friends with all at the International Centre for Sports History and Culture (ICSHC).

Jeff Hill also took over as Director of the ICSHC in 2001 when Wray Vamplew left for the University of Stirling. Jeff had to read through a final draft of my thesis in view of a somewhat fluid situation which meant I was without full supervision for quite some time. It is worth saying that the Director position of the ICSHC was very politicised. Jeff was unanimously agreed as the right man for the job. He was particularly adept at protecting research time against the Faculty's other priorities; and for being generous, and incisive.

I submitted the thesis and sat my PhD *viva voce* examination in 2002, with cricket expert and all-round nice guy, Jack Williams, as External Examiner. Jack was kind but the *viva* wasn't a happy experience. Simon cancelled our celebration dinner when I came home, threw up and went to bed. I was the first person in my family to go to university, and the first to get a PhD—hard won achievements. The internal examiner was so unprofessional she told me I had passed my minor amendment corrections a few months later while buying a birthday cake for her daughter in M&S. I was three tills away.

The SARS Pandemic Disrupts Women's World Cup 2003

In 2002, FIFA launched the João Havelange Research Scholarship established in honour of their former President, and I was one of four academics globally to win this newly branded funding. I had already begun to turn my PhD thesis into a book, *A Game for Rough Girls*, thanks to Simon Whitmore at Routledge, which was published in 2003. I continue to be grateful to Simon for his support. A keen runner and great asset to the academic publishing community, Simon Whitmore took a risk on me in 2002, for which I remain grateful more than 20 years on.

RADICALISED BY FIFA

I was awarded two Havelange Research scholarships in 2002 and 2003, into the international connectivity of the global women's football community at the time. This eventually found its way into another monograph, *A Beautiful Game*, released in 2007, with Berg. So, by the time of the second Los Angeles Women's World Cup, I would have my PhD, a research monograph and a promotion to Principal Lecturer secured—as well as prestigious international research funding. So, I was a lot clearer about the objectives and scope of the research, but also for the first time actually had some resources to carry out the work, instead of self-funding.

The João Havelange Research Scholarship is no longer available. The Brazilian stepped down from his role in 1998 in the election which saw Blatter come to power, but was already unpopular in 1994. Beyond his senior position at the International Olympic Committee, Havelange was recognised for his leadership of the Fédération Internationale de Football Association for 24 years from 1972, a term exceeded only by Jules Rimet who served 33 years. He was actually a double Olympian, having swam in 1936 and played water polo in 1952, a remarkable achievement. But he is now widely regarded as the initiator of the pursuit of profit over football development, especially in his connections with the Adidas company.

Blatter was in many ways Havelange's protégé, and worked closely with Horst Dassler at ISL. The work of journalists and broadcasters like Andrew Jennings can enlighten readers further on these and related issues, particularly the role of Seb Coe as Head of the FIFA Ethics Committee 2006 to 2008, when apparently nothing particularly serious happened to require his intervention.

I was not at the Los Angeles World Cup in October 2003 as a guest of FIFA, although I did attend some of the conferences and medical events, as I had the Havelange FIFA research funding. My experience was very different but the landscape had also changed. By the time of the hastily arranged 'hangover' 2003 Women's World Cup in Los Angeles the WUSA league would be gone. The WUSA league suspended operations on 15 September 2003, shortly after the end of its third season, with estimated losses of around $100 million.

In early May 2002, Michel Zen-Ruffinen, assisted by Doris Valasek, presented a dossier to the FIFA Executive Committee alleging on several counts that Sepp Blatter had conducted himself in a less than ethical manner. As Secretary General, a lawyer and a respected referee, Zen-Ruffinen was also Blatter's right-hand man whom he had described as being 'like a son.' Zen-Ruffinen's 21-page dossier was supported by 300 pages of internal FIFA HQ documented evidence, and he distributed it to all 24 members of the all-male executive committee.

Zen-Ruffinen must have been aware of the risk in making the allegations just before Blatter went on to win another FIFA Presidential election on 29 May 2002 by 139 votes to 56 over Cameroon's Issa Hayatou. Although legal action in Swiss courts was threatened against Blatter, the Executive Committee members instead decided that he could respond to the allegations in writing. In the intervening period, Zen-Ruffinen, who Blatter now referred to as 'Mr Clean' was relieved of his contractual responsibilities, but required to organise the Korea/Japan Men's World Cup until 4 July 2002. Urs Linsi succeeded him as Secretary General, until required himself to resign in 2007. The Swiss public prosecutor found no case for Blatter to answer.

The fourth edition of the Women's World Cup was due to be held in Autumn 2003 across four cities in PR China, having been awarded in 2000, beating a bid from Australia. At the time of the 2000 bid award announcement, the Australian Women's Soccer Association (AWSA) was still a separate organisation to Soccer Australia. The shock defeat, since women's football at the Sydney Olympic Games had been relatively successful, was thought to hasten a merger between the men's and women's administrations. The wildly successful Sydney Olympic Games had seen the debut of both Australia and Nigeria, firsts for Oceania and Africa, and the first time that all six confederations had been present at an Olympic tournament of eight national teams for women.

As we all know, Australia had a very healthy haul of domestic gold medals in Sydney, but the host women's football team failed to get out of the group stages, indicating a gulf in tournament preparation. Brazil came second to Germany in the group stages, and were then defeated by them in the third-place playoff match to the despair of Sissi, Pretinha and Formiga. China was eliminated in the group of death, although Sun Wen finished top scorer of the tournament with four goals. In a heavily Eurocentric tournament, Sweden was eliminated in the groups stages before Norway defeated the USA 3–2 in front of a crowd of 21,000.

Bidding in 1998, AWSA couldn't fathom the award of the World Cup to China two years later, especially after a successful Sydney Olympic Games, even though there had been very little enthusiasm, and no comparable bid from the Chinese FA. Blatter, however, wanted the Women's World Cup to return to Asia as part of the diplomacy of integrating China into world football. However, the first known cases of severe acute respiratory syndrome (SARS) occurred in November 2002, and spread to the 2002–2004 SARS outbreak, killing at least 774 people worldwide. This particularly affected Guangdong province. Some debated if the 2003 event would be held at all. The solution was to return to the US. A 16-team tournament was hastily put together, only three months before kick-off, ahead of a bid from Sweden. The Fall sporting schedule of the male-dominated US media had already highlighted traditional favourites such as baseball and American football. Meanwhile PR China was automatically handed the 2007 Women's World Cup and $1 million in compensation for organising costs already incurred.

The lie of progress in women's sports was shown in 2003, compared with 1999.

There wasn't even a mascot in 2003. No one at FIFA could be bothered to concoct one. Thirty-two matches, organised as 15 double-headers, except for third place and the final, were scheduled for minor venues. Instead of the Rose Bowl, fans were encouraged to go to Home Depot Centre, Carson for the final, a 27,000-seat capacity venue on the campus of California State University. Portland had new grass and more bleachers added. Venues on the West Coast included Foxborough, Philadelphia, Columbus and Washington. Giants Stadium, New York, could not host due to the impossibility of moving existing fixtures, and in all airports and stadiums, new security measures were in place after 9/11.

Argentina, France and South Korea made their Women's World Cup debuts in 2003, while China retained their place in the 16 by dint of being the original hosts. Controversially for historians, FIFA announced its Women's World Rankings which retrospectively calculated the outcome of 3,000 'official' fixtures dating back to 1971, and on which basis determined seeded groups going forward. A work of fiction, indeed, but an influential one.

Germany, and specifically striker Birgit Prinz were dominant in 2003. With seven goals she won the Golden Boot and the Golden Ball. Goalkeeper Silke Rottenberg won the Golden Gloves. Sonia Denoncourt, who had been so friendly in 1999, refereed the 3–0 shock defeat of the USA on 5 October 2003 in the semi-finals. After a Kerstin Garefrekes goal at 15 minutes, Germany just held on and on, the USA unable to break their defence, with Maren Meinert scoring again in the 91st minute, and inevitably Prinz in the 93rd minute. Even with powerhouse Abby Wambach backing up Hamm, Foudy, Lilly, Parlow and Boxx, and coached by April Heinrichs, Tina Theune led Germany to their inaugural victory as the first female coach to take the title. Germany beat Marika Domanski-Lyfors coached Sweden 2–1, after Hanna Ljungberg had initially taken the Scandinavians ahead just before half time.

Conclusion: Falling for Marta

Simon and I had a lovely time at the finals of what was such an underwhelming tournament, largely for reasons that really had nothing to do with the football. I got lots of professional contacts and did some wonderful research that I really enjoyed. For instance, in 2003, I first met sports medicine practitioner, Jiří Dvořák, at the FIFA symposium for Women's World Cup 2003, when he was looking for extant work on female soccer players' incidence of injury. A spinal neurologist by medical specialty, his work did not translate to biomechanics, especially of the female athletes. To that point much of his collaborative work focussed on the problems of defining anterior cruciate ligament (ACL) injuries and only looked at male youth players. There remain huge problems defining contact and non-contact ACL injuries, with many of the world's finest football players suffering a contact injury only for days, weeks, months later for it to end in a non-contact ACL injury.

The FIFA Medical Assessment and Research Centre (F-MARC) had been established during the 1994 Men's World Cup in the US. Thereafter led by Dvořák's leadership at FIFA, and F-MARC , studies placed an undue emphasis on collecting data via web-based methods, and in a youth-based, and US context. What we needed were elite studies, and I knew of several ex-England players who had had multiple ACL injuries. Age, menstrual cycle, neuro-muscular factors, body mass, mental health, access to recovery and injury prevention were all key issues—wider factors were rarely considered, or the player's journey.

I felt after talking twice with him in 2003 that many of the F-MARC interpretations offered for ACL injuries in women's football relied upon biological determinism (men's knees, hips, or whatever, are different from women's knees, hips, or whatever) regardless of the variance in male somatotypes and female body types. Peter Crouch is a very different-sized striker to Lionel Messi. Why essentialise the genders? I've carried on this work and how constructed narratives shape the collection of supposedly independent scientific data ever since. Sports medicine was not very well-developed at this time, and remained a mainly male academic field. The paucity of ACL injury research in women's football remains an issue. Jiří seemed very nice though.

Simon's relatives made it down to visit us, and we dined on the Queen Mary with them and went to the Aquarium. We had dinner with someone who used to work for us in the bar and who was now based in LA as a sound specialist, having worked in the US since 1998. We saw a very jetlagged Paul Weller play an acoustic set at the House of Blues with Gem Archer to about 500 people, and we joined Salsa Sunday on the Queen Mary with Jonny Polanco and his band. The main act, a Korean Elvis tribute artist, wanted to be our teddy bear.

My £25 M&S leopard print bikini was still going strong six years after it was purchased and I put it to good use swimming laps in the pool at The Standard Hotel. A seemingly innocuous phrase, but no one swam on the rooftop pooldeck at The Standard. Instead people got their hair and makeup done to be seen sitting languorously by the water. Good for the light apparently. There may be a casting agent. It was the sort of place where the receptionist by day doubled up as a DJ from 5 pm in a plexi-glass booth and there were no chairs, just beanbags or opportunities to lean on things. It was not intended as a place for those with sciatica or lower lumbar issues. To swim or not to swim, that was the question. By now my High Street two piece's cost of use per plunge was down to pennies. Such very good value M&S. So up and down I would lap. The water quality was lovely and the people-watching world-class. The hotel closed permanently in January 2022, not really recovering from the pandemic. So I guess the aquatic etiquette doesn't matter one way or the other now.

RADICALISED BY FIFA

Why mention all this tourism? Because 2003 was such a hangover World Cup, such an anti-climax compared with 1999, especially after the USA had departed and the WUSA league folded, that FIFA did not even bother to dignify proceedings. US Soccer struggled to host under difficult circumstances, but the naysayers appeared to have been proven right. Even four years after a zinger of a storyline, the crowds would not come in sufficient numbers, the media had other news, and there were other self-fulfilling prophecies. Never mind the systemic lack of funding, long-term planning or actual political will to place women centre stage. Even someone as invested as I didn't mainly go for the football. Average crowds were 21,000, much as they had been at the Sydney Olympics in 2000, and about 700,000 tickets reportedly sold, though how many people actually made it into the stadia remains unclear.

The declinist narratives continued. At the Athens Olympic Games of 2004, crowds averaged just 10,000 for a 10-team tournament in which Brazil's Cristiane matched Birgit Prinz for the Golden Boot, both on five goals. The USA were able to reply to Germany with a gold medal, won over Brazil in the final 2–1, with the Europeans in bronze medal position. Abby Wambach sealed her place in history with her performance. The great Nigerian playmaker, Mercy Akide, hung up her boots, as did China's Sun Wen, along with US gold medal winners Joy Fawcett, Julie Foudy, Brandi Chastain, and Mia Hamm. April Heinrichs, who had lifted the first ever Women's World Cup in 1991 as US captain won an Olympic gold medal as their coach, a unique double to that point.

Returning home from LA in 2003, I was deep into teaching Education Studies, completing the funded research project, and planning more publications. I was also falling out of love with organising local football leagues, clubs and so forth, and stood down from a lot of committees. There was meant to be a female coach mentoring scheme, which I joined, and did a couple of seasons with Loughborough University women's second team for elite experience, and Nottingham Forest FC Girls' academy to get some youth elite coaching in. By 2003, this scheme began to run out of money, and for want of time and resources, my coaching career stalled. Academia seemed a more negotiable bet. The actual football wasn't really getting me anywhere and was more a drain than a reward. I retired aged 40 while my knees were in good enough shape to enter the London Marathon (although I didn't get in that year but in the 25th edition. My young niece saw the commemorative 25th medal and thought that was my placing in the whole London Marathon. I didn't disabuse her.) Sporting challenges were sadly not as thrilling as chasing a ball with your mates, but kept me fit. I also had new care responsibilities due to family bereavement, so time was short.

I had been helped during the period of FIFA funding with language training so that I had a passable proficiency of French, Italian and Spanish to access archival data in different forms and make my own translations. However, in 2004 when I had travelled to Mexico in trying to explore some issues that were covered in more detail later in

THE HANGOVER WORLD CUP, 2003

Brenda Elsey and Josh Nadel's excellent book *Futbolera*, I found the national association in Mexico impenetrable. While I was able to access some of the community groups and individuals working in women's football in Mexico City, where I spent two weeks doing research, it was impossible to access the written record and speak to FA officials. It was a forewarning of the problems we knew were in place in the Mexican federation in regards to bad governance, and the effects that has on athlete welfare—especially female players. Those who became aware of this in 2023, with the Spanish federation after winning the Women's World Cup, were way behind what we knew was happening at the turn of the new century and shortly afterwards.

But the gloom of the 2003 hangover World Cup contained a nugget of treasure. And what a prize! In what seemed like a time of endings, long shadows, and goodbyes I was delighted on the 21 September 2003 to see someone who would become one of my football heroes play for the first time.

Although Juliana was the captain and Kátia the star striker amidst the galaxy line-up of Andréia, Formiga, Cristiane, (and others requiring only one name), the player who caught my attention with a 14th minute penalty over the Republic of Korea, in an eventual 3-0 win, was Marta. She was just seventeen years of age. Marta scored again against Norway in a 4-1 win over the previous world champions in a Brazil side full of confidence and strategy. Although they drew 1-1 with France in the group stages, Brazil topped group B over Norway France, and South Korea. Although Brazil eventually lost 2-1 to Sweden in the quarters, Marta was the one who drew a penalty from the keeper, and strode forward in the 44th minute to score the consolation goal from the spot.

Marta Vieira da Silva. Born in February 1986, and playing with the senior side since 2002, the lack of public awareness of how great a player Marta was, and is, somehow has made being a connoisseur of her career even more special, all the while wishing she could have been more celebrated and famous. It would have been nearly impossible for me, in April 2003 to see her Copa América matches, or the Pan American Games in August. But because of the 2003 Women's World Cup, however miserly in its ambitions, lowly in status, and mean in fan-experience, I got to see Marta and begin to follow her career. That has been a joy as golden as I have ever had from football.

How the three-pronged attack of Marta, Cristiane, and Formiga transformed the Brazilian women's football team at this time has received little critical attention outside of Brazil. Sissi now has her own documentary directed by Ana Rieper, written by Olga Bagatini and Paulo Silva Junior. I personally am here for the technicolour, star-studded cinematic opus that deserves to tell Marta's story as the lead of this trident. When Marta wins, we all win. When Marta cries...

There had been a growing antipathy to women's football in Brazil in the 1930s, as more teams grew. In 1941 sports like football, rugby, wrestling and others were banned for women by law so that they could have more babies, (yes, really) and remained in place, in the case of football, until 1981. There was football to be found, played by women and girls—but as an underground activity for 40 years. When developed, particularly from 1983 onwards the 'Futbolera', a type of woman who would play football, seemed to be a new thing when it was more visible, as Brenda Elsey and Josh Nadel's brilliant book of that title reminds us.

Three years later Marta was born, just as women's clubs were being formed more widely. For instance, the Clube Atlético Indiano, was organised by the sister of José María Marin, who went on to lead the Confederação Brasileira de Futebol (Brazilian Football Confederation), and who would later be charged in the 2015 FIFA scandal.

So, when in 1988 the Brazil women's national team went to the International Women's Football Tournament, organised by FIFA in China over 12 days in June, it was as the leading South American country which had, so far as its own governing body was concerned, only been playing football for seven years. Having lost to Australia 1-0, and beaten a strong Norwegian side 2-1, Brazil served Thailand a 9-0 defeat to finish top of their group. Having progressed 2-1 past The Netherlands, thanks to goals from Cebola and Sissi, and lost 2-1 to Norway in the semi-finals, Brazil won the third place playoff against China on penalties. This Norway rivalry has been a presiding confrontation, often essentialised by commentators as Scandinavian ice and Latina heat, but that does a disservice to both sides.

Brazil was then eliminated in the group stages of the 1991 Women's World Cup. And again in 1995. But in 1996 they finished fourth in their first Olympic competition. So, their third place at the 1999 World Cup was an enormous achievement, as has been described. Sissi's wonder goal in 1999, and winning the Golden Boot award, have been hidden largely from history as she never played a World Cup match again. A fourth place at the Sydney Olympics confirmed that Brazil was one of the world's best teams in 2000. Then there was the 4-1 defeat of Norway in 2003, and holding a very strong France side to a 1-1 draw, combined with a 3-0 win over South Korea. Sweden, who beat them in the quarters 2-1 would make it all the way to the 2003 World Cup final. At the final of the 2004 Olympic Games in Athens, the USA only beat Brazil in the 112th minute of added extra time, 2-1, thanks to Abby Wambach.

My point is, when Marta sat disconsolately in the golden ticker tape of the World Cup in China 2007, a runner-up rather than a winner, the trajectory had been to place her team in the final on a number of occasions since I first saw her play in 2003. She was by 2007 both the Golden Ball winner, and the Golden Boot, with seven goals. She would lead Brazil again in the Beijing Olympics of 2008 to glide 2-1 past Norway, and a thumping 4-1 despatch of Germany in which Prinz could only score a consolation. Then, heartbreakingly in added extra time of the final against Pia Sundhage's USA team, Carli Lloyd scored a single goal to which Marta could find no reply.

It had been the fourth consecutive Olympic semi-final for Brazil and their third consecutive final of an Olympic or World Cup tournament. Marta and the Brazil team would leave the field in tears. Sissi was incredible in 1999. Cristiane has had arguably a larger influence on the team, just not such an effect on me. Formiga is impossible to define in terms of a position because she is *everywhere*, all the time. What Marta, as talisman, changed was an expectation of being there, or thereabouts of winning the thing. The outcome of a loss while watching Marta play is one of those football experiences which make us resent the tournament context, because why should there be losers?

Unlike pre-rehearsed drama, the fluidity of football is about the unrepeatable moment and consequently human. Ultimately a romantic idea, each second Marta plays is about what is humanly possible. It is as difficult to write about great football as it is about dance, or music, or beautiful scenery. A present and near future that can almost be grasped, but in that act of distillation, missed.

When Marta plays there is not just the possibility, but the distinct probability of greatness. It's fine if Germany or the US, or whoever, wins—but then we lose the transcendental moment, because Marta is art. Larger than us, yet amongst us. For a split second in time, her skill, anticipation and intention coalesce in a single moment of control, (a strike, a pass, a dummy), and then dissolve.

Gone.

CHAPTER III
THE INVISIBLE WORLD CUP, 2007
Introduction:
Lunch with Sir Bobby and Sepp Blatter

The next time I met Sir Bobby Charlton was on my turf in 2005, but I was so mortified by the occasion that I could not eat my lunch. A very rare occurrence.

De Montfort University gave Sepp Blatter an honorary Doctorate in Arts and Humanities at a special ceremony in 2005, and Sir Bobby was the guest of honour. Someone had floated the idea in 2004, and it had percolated. There was a rash of celebrity honorary doctoral awards and a connection with FIFA was a unique selling point for an ex-polytechnic, so it perhaps seemed too good an opportunity to miss. To deliberately mix a metaphor, as own goals go, it was the gift that kept on giving.

The current Dean of Humanities at De Montfort at the time of the Blatter award was a football fan. He was once known to attend a University of Leicester versus De Montfort University Varsity match in his trademark headgear, only for the opposition supporters to begin rowdy choruses of, 'Who is the twat in the hat?' It was rumoured that some staff and students from De Montfort joined in. I couldn't possibly comment.

Given my experiences in relation to Michel Zen-Ruffinen and Doris Valasek between 1998 and 2002 I was surprised by Blatter's conferment, to say the least. The citation read out by the Vice Chancellor at the ceremony said that the university had made the award to Blatter because: 'he is forthright, visionary, ethical and, above all, professional… It is these qualities which have driven the development of the sport to the international position it holds today.' Little wonder that I felt queasy even without attending the conferral of the degree itself.

But at the lunch afterwards seated on the table with Sir Bobby, which was a very generous gesture by my colleagues as I was still leading Education Studies at the time, it seemed that the Vice Chancellor had been briefed that somehow the England and Manchester United stalwart had a strong Leicester City connection, and had possibly played for the team.

Sir Bobby's Leicester City career was airily being cast as a possibility for quite some time. I grew increasingly embarrassed, and could not stomach my food. I wished, quite frankly, that I could pass out. Where's oblivion when you need it? Given the impending 2006 Men's World Cup in Germany, and the doomed England bid, Sir Bobby attending as Blatter's special guest must have already been difficult for him so maybe he didn't notice the fictitious connection with Leicester, or my discomfort. Sir Bobby went on to become one of the course patrons for the FIFA MA. A good choice.

I often wonder what those involved made of all this in 2015 when the university revoked Blatter's degree. It did so quietly and with only a flurry in the press. I did hear that Blatter had written to the Vice Chancellor in 2015 begging that his Doctorate would not be revoked, but I have no documentary proof. To be fair to De Montfort, the Oxford Union website still lists its invited 'thinkers and influencers' in the following order, 'Malala Yousafzai, Sepp Blatter, Nancy Pelosi' so there is that.

Shortly after the Blatter Doctorate debacle, multilingual Kevin Tallec Marston who had graduated the FIFA MA programme in the 2003 session went to work for CIES and co-ordinate the academic FIFA MA programme as a whole. I continued to work with Kevin as second supervisor on his PhD until 2013 when he completed it, and he has since published widely while at CIES, including most recently on women's football in Asia. He's a lovely person, a great academic and has helped me personally on a number of occasions.

A second major event for my career in 2005 was when the FA hosted the Women's Euro competitions for the first time. Previously the Women's Football Association (WFA) had held the final of its predecessor tournament, the European Competition for Representative Women's Teams, at Luton Town in 1984 in a two-legged defeat to Sweden on penalties which became known as the 'Battle of Kenilworth Bog' because of the state of the pitch.

In 2005, the FA would host the whole thing in 15 matches held from 5 June to 19 June, in five venues across Lancashire, and Cheshire. England were a poor side as hosts, beating only Finland 3–2, and losing to both Sweden and Norway in the group stages. The average attendance was under 8,000 spectators per game. As the old joke goes, Germany won. In fact, the 3–1 win over Norway was their fourth consecutive win in the Women's Euros history, plus their two European Competition for Representative Women's Teams titles. The FA judged the tournament a success, even though they had paid a consultant to draw up a legacy assessment which reported that there wouldn't be much of one. He was right. Media interest certainly grew by a small margin in women's football during 2005, but the benefit was limited in geographical scope and short-lived.

I gave keynotes at the University of Central Lancashire International Football Institute (IFI) led by the wonderful Professor John Hughson and with Dr Jessica Macbeth, who wrote an important PhD on the history of women's football in Scotland, her mother having also played for the England team, Fodens, in Sandbach. Dr Kevin Moore, founding Director and CEO of the project to set up the National Football

Museum in Preston, England in 1997, was also associated with the IFI. The permanent home of the FIFA Collection, this £15 million National Football Museum opened in 2001 and attracted over 100,000 visitors each year in Preston, before moving to Manchester in 2010.

Things changed somewhat in 2006 when a colleague left, creating an opportunity for a Senior Research Fellow in the International Centre for Sport History and Culture which was still led by Jeff Hill. There had never before been a woman in post in the ICSHC, let alone full time. There hadn't been a woman in the History department at De Montfort until this point, so I knew this was risky. As a Principal lecturer anyway, the salary was much the same, but being a Senior Research Fellow would facilitate more research time and access to PhD supervision that I was unlikely to get in Education Studies. It is said women often don't apply for jobs if they don't meet every criterion, and men apply if they meet some of the job description. I thought on balance it could be a bit embarrassing if I wasn't short-listed, as my first degree and MA were in English, not in history, but why not?

Having been asked to contribute to the History submission for the Research Assessment Exercise (RAE) of 2008 due to having one book and three longish articles published; plus two external FIFA grants; sustained internal funding; and another book in progress, I felt I'd enough behind me to apply. The primary purpose of RAE 2008 was to produce quality profiles for each submission of research activity under broad subject headings, in this case—History. We didn't have enough of a research culture then to enter for Education Studies. The results were used by the four UK funding bodies to determine the level of funding for research, based on good value for money. I had a better RAE profile personally than many of the men being entered in the History submission at Leicester in 2008, or, to put it bluntly, I would not have been invited to have my work assessed. A lot of the guys watched daytime television and could always tell the scores of the cricket, darts or what have you. I didn't have that luxury. Being submitted for the RAE was also an indicator of research quality through peer review.

If I didn't get the Senior Research Fellowship, I really loved the Education Studies students and their sense of purpose anyway, even if being Subject Leader was a complete pain due to various staffing issues. As an example of how amazing these students were: I ran twilight Access to Higher Education courses, for those without qualifications to get into university. Two mature students on one course wanted to get into education professionally as they both had children and found the system was not working for them. Having passed the Access course, they both did extremely well on their Education Studies degree, completing it part-time, and found employment, one as an educational psychologist and one working with children with special educational needs. At least one of them continued to an MA. It felt like a huge privilege working with such students.

There were lots of examples like this as our intake trebled and diversified. I had been awarded small pots of internal funding, such as £6,000 for me to digitise the archives of Bedford College, a 19th century physical education establishment for women, which predated the Bedford Campus of De Montfort University. I also won external funding for pedagogical development. ESCalate, The Education Studies subject centre, funded a £5,000 project to embed and evaluate reflective practice in undergraduate employability modules. It was incredibly rewarding work in Education Studies. But juggling this degree of pastoral care and teaching with doing any level of detailed research was tough.

I got the post of Senior Research Fellow joining the ICSHC at the same time as Pippa Virdee completed her PhD at Coventry University and joined the De Montfort History department. So, there was a year when Jeff Hill was Centre Director that was joyful in which to work. There were two women in what had been an all-male History department to that point. Virdee's interests were British India: 1857-1947 and post-colonial history of India, Pakistan and Bangladesh. Furthermore, from October 2006 to August 2009 Daphné Bolz joined the ICSHC as EU Research Fellow, to progress her work on Olympic research. This was not a permanent full-time position but was a new form of prestigious funding, and as such Daphné was accorded a good deal of respect. She was also fluent in several languages, working across a range of projects with European partners. Daphné is quietly impressive, and very rigorous in her work. We had a lovely time in the oddly amateurish archives of the British Olympic Association (BOA) in London conducting our research, although the terraced house in which the documents were kept at that time flooded regularly.

London was awarded the 2012 Summer Olympic Games on 5 July 2005, and there was an expectation that the Olympic Games would feature more in our publications, and new teaching loads. I was also working through the book manuscript for my FIFA-funded research which ended up as A Beautiful Game with Berg.

In helping understand Olympic history, it was great to see how Daphné approached her archival work, which I had done before only in isolation at the FIFA archives in Zurich. Having covered the history of football for some time now, the whole literature on Olympism was huge, and new. So, it was very jolly to have train journeys with Daphné to chat about different aspects, and, if she wasn't already impressive enough, she found she was expecting her first child, so her resilience was all the more awe-inspiring.

I had taken over with Dilwyn Porter the MA Sport History and Culture as course leader in 2006, so I was trying to move from Education Studies undergraduate teaching to postgraduate history teaching. It was very different. History seemed less socially engaged than Education Studies, and much more male in its curriculum and in its ethos. Over 60% of full-time permanent posts in UK academic history departments today are held by men. Back in 2006, things were worse. I later learned this was a subject of an academic study project. While in the UK there is a small majority of female students in history at A-level, undergraduate level, and on taught postgraduate programmes, women remain underrepresented at more senior levels. Just 40% of academic staff in history are women, and only 26% of history Professors are female. Female historians are also more likely to be in temporary, fixed-term, or part-time posts.

Many women historians stall in mid-career, and at all levels report gender inequality in conference programming, keynote lectures, publishing, and teaching. Try then specialising in sport. I cannot tell you the number of times I casually dropped into conversation that I was married on FA Cup final day 1986, only to have a male student, colleague, or conference delegate try and correct me as to who played and what was the score. The male entitlement is *extraordinary*. Toxicity takes many forms, both subtle and overt.

This would be my career for the next 10 years. If I was going to make the promotion to Reader, then Professor, it was going to mean a lot of evenings, weekends and annual leave swallowed up in work. Why are there so few women professors? Because there is a lack of institutional will, in spite of campaigns like Athena Swan. But I am relatively entitled. If we look through an intersectional feminist lense at the issue—if you are a black, Asian or a non-European woman, trans, have a disability, or are diverse in terms of sexuality, that 26% Professorial figure reduces considerably. Similarly for non-white males, and LGBTQ+ male identities History is very conservative. History of Sport is moreso hostile than the broader occupational culture. Having taught history of education modules, including gender in HE, I knew I had my work cut out. Bring it on. I always preferred literature anyways.

Because of my Education Studies background I was able to make curriculum changes that placed the ICSHC on a surer financial footing. We changed the mode of delivery of the MA Sport History to a blended learning environment of in-person and online pedagogy but this meant between 2006 and 2008 that the whole course had to be re-written for an online offering. The IT system by which this was to be delivered was new to the university, so that was particularly challenging. There was a whole literature to assimilate ahead of those curriculum changes from the Olympics and cricket, to tennis, rugby codes and so forth. The university was not used to teaching by distance learning, but as a graduate of the Open University and with some curriculum development experience, I could envisage how we could change the way the MA was taught.

It was time-consuming, fraught with committee-work, and misunderstood. The MA would ultimately prove very successful, and we became victims of our own success in terms of turning a course which had two or three students annually into one which recruited 18 to 20 people of all kinds, but that was in the future.

THE INVISIBLE WORLD CUP, 2007

The MA became the main pipeline of PhD students into the Centre, and we literally 'grew our own' postgraduate cohorts and Doctoral numbers. I took over as sole course leader in 2008, and I have to say the exam boards were some of my all-time favourite days in academia. Not just the sense of helping people to change their lives but also our External Examiner, Roger Munting, was extremely professional, while also seemingly out of a Tennessee Williams play.

It helped that it was always summer of course, but Roger would arrive resplendent in a cream linen suit, with elegant manners and a keen interest in the students' welfare and work.

I was strict in holding the exam boards for one hour only from 11 to 12 when we would retire for lunch. This was not a small undertaking because at University M level, every student is important and treated as an individual. The progression of each one was discussed in turn, and then Roger would make some suggestions about how we could improve across the whole cohort. I was sorry not to be able to offer something cold and refreshing on a veranda, but the local Bistro Pierre sufficed and we would talk shop, having a jolly time.

With all this going on, there was no way personally or professionally that I would make the 2007 Women's World Cup in PR China which was held between 10 and 30 September, just as most universities induct new students, known as 'Freshers'. I also had care responsibilities for a vulnerable older relative which involved frequent trips to hospital, and, although I could have asked someone else to stand in, I am glad now of the decisions I made. Sitting in hospital waiting rooms actually proved quite useful for following world cup matches between appointments. You take joy where you can in the midst of misery.

Sixteen teams were represented at Women's World Cup 2007, from five confederations, and unlike 1991, five cities were used as hosts, moving outside Guangzhou for the first time. These included Tianjin, Wuhan, Hangzhou, Chengdu, and Shanghai. So, I followed and covered it from a distance as much as I was able. I watched a lot on my laptop while in hospital waiting rooms, with the sound turned down. To most people though the Women's World Cup in China in 2007 was invisible. While it was clearly a FIFA priority to use Women's World Cups to develop greater connection with Beijing, it didn't make sense from a fan perspective. But it was also assumed that there wasn't really a fan market for women's football.

The media diet was so different that not even the BBC covered basic aspects, the time difference was a big factor, and social media was only 10 years old. The Chinese-language channel CCTV-5, broadcast over the internet via TVU Networks but this was hit and miss to access. If you hadn't set up on Six Degrees, Friendster, or MySpace, then there was very limited connectivity. Facebook, founded in 2004, was not that relevant in the UK at the time. I also didn't have any direct funding to go to China, and we were renovating the old house that we had bought. In being unable to go in person, I missed seeing with my own eyes the world's greatest woman player, one of the global icons of 21st century football, at her finest. Regrets, I have a few…

Marta's World Cup

Spoiler alert: Marta practically won the 2007 World Cup for Brazil single-handedly. Golden Ball. Golden Boot. With seven goals. There are other historical interpretations available. Just not in this book. Cristiane may feel that this is harsh, and I declare my bias. In fact, the contribution of Cristiane and Formiga with Marta was the defining genius of this Brazil team and for balance it's important to say that. It made the dismissive treatment by Pia Sundhage of Cristiane and Formiga ahead of the 2023 Women's World Cup seem all the more egregious, and I love Pia, as you know.

The Shanghai opener saw Group A opposition Germany beat Argentina 11-0, a record which stood until 2019. Tinajin Olympic Centre stadium and Wuhan stadia had capacities of 60,000 each, with the Yellow Dragon Sports Centre in Hangzhou on 50,000, Chengdu 40,000 and Hoingou Stadium Shanghai 33,000. With this the organisers claimed an average crowd of 37,000 fans and an overall attendance of 1.2 million spectators over 32 matches. The latter figure is especially to be treated with caution, as some crowds were recorded as low as 6,000 for USA group games. There were 111 goals, an average of 3.47 per match, scored with the branded Teamgeist football. The matches were also fiercely contested with 77 yellow cards and two sendings off.

For Hope Powell's England team, it was a dramatic change from the last time England qualified in 1995. Drawn in Group A, Kelly Smith scored a brace to draw 2-2 with Japan, before a scoreless draw ruined Germany's otherwise perfect start, followed by a 6-1 victory over Argentina. Scorers were Jill Scott, Fara Williams, two from Kelly Smith and Vicky Exley. To give an idea what a fraught match this was, both Williams and Exley scored from the penalty spot, and Eva González scored both an own goal on nine minutes, and Argentina's only other strike on 60 minutes. Both Fara Williams and Alex Scott received yellow cards, as did Catalina Perez and González. England therefore advanced as Group A runners up with five points behind Germany on seven points, the latter having beat Japan 2-0 after defeating Argentina.

With the USA on fantastic form to win group B, largely due to Abby Wambach's goals, North Korea also progressed having held the US to a 2-2 draw, and a 2-0 win over Nigeria. Sweden defeated North Korea 2-1, but had scored two fewer goals, and so finished third overall in group. Norway led group C on seven points, followed by Australia on five. Even Christine Sinclair could not lift Canada out of third place,

THE INVISIBLE WORLD CUP, 2007

and Ghana lost all their matches.

Only Brazil won their group with the full nine points, three wins from three matches taking Group D with a 5-0 victory over New Zealand, a 4-0 win over China, and a 1-0 triumph over Denmark. Of the 10 Brazil goals, Marta scored four and Cristiane three. It is worth noting that some group stage games were played on 12, 15 and 20 September. Others were 11, 14 and 17 or 18 September, a schedule of matches that did not allow much time for rest and recovery. There were expected weather problems and domestic cultural reasons for adapting the original schedule, and many games kicked off at midday to facilitate television coverage, but even so the schedule was amateurish and chaotic.

In the quarter finals played over 22 and 23 September, Germany despatched North Korea 3-0, matched by the USA's 3-0 defeat of England; Norway's 1-0 win over China; and, tightest of all, Brazil's 3-2 dismissal of Australia. In the latter match, Formiga had opened the scoring on four minutes, followed by a Marta penalty conversion. Lisa de Vanna drew one back for Australia before half time, and Lauren Colthorpe equalised after the break. Enter the great number 11 Cristiane to score on 75 minutes to send Tom Sermanni's team home. I hope you have noted the balance of that last sentence.

This set up semi-finals where Germany defeated Norway 3-0, led by an unfortunate Norway own goal and strikes from Kerstin Stegemann, and Martina Müller. But Greg Ryan's USA was stunned when Leslie Osborne's 20th-minute own goal was followed by a 27-minute howler from Marta, and further goals from Cristiane and Marta in the second half for a 4-0 win overall. The 79th-minute strike by Marta was played by FIFA in 2023 when announcing a new award in her name to be given to the best strike by a woman player annually.

Six yellow cards were issued in the USA versus Brazil game. This left the USA to take the third place match 4-1 over Norway. Captain Birgit Prinz led Silvia Neid's Germany to a 2-0 win over Brazil in the final, scoring the first goal after half time, before Simone Laudehr sealed the win in the 86th minute. The great keeper Nadine Angerer therefore went the entire tournament without conceding a goal. Meanwhile Marta won both the goal of the tournament for her 79th minute strike against the USA in the semis, and Brazil were voted the most entertaining team.

The winning team were given $1 million, and for the first time in Women's World Cup history, right down to those exiting from the group stages, there was some financial recompense, but a very modest return. Prinz became the first woman to play in three World Cup finals—in 1995, 2003 and 2007. Silvia Neid, who had been Tina Theune-Meyer's assistant in 2003 when Germany had first won the title, showed how investing in elite coach development could bring forward women leaders. Unlike Prinz, this would be Marta's only World Cup final. I can still see her sitting alone disconsolately in the golden ticker tape after the final whistle. She looked like a broken rag doll.

The loneliest person on the planet—so close but so far from the prize.

What an achievement for a women's team ignored, derided and underfunded by the national association. The Brazil players held up a hand-written banner on cardboard, Brazil we need your support. The most famous footballing nation in World Cup history had pretty much left its women's national team to fend for itself, and they had made the final.

Conclusion: The unseen GOAT and disappeared women players

Just 11 months after the 2007 World Cup in China, the Beijing Olympic Games again placed a high-profile international women's tournament in the country. Brazil would again reach the final by dint of outperforming Germany in the group stages, through a superior goal count. Jorge Barcellos remained in post as coach for Brazil for the Beijing Olympic tournament, showing how little the national association cared for its women's team. The two countries tied in a 0–0 draw in their match on 6 August. After defeating Norway 2–1 in the quarterfinals, Brazil beat Germany 4–1 in the semi-finals after Birgit Prinz initially put the world champions ahead. Goals from Formiga, a brace from Cristiane, and Marta took Brazil to the final where it took until the 96th minute for Carli Lloyd to put the US ahead. Hope Solo in goal also had a fantastic final. Very few journalists were talking about this, but as academics we had debated how Brazil could squander the richness of its playing talent with lack of investment.

So, with back-to-back Olympic finals, and a World Cup final, this run by Brazil was quite incredible given the lack of backing from the national association, especially when compared to the likes of Germany and USA. Cristiane won the Golden Boot in both 2004 and 2008 Olympic competitions. The whole thing was a fresh start for the US team under new coach Pia Sundhage and the Olympic gold medal campaign she again matched in 2012. In this sense Sundhage was the first foreign coach to win an Olympic title, it had not been done in a World Cup at that point, although Jill Ellis was an assistant coach to Sundhage at this time.

For Brazil a victory in any of these finals could have proved pivotal domestically, although Marta's achievements were recognised by having her feet imprinted in the Maracanã's Hall of Fame. As one of the greatest of all time (or GOAT), one had to be very curious to witness Marta's greatness.

In terms of my professional life, Arsenal had won the UEFA Women's Cup in the 2006/7 season and I was doing some research on how they viewed this precursor to the Women's Champions League. This was the first and only time a British women's club had taken the title. I was also in London at another conference, this time on the forthcoming Olympic Games, when the 7/7 bombings took place, and felt the panic around the city, unlike my time in New York. There were some concerns that the Olympic Games might be affected in 2012, a worry that was unfounded.

Jeff Hill and I organised an international Sport and Literature conference at De Montfort in 2008, managing to leverage £10,000 funding from the Faculty to bring Mike Oriard over as keynote speaker, and several international guests. Convening a three-day international conference is a major milestone in an academic career—but goodness, this one had a number of challenges.

Iceland practically went into a volcanic meltdown, and bankruptcy, while we were in process. One delegate lost their passport. Twice. Another insisted on booking their own accommodation and obtained a room in a well-known Leicester sex facility. The conference dinner was augmented by a speaker who had invited their friends, who ordered lots of extra bottles of wine before disappearing, and we overspent by £170 on the planned bill. People overslept and were late for their papers. I presented on the rules of Quidditch and Harry Potter. It was a fun couple of days!

I also presented at an international women and sport conference in Finland while the country hosted the 2009 Women's Euros, in which England reached the final for only the second time since 1984. A group of Japanese women joined me in the Helsinki hotel sauna, where, unused to bathing costumes being worn in spas, they tried to relieve me of mine! Back at the football, Germany's Birgit Prinz scored first, and then in quick succession, a goal from Melanie Behringer before Karen Carney responded for England. At three goals to one Kelly Smith was able to score, but then England seemed to lose heart, and lost eventually 6–2. Smith and Eniola Aluko tied for three goals each while Golden Boot winner, Germany's Inka Grings had six. Silvia Neid therefore took her first Euros title as Head Coach having worked with Tina Theune Meyer for almost a decade. There were just 16,000 fans in the Olympic stadium in Helsinki. Unlike the previous England players who had wanted to become coaches, Germany actually had a system in place to mentor and develop their women internationals.

The news of England's 2009 Euros final run hardly registered with the British press, although it would stand as a key date, along with 1984 until it was surpassed in 2022 on a glorious day in July. But there were other heart-rending stories in the world of women's football that reached the newspapers in 2009. Annie Kelly, writing in *The Guardian* covered the murder of one of South Africa's high-profile stars, Eudy Simelane. The violence of the murder—Simelane had been stabbed 25 times, following what was described as a 'corrective' gang rape—was absolutely shocking in a country that would host the 2010 Men's World Cup. That the country did not prioritize policing the increase in rape and assault in the approach to the tournament reflected a wider macho, misogynistic culture, but also one where women's safety was not a day-to-day priority.

Other lesbian players reported being assaulted on their return from training, prompting thoughts about the correlation between playing football and being targeted for their visibility.

A high-profile equal rights activist who lived openly as a lesbian in Kwa-Thema, Simelane had been attacked by men who thought that by assaulting her, she could be 'cured' of her sexuality. The crimes were being ignored by the state although Eudy Simelane's two assailants were eventually jailed.

The idea of being a well-known openly lesbian female football player, and living authentically, remains in many parts of the world so challenging that this murder is sadly not isolated. In October 2018 Marbella Ibarra, the Mexican women's football pioneer, was kidnapped, tortured and killed, her body found wrapped in plastic, dumped in a public place, as Simelane's had been.

Symbolically, the violence of these attacks disputes that a woman has a right to determine how she uses her own body: a long-held contention across religions, societies and cultures. These murders are ultimately an assault on the freedom to be female in the ways that one chooses. There are probably more such stories about which we do not know, and that have not made the international media outlets. But we should keep the names of these women in our thoughts as having paid the ultimate price for being themselves, and playing a sport which they loved. Male commentators new to women's football have pointedly asked at world cup press conferences since 2007 about the sexuality of women players and how they negotiate laws which prohibit gay relationships in society in ways that place the individual in danger. This is not theoretical harm, nor is it a matter of private choice when women are killed for being authentically themselves.

Eudy Simelane, Marbella Ibarra. How many more?

CHAPTER IV
THE 'TIE IT UP WITH A BOW AND GIFT IT' WORLD CUP, 2011
Introduction: Free Lunch

As I sat on the banks of Lake Geneva in July 2009, on the terrace of the cafeteria of the UEFA offices in Nyon, I was enjoying a free lunch, in good company, and basking in summer sunshine. In 2009/10 I won one the of inaugural four UEFA academic research grants, becoming the first academic to win both FIFA and UEFA funding streams, and joined the staff of the European confederation for lunch on that July day, enjoying healthy, nutritious subsidised meals. I sat with the other awardees and we discussed our projects at length. Quite a difference, this lunch, as most time-poor academics in the UK seize a sandwich midday to eat at their desk.

For those not aware of the history of UEFA, the Union of European Football Associations, it is worth pausing to mention the effect that the pugnacious Stan Cullis of Wolverhampton, pioneer of so much sports management and journalism, had on his European counterparts. Cullis, a gifted centre-half, had become England captain aged 22, and at Wolves, under manager Major Frank Buckley, would have had a better playing career had the Second World War not intervened. He then went into management, notably at Wolves, with a talent for self promotion and a pithy soundbite to spare.

Since there had been a long history of Eurocentric-assumed superiority in regards to international football, particularly since the advent of the Fédération Internationale de Football Association (FIFA) in 1904, there had never been a European Football Confederation until 1954. No one had much seen the need, since FIFA had been led by four European Presidents to date: Robert Guérin (1904–6); Daniel Woolfall (1906–18), Jules Rimet (1921–54), and Rodolphe Seeldrayers (1954–55). There had been a number of European international club competitions before, but under the management of Cullis the great Wolverhampton side of 1954 beat Hungarian side, Honved 3–2 under floodlights to be declared by some British newspapers 'Champions of the World'.

As manager of Wolves, the 1954 win over the Honved squad included forward Ferenc Puskás, and several of the Hungarian internationals who had decisively beaten

England twice in 1953. Cullis was in a mood to celebrate. This grated with French journalist and editor, Gabriel Hanot, who opined that Real Madrid would have a greater claim in *L'Equipe*. With that, European club championship football, now better known as the Champions League, was created as much by the newspapers—who knew it would be good for sales—as football governing bodies. A colleague of Hanot, Jacques Ferran wrote the rules, and Jacques Goddet, who had previously promoted the Tour de France, supported the new competition as owner of newspaper, *L'Equipe*. This occasioned for the formation of UEFA on 15 June, 1954 in Basel, Switzerland, with 25 members present and from where more far-reaching European-wide competitions became coordinated.

At the time of being awarded the research grant in 2009, UEFA had 54 members, and now, at the time of writing in 2024, has 55, which is an over-broad definition of Europe involving many transcontinental states. My project was one of the first global attempts to: 1) Look at the status of women's football in each member national UEFA association; 2) Assess different patterns of professionalisation into, and out of, Europe; and 3) Theorize types of female player migration into and out of Europe, looking at donor countries and nodes of inward resettlement, with a chronological model developed of short-, medium-, and long-term migration, with varied levels of cultural engagement. In this I also interviewed key players turned coaches, and investigated the working conditions of players, particularly as the Women's Super League was just about to be launched in England. I was particularly grateful to Kelly Simmons and her team at the FA for interviews on this topic.

The lunch was to welcome the four inaugural grant holders and to set out our body of work for the year. It was hosted primarily by a new head of education and research. He was a very nice guy but didn't have a PhD, let alone publications. In my dealings with the program, I found a profound anti-intellectualism in the UEFA research and education programs. It lacked academic rigour, favouring instead market research. The UEFA archives were exploring how, and in what ways, the collections could be monetised. There was a suggestion that universities would in future pay to subscribe to the holdings, although I am not sure that this went ahead. I was told at the time that the archives would not be open to academic researchers on a free basis from then on, and so it was an urgent schedule to look at all 54-member national associations before losing access to centralised data. But obtaining data on 54 countries in 9 months was no small undertaking, and records were patchy, to say the least.

International research on such a scale is tiring. Between 2002 and 2009 I calculated I had spent the best part of a month in Geneva airport, if all the hours of arrival, departure and delay were consolidated. By the time the London Olympics came round in 2012, it felt like I'd been there for two months solid! The two FIFA grants, 2002-4, presenting the final data sets and negotiating the publication schedule of that work, had

THE 'TIE IT UP WITH A BOW AND GIFT IT' WORLD CUP, 2011

seen me criss-crossing into and out of Geneva airport—at that time more accessible than Zurich by the cheap airlines preferred by university travel agencies. Then slogging three hours by train to the FIFA archives and HQ. Olympic research to the International Olympic Committee (IOC) archives in Lausanne was, thankfully, just an hour by train. I'd found a tiny, odd little hotel where the rooms were only 12 ft across right by the railway station, but spotlessly clean. What with Final project assessments and graduation for the FIFA MA at Neuchatel, the UEFA project, and the fact that there was a 30-year moratorium on Olympic material which was released on a rolling basis upon request, Geneva airport became like a pair of old slippers.

It was a particularly auspicious time to be researching in the UEFA archives, as the confederation prepared to host Germany 2011, Europe's second Women's World Cup only, since Sweden in 1995. The status of women's football had changed during the intervening 16 years, but not so radically as it would by France, 2019. Budgets were still small and the finals tournament for 16 nations was held in a little over three weeks from 26 June to 17 July. But the UEFA connection enabled me to attend various women's football conferences in Switzerland, Women in Sports Law events in Zurich, and a development symposium at FIFA House in the run up to Women's World Cup Germany, 2011.

So, why have I titled this chapter the 'Tie It Up with a Bow and Gift It' World Cup? Because, the currency of World Cup and event bidding had by now included women's events as part of the soft diplomacy. This wasn't new, as I have indicated in FIFA's choice of China in 1991 and 2003 (postponed to 2007), but there were novel nuances. The German Football Association had originally announced its hopes to host the 2011 Women's World Cup on 26 January 2006, with support from Angela Merkel, the German Chancellor. Six nations, including Australia, Canada, France, Germany, Peru and Switzerland submitted bid dossiers by 1 March 2007 to FIFA. Soon after, Switzerland withdrew, citing that a third European bid after France and Germany appeared futile. France then withdrew, as a thank you for Germany's support for their bid to host the men's UEFA Euro 2016, which was successful.

Later Football Australia withdrew their bid soon after entering into a memorandum of understanding in September 2007 with the German FA, led by Franz Beckenbauer who was assisting the Australia bid for the 2018/22 Men's World Cup. Then Peru voluntarily dropped out as well, leaving only Canada and the favourite, Germany, as the remaining candidates. In October 2007, the FIFA Executive Committee assigned the 2011 tournament to Germany, and, at a later date, Canada was awarded the 2015 Women's World Cup.

It is naïve to think that the 'best' country wins a Women's World Cup bid any more than the most outstanding men's bid is successful. Like the French withdrawal in reward for support for a men's Euro in 2016, the Australia bid particularly demonstrated the aspirations of the national association to host the Men's World Cup in 2018 or 2022. Franz Beckenbauer, a FIFA Executive Committee member, and his associates, Fedor Radmann and Andreas Abold, were meant to help Australia obtain the Men's World Cup. But the triumvirate so important to the 2006 Men's World Cup did not assist Australia very much, for reasons outlined in former head of corporate and public affairs for Football Australia (and FIFA whistleblower), Bonita Mersiades' 2018 book, *Whatever It Takes - the Inside Story of the FIFA Way*.

So, Australia's forfeiting the women's tournament bid for 2011 is instructive to remind ourselves that World Cups (men's or women's) are not won by hosts on merit—but more on a variety of political negotiations. In these acts of soft diplomacy, 2011 was tied with a bow and gifted by other national associations to Germany, as each sought to develop their own large event bids. Unlike France where the Men's Euros 2016 were a great success, it was not a happy outcome for Australia, which secured a single vote for the $50 million spent on its 2018/22 Men's World Cup bid—and that vote did not belong to Beckenbauer.

Karla Kick, and Germany 2011

I urge you to look up Karla Kick, the Germany 2011 mascot, online. She is a wide-eyed kitten who plays football for fun. Her head is disproportionately large to her body, in order to accommodate huge eyes, complete with artificial eyelash extensions, a cute pink snub nose, and stripes of the colours of the German national flag on each cheek, like a festival-goer. Looking off to the left in her posters, Karla is punching the air with her left fist/paw in anthropomorphised excitement at the approaching kick-off. Sure, she has on football boots and socks, and a recognisable football strip, but as sexualised mascots of Women's World Cups go, Karla Kick is particularly spooky, and the Disneyfied large-eyed style was to remain a feature of mascots in all future women's events. Even kittens can be sexy if it sells football.

FIFA had considered the prospect of increasing the number of teams in Germany 2011 from 16 to 24, to reflect the game's growing global popularity. But in 2008, the FIFA Executive Committee decided to keep the number of participants at 16, concerned that more teams would show the disparity between national associations. An experiment with 20 teams was briefly considered, but ruled out as logistically impossible. Other FIFA critics cited the opening game of the 2007 tournament, where Germany trounced Argentina 11-0, as evidence that 16 teams would be a better spectacle. In 2011, only five games would have a gap of three goals or more, a sign that the tournament could perhaps have been expanded sooner.

Of the 16 qualifying teams, Asia by now had three berths, perhaps in recognition

THE 'TIE IT UP WITH A BOW AND GIFT IT' WORLD CUP, 2011

that PR China had played such a pivotal role in hosting two World Cups, and also in part because in 2006 Australia had moved after four decades from the Oceania Confederation to the Asian Confederation. This meant that Australia, Japan and North Korea would qualify for 2011 from Asia.

With the exception of 1991 and 1995, Communist North Korea would have a more successful record of qualifying for Women's World Cups than its neighbour, South Korea. This is hardly mentioned in the West, but is an astonishing achievement in world sport. After five of the players failed doping tests in 2011, North Korea would be fined $400,000, as well as banned from qualifying for the 2015 Women's World Cup in Canada. However, the IOC took a different view, and North Korea played in London at the 2012 Olympic Games. As I said, the politics of the situation can sometimes be opaque.

North Korea rose again phoenix-like. By 2019, the senior team was practically inactive and this was exacerbated due to the pandemic. But as Samantha Lewis has written in her recent piece, from 2017 foreigner-managed youth age teams allowed the women's program to return, and North Korea to qualify for the 2023 World Cup. A recent game against Japan, moved to neutral Saudi Arabia, saw them score 0–0 in trying to obtain the final available berth at the 2024 Olympics. The development of women's football in North Korea between the 1999 Women's World Cup qualification, and now, remains a fascinating and virtually untold story.

Back in 2011, Oceania had a single allocation: New Zealand. The two South American teams were Brazil and Colombia. The goalkeeper Yineth Varon from Colombia was also suspended for doping violations for two years during the 2011 tournament. The two African teams were Equatorial Guinea and Nigeria. The Central and North American countries were Mexico, Canada and the USA, who beat Italy in a play-off to take 16th spot. This meant that five berths remained for European teams including the hosts, England, France, Norway and Sweden. This meant that Colombia and Equatorial Guinea made their debuts. PR China failed to qualify—the first time they were not included. Brazil, Germany, Japan, Nigeria, Norway, Sweden and the United States had now qualified for all six Women's World Cup tournaments.

The great centurion defender, and World Cup winner in 2003, Steffi Jones was President of the organising committee, and there was considerable domestic optimism at the UEFA events where I met her in 2010/11. Jones put together a team comprised of those who had experience in hosting the 2006 Men's World Cup, such as Ulrich Wolter, and Jens Grittner. In addition, there were prominent figures in women's football— Doris Fitschen, Winfried Nass, and Heike Ullrich who held a degree in Sport, Business & Law. Ullrich has, since July 2020, subsequently become Deputy Secretary-General of the German Football Association. The under-20s Women's World Cup held in Germany in Summer 2010, and won by the hosts—with striker Alexandra Popp as Golden Boot

(10 goals) and Golden Ball, acted as a warm-up event for many of the logistical, media and fan experience strategies developed for the senior tournament in 2011.

Germany was expected to complete the hat-trick of Women's World Cup wins in 2011 as hosts, but it was to be Japan who took the title—a shock, as the first Asian country to win it. Although as David Hanley has written in his history of women's football in Japan, the sport had a longer history particularly in educational institutions; the Japanese came over to a women's match in England held at Leicester City in the early 1980s where they were impressed by the professional atmosphere and detailed organisation. The FA of Japan invited several European teams, Denmark, Italy and England included, to the Portopia tournament in 1981. Portopia was a commercial trade exposition, or Expo, on man-made Port Island, off the coast of Kobe. The island was completed at considerable cost, and celebrations to open the facilities funded the trip, in which domestic and international teams could compare their relative strengths. Given that the amateur national league was then set up in Japan in 1989, to win the Women's World Cup less than 30 years later was a considerable achievement.

This was even more impressive given that on 11 March 2011 Japan experienced an earthquake of magnitude 9.3—the fourth most powerful in history to date, with almost 16,000 deaths. Many of the casualties resulted from a tsunami which reached 100 kilometres inland, and took out three reactors of the Fukushima Daiichi Nuclear Power Plant. Having beaten the hosts in the quarter-finals, and the USA in the final, led by the tournament's top scorer Homare Sawa, 'the Nadeshiko' (the standard of Japanese female beauty) as the Japanese team was nicknamed, gave some good news to their devastated nation. The team paraded banners thanking their friends around the world for their support.

The media coverage in Germany 2011 was unprecedented, including the use of spidercams and in-goal cameras. But the overall fan experience was disappointing. In spite of wishing to host a multicultural festival, many of the stadia were chosen because there was the anticipation of difficulty in filling the crowds to capacity, a vital element of the media's diet. Across nine cities, smaller stadia included Bochum (21,000), Augsburg (25,000), Dresden (26,000), Sinsheim (25,000) and Wolfsburg (26,000) and Leverkusen (30,000). Frankfurt, Mönchengladbach and Berlin were larger.

A capacity 74,000 crowd in Berlin was not repeated because the stadium was used only once, for the host's opening game against Canada. This match in Group A was notable for Alexandra Popp coming on in the 56th minute for injured German Captain Birgit Prinz, who retired as the leading all time Women's World Cup scorer to date, with 14 goals. In her World Cup and Olympic career for Germany's senior team Prinz scored 24 goals in 43 games. Another legend, Canada's Christine Sinclair, playing on with a broken nose, scored a consolation free kick in the 2–1 defeat to end goalkeeper Nadine Angerer's unbeaten World Cup run of 622 minutes without conceding a goal.

THE 'TIE IT UP WITH A BOW AND GIFT IT' WORLD CUP, 2011

The final was held in Frankfurt. In the smaller stadia, the overall average spectatorship was 26,500 and nearly 850,000 tickets were sold overall, many at low prices to encourage families and children to attend. In Group B, England drew with Mexico 1-1, then defeated New Zealand 2-1, before winning 2-0 against the future world champions, Japan, to top their group. This was a reminder that they had been in the finals of the 2009 Euros, losing 6-2 to Germany in Helsinki, Finland. Group C was no forgone conclusion. Sweden proved that the USA could be vulnerable by defeating them 2-1 to record the Americans' first ever group stage loss. In Group D, Australia inflicted another shock victory in their group over Norway, with 16-year-old Caitlin Foord instrumental to Kyah Simon's two goals, and Lisa De Vanna influential in changing the game. Tom Sermanni, having managed Australia women from 1994-1997 (and 2005-2012) therefore led them at his third World Cup.

For those paying attention, Japan's defeat of Germany in the quarter-finals on 9 July showcased many experienced players, none more so than Karina Maruyama, a veteran of the 2003 Women's World Cup, who scored an extra time winner in the 108th minute. Ayumi Kaihori's fine goalkeeping played its own part in the game ensuring it went to added extra time. As France despatched England on the same day, a game which ended 1-1 in added extra time and so went to penalties, there was a consolation for Jill Scott. Her 59th-minute strike would be the 600th goal in FIFA-organised Women's World Cup history. But the satisfaction was short-lived as Élise Bussaglia matched her efforts for France in the 88th minute, followed by an agonising period of added extra time— and defeat on penalties. Although Camille Abbily's first penalty was saved by Karen Bardsley, Kelly Smith, Karen Carney and Casey Stoney were subsequently outmatched by Bussaglia, Gaëtane Thiney, Sonia Bompastor, and Eugénie Le Sommer. England substitute Clare Rafferty pulled hers wide, captain Faye White hit the woodwork. England had never won a shootout in a competitive women's final at that point.

England had last beaten France 2-0 on 7 November 1974 in Wimbledon, and had subsequently drawn in 1977. In 2011, only 37-year-old French Captain Sandrine Soubeyrand was alive to witness the last England victory. Her record as the oldest player in a Women's World Cup stood until 2015—perhaps evidence of better player welfare regimes at club and national level. France had gone to the 2003 Women's World Cup at England's expense, and the latter had returned the favour in 2007. So, in exiting England in 2011, France maintained a rivalry that had endured since unofficial internationals, dating back as far as 1920.

On 10 July Sweden dumped out Australia 3-1, and Brazil almost, almost squeezed past the USA with two goals from Marta, after an own goal from Daiane after two minutes, and an Abby Wambach goal 120+2 minutes into added extra time to draw 2-2. Penalties by Cristiane, Marta and Francielle were no match for the five for the USA. This was bitterly close. Rachel Buehler (later Van Hollebeke) was sent off with a red card for a foul on Marta, and the USA had a further four yellow cards to match Brazil's. A Hope Solo save from Cristiane's converted penalty was deemed subject to encroachment. In scoring the retake, and a 91st-minute goal, Marta joined Birgit Prinz as the all-time WWC record scorer.

France fell to the USA in the semi-finals 3–1, and Japan overcame Sweden 3–1. In the third-place playoff, Sweden were victorious 2–1 over France—in spite of a Josefine Oqvist red card.

The final had all that could be wished for. It opened with US coach, Pia Sundhage, singing Simon and Garfunkel's 'Feelin' Groovy' to the world's press. In three and half years Sundhage had won Olympic gold and regained the American's reputation as the world's leading women's team. Normally the USA were characterised as the more physical team, and Japan as technically refined, but each battled for a 0–0 draw at half time, Japan charging in as much as the USA finessed its passes. Substitute Alex Morgan made the difference in the 69th minute, a feat matched by Aya Miyama nine minutes before the whistle. In added extra time, first Abby Wambach scored for the USA, then Homare Sawa for Japan.

Yūki Nagasato had her penalty saved by Hope Solo; Shannon Boxx and Tobin Heath were both saved by Japan's keeper Ayumi Kaihori, and a Carli Lloyd spot-kick opened the way for a new star, Saki Kumagai, to score the winner, after Miyama and Mizuho Sakaguchi converted their opportunities. Homare Sawa took home the Golden Ball and Golden Boot, Marta the Silver Boot (narrowly from Wambach). Australians will rejoice in the Best Young Player title being awarded to Caitlin Foord. Japan won the Fair Play award, and even players on the USA squad thought that, on balance, this win would bring some good consolation to a country devastated by natural disaster.

London 2012: The Second Austerity Olympics

In 1948, the second London Olympic Games, 40 years after the inaugural 1908 Olympics in that capital, was known as the 'Austerity Games' because of the disruption and rationing of the Second World War. These were still very much in place in 1948. But the 2012 Olympic and Paralympic Games were also affected by austerity, this time of a political nature orchestrated by a Conservative government who wished to undo much of the reform enacted by the Welfare State.

Although originally won in 2005 when Labour's Ken Livingstone was mayor of London, and Conservative peer Lord Sebastian Coe collaborated on the successful bid, the Games themselves took place under a Tory-led coalition government who argued that grassroots sport would be the largest legacy benefactor—as they put it, to 'Inspire a Generation.' However, London 2012 exposed fundamental contradictions between austerity politics in the form of rolling back state support for education, health and welfare, and securing increased participation as a result of hosting costly mega events. In fact, by 2012, mechanisms that supported increases in participation had often already been reduced or eliminated. Not least, to fund an Olympic tournament that ran over its projected £9.3 billion budget at a time of fiscal cuts.

This said, the London 2012 Olympic and Paralympic Games innovated new tournament forms. England, Scotland and Wales all hosted Olympic matches, and special dispensation was given to the formation of a Team GB women's football team, as hosts. But this was historically contentious, and while Scotland, Wales and Irish football associations were not willing to actively take part, they did not boycott the idea either. While the IOC views Team GB as one nation, FIFA views each of the national members' football associations as independent, so it was some compromise. In the end it was window dressing. No such collaboration for the men's football teams would be forthcoming.

The women's football team for GB was almost exclusively drawn from England with only Scotland's Kim Little and Ifeoma Dieke forming part of the squad. Since the World Cup formed the qualifying route for the Olympic Games, the two top European sides were Sweden and France, who had competed for the third-place playoff. Hence, 2012 would be the only time that Germany failed to qualify for either a World Cup or Olympic tournament. China also failed to qualify, leaving Japan and North Korea as the Asian representatives. Nigeria was another absentee, in favour of Cameroon and South Africa. New Zealand took the lone Oceania Football Confederation (OFC) berth. Colombia beat Argentina to take the second South American spot behind Brazil. The USA and Canada completed the 12-team roster.

Consequently, 11 teams plus hosts Great Britain contested the event. But what constitutes a host nation? London, Cardiff, Coventry, Glasgow, Manchester and Newcastle acted as football host cities, this was the first major female-centred FIFA tournament in the United Kingdom. It also became the first tri-hosted FIFA women's tournament. In all across the Olympics and Paralympics, around 10,500 athletes from 210 national associations took part, making it the largest multi-sport event ever held in the UK, beating the Austerity Olympic Games in 1948, and the original London Olympic Games of 1908 by some scale.

Compared with the 16-team men's Olympic tournament, which is limited to under 23 national squads, with three over-aged players allowed, the women's football tournament is a senior discipline. Even though Men's World Cup football grew out of the popularity of the Olympic tournament back in the 1920s, FIFA is now keen that the Olympic Games do not overshadow their own main festival of world football.

Perceived as still developing internationally, women's football does not have the same challenge.

Twelve team tournaments are notoriously difficult to arrange logistically in a way that fosters exciting play, but the seeding of Great Britain, Japan, and the USA left only Pot 2 of Cameroon, South Africa and Colombia without a seeded nation. The Olympic match format for women was double headers, the first two in Millennium Stadium in Cardiff on 25 July. Steph Houghton scored the winner against New Zealand in Cardiff, in Team GB's 1-0 victory, and a few hours later Brazil ran over Cameroon 5-0, including a Marta brace. Having defeated Cameroon 3-0, Team GB topped the group by despatching Brazil 1-0, again a goal by Steph Houghton.

There was almost a diplomatic incident over the Hampden Park game on 25 July because the South Korean flag appeared in error on the scoreboard at the Columbia–North Korea tie in Glasgow. The North Korean team walked off the pitch in protest. The apology failed to use the correct terms, Republic of Korea and Democratic People's Republic of Korea, and there was an hour's delay. It was an embarrassing oversight for the local organising committee.

In the quarter-finals, Canada dismissed the hosts 2-0, the USA sent home New Zealand 2-0, France defeated Sweden 2-1, and Japan overcame Brazil 2-0. In the semi-finals, 61K people watched Japan defeat France 2-1 at Wembley, and 26K punters at Old Trafford, Manchester saw a Christine Sinclair hat-trick for Canada, that wasn't quite enough when the USA scored a fourth in 120+3 minutes in added extra time, thanks to Alex Morgan. A time-wasting call against the Canadian goalkeeper, and a handball in the penalty area remained contentious refereeing decisions, and Christine Sinclair disputed the judgement. Otherwise, the tournament was relatively evenly contested with only one red card for North Korea, and Colombia's Lady Andrade given a two-match ban for pushing Abby Wambach, (who was fairly assertive herself and lucky to escape censure).

A Carli Lloyd brace won the Wembley final against Japan 2-1 for the USA. A number of the US team had been in the 2004, 2008 and 2012 winning teams, such as Christie Rampone and Shannon Boxx. It was Japan's first Olympic final. Undoubtedly the profile of the women's game was helped by large celebratory crowds filling major stadia, something that would not be repeated in England, at least, until the Women's Euros in 2022, a decade later.

London was the USA's fourth Olympic title (1996, 2004, 2008 and 2012), and Japan finished runners up. Canada's Christine Sinclair finished top scorer, with six goals. As fans of women's football looked forward to Canada hosting the competition in 2015, the controversy over the use of artificial surfaces, the first senior World Cup to be played entirely on artificial turf, continued to build from 2012 onwards.

Brittle Academic Masculinity

My sunny Swiss interludes, and an enjoyably diversifying research agenda, would soon be interrupted. Higher education was entering a new 'audit-phase' as opposed to being based on educational principles. The major review bringing in changes to UK Higher Education in 2010 came from the Department for Business, Education and Skills. It was led by Lord John Browne, who had worked almost exclusively for oil giant BP, becoming its Chief Executive. Browne's management style was epitomised by cost-cutting, acquisition and his own six figure annual salary. Not therefore an expert in *education* by any means, Browne's findings were that the cap on student fees at £3,290 should be abolished in favour of universities setting their own fees. Having studied at Cambridge and worked for BP (following his father into the oil business), he argued that working-class students would not be deterred by debt. I don't suspect Browne had dealt with many working-class families for whom debt was to be avoided at all costs. My own included. My parents would not have used hire purchase, and did not even own a credit card. As one of five children, how would I have gone to university had there not been free school meals and then a full maintenance grant? And how many times over had this investment been repaid to society by the sheer volume of state-educated students I had then gone on to teach?

After an about-turn by the Liberal Democrat party who then entered into a coalition government with the Conservatives, the new fee structures commenced in September 2012. This marketised Higher Education in an unprecedented way, with universities treating prospective students as consumers. We even had a session in 2012 where John Lewis executives came and shared their customer service ethos.

Whatever the complicated specifics and wider context, I was under pressure to do more undergraduate teaching in History. Most parents do not realise that for their £9,000 in fees their offspring will most likely be tutored in their first year by PhD students. I did not particularly want to give up winning large bids and working in a research-intensive centre, in order to do more undergraduate teaching. I had by then taught thousands of undergraduates during my career, if the large classes in Combined Studies and Education Studies were taken into account. Many of my male colleagues wanted to be taken more seriously as historians, more aligned with the history department. I felt the sport history research centre focus was diluted by those aspirations because our time was being continually cut by various teaching time allocation reviews. The beginning of the end at De Montfort hoved into view.

In late 2010 De Montfort University appointed a new Vice-Chancellor, Dominic Shellard, and initially I really wanted to like him. He was young, openly gay and seemed to have progressive politics. However, in my opinion, he didn't quite have the emotional maturity to cope with the job once in the post. He cultivated a group of insiders who agreed with him and this was not healthy.

It became clear soon after he arrived that, as a fan of QPR, Dominic felt he had an insight into the football industry unmatched by those of us who had spent a decade or so actually studying the topic.

By the time I left in 2016, earning less than £60,000 as a Professor with almost 20 years' service at the university, Shellard's salary was £286,000. According to documents in the public domain and reported by *The Guardian*, the following year it rose to £350,000. This was in spite of findings of systemic and significant failing of governance by the Office for Students (OfS). A 39-point action plan was required to address governance issues after Shellard left in 2019.

Though the direct effect on me in 2010/11 was small, mainly because I was often doing research abroad, the emphasis that was placed on agreeing with the Vice Chancellor was evident. Staff were briefed not to ask questions in meetings. He ignored raised hands in meetings that might lead to uncomfortable questions. We were asked to 'Like' his Tweets.

When he arrived in 2011 as the new centre director, Tony Collins undertook to deliver for Dominic Shellard a BA undergraduate course in sports. The VC had already made a commitment to the Board of Governors, with no particular vision of how to deliver the curriculum. Two short years later, in 2013, Tony stood down as Head of Centre, leaving those of us who remained full time to carry on with the validation.

The market research did not support the need for such BA provision, but the VC had a 'build it and the students will come' mentality. Eventually we did build it—and they stayed away. I can't remember now whether the first intake was six or eight students, but the two female first years had left by Christmas. It dwindled, and frizzled out with a whimper.

As this began to unfold, I was asked to lead on the validation of the new BA course. But I was not the person who had made the promise to the VC, that was up to Tony. Up until 2012, I had laughed when male colleagues would wander into my office, waving paperwork in hand that they didn't know how to complete—or didn't want to try, saying, 'Jean you're awfully good at this, could you possibly....' It was damning my ability with faint praise, and false flattery to avoid a boring task. It also demoted me to their personal assistant. Often I agreed, as it took about five minutes. Always ask a busy person to do a job, as they tend to pull in 'one more thing.' This time I declined to lead on the BA validation. I wasn't the best man for the job and I hadn't been head hunted to be Centre Director. Over to you guys! If the chaps had their way my gravestone would read, 'She was awfully efficient at administrative tasks, and Chaired meetings to time.' Thankfully, I get to author a more interesting history.

THE 'TIE IT UP WITH A BOW AND GIFT IT' WORLD CUP, 2011

When colleagues persisted, things escalated. I cited my extant funded research commitments and my teaching load, also leading the MA Sport History with very healthy annual intakes, and with a role on the Faculty Senior Management team as Head of Postgraduate students. I was writing up much of the UEFA documentation in 2011, and involved in Olympic work in 2012. I also spent most of the academic year 2011/12 on a funded research project on sportswear, Fashioning the Body for Sport, with a Professor of Dance and staff from Fashion. Developing this object-based research, I had managed to obtain grant support to go out in January to the Fashion Institute of Technology, New York, to look at sportswear in the archives, and a related exhibition. This was a very new way of working for someone who has been text-based all their life. I'll sit and read the back of a cereal box. But the archivist bought out garments first, which we then decoded and analysed, suggesting lots of questions about design, production, material, embellishment, consumption and finally storage as an archived object no longer in connection with the body.

There was a lot of exciting work going on, and small pots of Faculty money to bid for, in which I was successful both as an individual and mentoring Dance and Fashion staff who were less research-active. So, my general policy was to keep my head down and do interesting work. This later came out as a special edition of the journal, *Sport in History* and as a book, *Kit: Fashioning the Body for Sport* with Routledge.

After I declined to lead the validation for a third time, an attempt was made to take over my research funding, which was unprecedented. If someone else owned my research funding they could choose how it was used, and I could be obliged—even directed—to take more of a role on the validation. The day I found out someone was trying to control the funding that I had won as a Principal Investigator, I had a panic attack in the car on the way home and thought I would crash. Seeking help from my GP, I was given medication that just knocked me out. I couldn't afford to take time off. So, I soldiered on, and took out a grievance guided by my male Head of School, who was an absolute lifeline. I won't mention his name because I sensed at the time he had a difficult situation going on, and he retired early soon after. But I would like to thank him. He will know who he is. With his help, we secured control of my funding.

Relationships with Centre colleagues never really recovered. They particularly did not like that I could use the university human resources policies to defend my position. This is a relatively well-known practice in education, but was not so common then in higher education. Time and again when they went straight to the Head of School to complain about this, that or the other, brittle male colleagues used to speaking man to man found that they had already contravened the grievance procedure of speaking to me about whatever it was first. I always tackled them head on individually or as a group before going to the procedures. With the funding secured and the validation lead declined, I was told I wasn't a team player. Never mind that I had led the expanded MA

Sport History teaching team since 2006, was forming new research groups all the time, and serving on the Faculty Senior Management. By not complying in doing someone else's work and in sticking to my own agenda I had become that well known work figure, the difficult woman.

At this point I was working 70-and 80-hour weeks. I was so ill by the weekends that Simon would drive me to the Staunton Harold estate where we would buy pick 'n' mix, walk with his support around the garden centre for half an hour, then come home. The rest of the weekend I slept, recovering. Having to continually fight for being treated decently, I'd given up exercise which is normally how I manage my mental health, because I was so exhausted. I wanted to give the increased number of students we had on the MA Sport History the best experience we could offer, but that meant a lot of individualised learning. I was also maintaining my PhD supervisions, and funded research. The only solution, in the face of cuts to teaching hours, was to work longer unpaid hours.

There were still collegial times and it wasn't all difficult. In July 2012 a group of us, including Simon, went out to the North American Society for Sports History conference in Berkeley, California. Mike Cronin had obtained a reservation at Chez Panisse. It was a lovely evening, and very generous of Mike to arrange it and invite us.

But larger changes were on the way. Rob Colls joined the Centre in 2012. The nicest thing I can say about Colls is that he enjoyed being a Geordie in exile. While extolling the virtues of his home town, South Shields, to anyone who would listen, he neither wanted to live nor work in the north, having come to Leicester in the 1970s. Like most left-leaning men of a certain vintage who take themselves very seriously, Colls had written a book on George Orwell. Further cementing his legend as a 'Prince of the North', Rob had an acquaintance in Melvin Bragg who would say nice things about his books.

Some of the chauvinist hostility Colls brought with him was low level schoolboy stuff. He would send out emails beginning 'Hi guys' and mansplain women's Olympic boxing to me. Pretty mundane. However, the previous paragraph is dedicated to a Doctoral student of mine to whom Rob was needlessly cruel in an annual review as the independent assessor. The job of an independent assessor is to ensure fairness and rigor in how the student is progressing. Rob instead showed off. A mature writer of considerable skill and experience, the student had graduated the MA Sport History and Culture with a Distinction, and was doing equally excellent second year Doctoral work until our meeting with Professor Colls. The unkind comments nearly caused the student to withdraw, but were not ultimately successful. I hope that the characterisation above makes the now successful Doctoral candidate chuckle.

Dick (Richard) Holt may have stood down as Director of the Centre for Sports History and Culture, but he liked to orchestrate. He could be generous and kind. He loaned me an interview he had done with Audrey Brown, for my Olympic book. Simon and I were invited to his 60th birthday in Paris, and attended. He also read an early draft of my Olympic book and made some key suggestions. He was great when Daphné had her first child in Leicester. On a daily basis he was a very charming person with whom to work.

But the only consistency was inconsistency. One time, Dick booked a hotel room at Birmingham airport to fly out early the next morning to Milan to meet Dino Ruta, a Professor at Bocconi School of Management, sharing a room with Professor Chris Young whom he'd also invited to contribute. I was told there was no money in the 30,000 Euro project budget to get me a room or a flight but I could use some of my own funds. In a snowstorm so heavy the runways were closed, I got up at 3am to drive to Birmingham and wait with Dick and Chris for the 6am flight. By 11am it became clear that my plan, to fly to Milan and back in a day, hence no hotel bills, would simply not work, and I abandoned the trip, leaving them to it. Publishing a chapter on China and mega events in the resulting output, I remained unclear, other than a short one-day conference in Leicester, how that pot of money was spent.

Another example: We were going to celebrate the graduation of the FIFA MA students in Neuchâtel, in July 2013, after I had supervised a group of all-female students in the final projects. The students had obtained a Distinction. In the hotel lobby with the Dean of Business and his personal assistant, we gathered as we were going out on the lake on a boat for drinks at sunset with the students and their parents. Dick and a member of professional services staff, lets call him JP, dressed in matching grey suits.

The Dean of Business was in a blue summer linen suit. His female PA was in a loose jumpsuit. In front of everyone in the hotel reception, Dick chastised me at some length for what I was wearing, saying he didn't think it was appropriate for a 'smart do.' Simon had bought me black capri pants and a white silk shirt, over which I wore a light leather jacket (all from Reiss), and pink sandals from Pelle Moda. I patiently explained how much each piece had cost, and that three pieces had been bought expressly for this 'smart do.' Allowing that individuals have different interpretations of smart casual, this was unacceptable.

This occasion in Neuchâtel was publicly humiliating, and deliberately so. As we left the hotel lobby to get in the taxi, the Dean's assistant asked me, 'Wow, is that what you have to put up with every day?' and I silently nodded, yes. The Dean of Business looked visibly shocked and we spoke about it out on the water. I had a glass of champagne with Natalie Smith and her parents on board an immaculate white vessel as the sun descended, whizzing rather genteelly around Lake Neuchâtel.

So, the point of including this example is to make a point about male toxicity that extends way beyond academia. Criticising a woman's appearance in public is not actually intended to be helpful. It's not designed to help the individual improve her haircut, or her weight, or her choice of clothing. No one actually expected me to change my outfit. And I was unable to change being female.

The low-lying fruit of misogyny, criticisms of a woman's appearance, reveal deeper truths. What had actually led to the frustrated comment was that I was there at all. The clothes were an opportunity for male colleagues' to be offended, by my taking up space, having an opinion, enjoying my female students' success, and my own. By being good at my job. Irritatingly, I seemed to manage to keep turning up. So that's exactly what I did.

There were many similar occasions not witnessed by others, and so over the course of ten years in the Centre, I'll leave you to do the maths on the effect of the insular male tribe 'othering' me as an individual woman. I didn't want to be exceptional, except at my job. I just wanted to turn up, do my work to the best of my ability, and go home to my Simon, the cat, friends and family. Systems of male privilege need to be constantly reconstructed, reinforced and reinterpreted because that sense of masculinity is so brittle. That's a lot of psychic and emotional work. And so those involved need to be really invested to keep recycling, and escalating that privilege.

Now I don't pretend, would not want, to be an angel. Around this time, I had my first meeting with a new authoritarian middle manager, a Head of Department I think was his title. I cannot be sure as there was so much restructuring. I was wearing a Jigsaw silk linen dress and a pair of Doc Marten shoes on the day of our appointment. The Docs were burgundy crushed velvet with cream flowers on them. The new guy took one look at my shoes as I walked into his office, and asked how things were at home. I was flummoxed initially. Then he started asking did I have a partner, did I have children, what did I do on the weekend and so on. Eventually the penny dropped. I studied women's football, I wore Doc Martens, ergo I was probably a lesbian.

For a couple of seconds this made me inwardly chuckle. What? I spent a split second seriously considering confecting a whole other exoticized life for myself where I spent the weekends in lesbian hot spots, (Brighton, Berlin, Hebden Bridge), working my way through an array of pansexual amours. But, in the end I mentioned Simon, the cat, and my family to make my life just a bit easier with this guy. Regrets, I have a few.

The specifics of De Montfort intersected with wider academic networks of sport often populated by male fans who have obtained a PhD. Such collectives can bring male tribalism into their professional work. I lost track of the number of edited collections whereby a group of male friends with Doctorates had decided to publish together, and then realised only afterwards it was pretty obvious what they were doing, so asked me to write a chapter as 'balance.' Of course, I would point out that a single chapter by a white woman was not balanced. There were rarely chapters by black and Asian academics or female early career researchers or any number of diverse voices in these edited collections. There I went, being difficult again instead of just shutting up and being thankful to be invited.

By churning out one edited book after another in this same format, the systems of masculine academia tended to help the friends to progress through their careers through mutual reinforcement. In challenging what I laughingly theorised as 'publishing edited academic collections with your football mates' I recently had a younger white male academic accuse me of not being intersectional in my approach because he had a working-class background. When I indicated that I am working-class and female, he had a tantrum and said we couldn't work together anymore. I didn't know that we ever did. He still continues to publish with the same three or four friends now. So why ask me to review your new edited collection, very similar to your last edited collection, dude, if your work isn't going to evolve?

There have also been occasions when male entitlement makes itself evident when least expected. At a conference on women and sport in Africa, organised by Michelle Sykes and John Bale, we had a series of papers in Oxford during the day. Simon had travelled with me, and spent the day at the Ashmolean and Natural History Museum so was not around during the conference. That evening Simon sat next to me for dinner at Browns when a professor who had been at the conference walked in and began massaging my shoulders. Warming to his theme, he became more vigorous. I let this go for about a minute before saying, 'Hello. Please meet my husband, Simon.' To which he turned scarlet and went and sat at the other end of the table, not speaking to either of us again for the rest of the evening. A well-known predator, he tended to have to move continents, let alone institutions, when complaints were made by women students and staff. Rather than risk reputational damage, institutions often move such individuals on quietly, and also avoid having to acknowledge student and staff complaints beyond individual cases. So, the wider industrial complex can tend to reinforce misogynistic behaviour.

Back in Leicester, at the same time all this was going on, Clare Balding, who had met Tony while doing some work on Rugby League, his big passion, arrived. A 30-part Radio 4 Series was commissioned over 2011/12 and eight of us (Tony Mason, Dick Holt, Tony Collins, Mike Cronin, Dil Porter, Neil Carter, Matt Taylor, and myself) wrote the episodes, each leading on three and co-writing others. The title of Dick's book, *Sport and the British* was used. As well as Olympic content, Clare was particularly keen to have a programme on women's football, which I wrote. I recorded interview content in London and at Radio Leicester. Working on research at University of Bath special collections on field hockey in the summer of 2011, I was asked to record more detailed content for that episode at BBC Radio Bath. It was a very hot summer day, stifling in the recording studio, and the Friday of a Bank Holiday. I remember it very clearly, staying late until nearly 6pm before driving home until my car broke down and I had to spend the rest of the journey in a recovery truck, with the driver and his dog. It felt portentous.

When the episode on women's football aired, I was standing in my kitchen with Simon who wanted to hear what had been done. I cried in shock. I had been cut entirely from the recording and another woman voiced the points I had made in my previous interviews, and using the script that I wrote. When I asked about this, I was told that the BBC wanted diverse voices and Scottish voice was part of their diversification in broadcasting.

It may have been that, of course. However, there was no voice in the entire thing from a woman in Leicester where De Montfort was based. Maybe it was after all another coincidence. But if it was, it was also the case that the male writers' episodes were not similarly thought to need a sustained Scottish accent, although there was a bit of a Hugh McIlvanney clip if my memory serves me correctly. Instead, my male colleagues appeared in their own right. I had been prevented from speaking about my own area of expertise by academic and media colleagues, none of whom was willing to be brave enough to admit their part.

I cannot have been so terrible in media interviews, because I filmed onscreen with Clare on later documentary films, such as *When Football Banned Women*, and saw her again at the Icons recording, judging the biggest sporting Icons of the Twentieth Century. Colin Jackson was part of the Icons panel; he was both nice, and very bright, asking a lot of questions. He also really listened in a considered way. I went on to media recordings with some of my own heroes in the future, and I guess the incident was instructive to make my own opportunities.

Clare treated us all to lunch, telling us about having a Nando's black card after a *When Football Banned Women* session, the second celebrity after James Cordon to do so, apparently. Those who wrote the *Sport and the British* radio series were going to co-author a book with her in which, as the big name, she would take two-thirds of the fee and we eight would share the rest. I was in favour of using the combined material for a textbook which would have been great for the MA Sport History, but it didn't really go anywhere. The Radio 4 *Sport and the British* slight was entirely unnecessary, but typified the atmosphere in the Centre, where the aggressions were no longer micro.

Sadly, it was not just staff who were affected by the strained relationships in the end. Two female PhD students, one who had come up through the MA Sport History, and another on a funded bursary, began to call themselves, 'Tony's Terrors'. Both were at least late 20s, and one recently married, but it can happen in Higher Education when a student over-identifies with a particular academic. It does tend to be female students and male academics because of the power imbalance.

I was second supervisor to both women and thought their work was great. But alarm bells began to ring when the annual review of one of them came around, which involved the whole supervision team making written comments during an in-person meeting with an independent assessor. I was not invited to the annual review, nor told of the date, and was sent the documentation after the fact. This was odd, since at that time handwritten signatures were still part of the process. How could the paperwork be completed without my signature and accepted by the Research Degrees Office?

An independent reviewer of the supervision team also makes comments, so I asked that person, why I was not told of the meeting. He replied he didn't know the second supervisor should be involved. He was himself a second supervisor, so knew the process. I had also mentored him on his PGCE qualification so we both knew what was expected in collegiate behaviour.

Then I wasn't invited to the annual review of the second student a couple of months after I had complained about the oversight with the first. So, there was a pattern of behaviour involving the same two male members of staff. When I raised a grievance, it was clear that the behaviour had been repeated. Since the incidents with the two students were the only times this has happened to me in my whole career, it was just bizarre.

I had been supervising Doctorates since 2006 and it had not happened before. I completed my last PhD supervision in 2024, helping in all about 20 people to obtain Doctorates, and it has not happened since. Any educator can only help a student who wants assistance, so I removed myself as second supervisor from the guidance of both and did not hear from the them again, and I am not sure what they are doing now. I am not sure how the incident helped them with their studies, but it was not nice that students felt they had to choose sides. With the next round of MA graduations, I picked up two PhD first supervisions and the example shows when it is right to let a situation, and some people, pass.

Even after he had stood down as Director, Tony's behaviour had wider effects. He held a Sport and Literature conference in 2014 in conjunction with one of 'Tony's Terrors', without inviting myself, Jeff Hill or anyone from the previous Sport and Literature conference in 2008 to be involved. Given Jeff and I had published most prolifically in this area, it was plainly a snub. Tony Bateman, a great friend of Jeff and a very fine writer, was not invited—nor John Bale and many of those who had written articles on the topic. The Sport and Literature conference caused the Faculty quite a few headaches. Jeff, John Bale and Tony Bateman asked me why we were not invited. Where to start?

So why not get out and get a job elsewhere? Firstly, there are few sports history opportunities in humanities departments, and even fewer in Institutes of Sport, or health schools, which tend to focus on science and technology elements, with some sociological specialisms. Secondly, why should I? I had been through a recruitment process to get my job, and was entitled to a collegial working atmosphere.

To give an example of how difficult it was to get out, I'll give an example from an interview for a Professorship I attended at the University of Brighton, which had a sports research cluster at the time called the Chelsea School. Ironically the Chelsea School had been founded in 1898 by Dorette Wilke, one of the pioneers of physical education for women and girls, and operating independently until 1979 when it became part of the University of Brighton at Eastbourne, under the former Brighton Polytechnic.

At the time of my interview, sometime in 2013/4 academic year, I was still a Senior Research Fellow. Dr Paul Dimeo was another candidate, widely known for his work in anti-doping, but not yet on the Professorial scale. Paul and I were then both in our late 40s. Then there was Professor John Nauright, working at George Mason in the US, and Professor John Horne who was working at University of Central Lancashire. We were all to stay at The Devonshire Park Hotel, Eastbourne, overnight and meet with some of the interview panel for dinner, led by sociologist Alan Tomlinson. I had been invited to bring along Simon, and if memory serves correctly, John Horne bought his wife along too. So, I wasn't the only woman, but I was the only woman being interviewed for the post which was advertised as a Professor of Sport and Leisure Management. During the meal, it became clear that Horne and Nauright were competitive even in casual conversation. Entertaining, but the appointment was evidently also considered by them to be a two-man race. Simon and I ducked out to watch England women play an international.

Although we met female members of staff the next day in a variety of meetings, and I already knew several, the interview panel comprised eight male professors. Each asked a question in turn around the table and then as candidates we answered that person. There were seven white, and one Asian, all male interviewers, all over 60, many nearer 70, or looked it anyway.

I then heard that Horne had been previously offered the post already before the negotiations had become unacceptable to him and he had turned it down. Perhaps Horne had thought he might have been able to improve the offer he'd been made at a second attempt. Who knows? As such, this was a re-advertisement of the original vacancy. Nauright had been flown in specially from the US. Sure enough, he got the job.

Simon and I had a couple of jolly days in Eastbourne, and saw an Amy Winehouse tribute on the lovely Art Deco bandstand. The Chelsea School brand was abandoned soon after Nauright was appointed, and the Eastbourne campus eventually closed. So, getting out of De Montfort was difficult, given the wider governance and recruitment practices of the industry.

Defying Clarity

It is a truth universally acknowledged in academia that with the appointment of a new Vice-Chancellor/Dean/whatever, there will be a restructuring. That reshuffle is like moving the deckchairs on an ocean liner—largely pointless and resource-intensive, but it *looks* busy.

From Faculties, to Schools to Departments, the introduction of a new layer of middle management will also inevitably lead, a year or so later, to a round of redundancies of middle managers. At De Montfort I was by now sitting in on strategy meetings about how to model our progress from being 48th in the University rankings to become a top 30 or 20 institution. What should our strategy be? Resources that had previously been used in teaching students went into strategizing. The wisdom of this was proven when the university had slipped to 68th in the ranking by the time Dominic Shellard left.

Humanities departments were increasingly under pressure at this time and by 2013 the new Dean of Humanities, Barbara Matthews, moved from the arts sector into higher education. Favouring Monday morning meetings, paper bag lunches, and other management tools over collegiality, Matthews had attended Stamford and Uppingham having gone on to an undergraduate degree in Chemistry at Durham. In Humanities, the highest achieving, and most research-intensive Faculty in the university, Barbara was the first Dean I had worked with who wasn't also a Professor. She didn't even have a PhD. Obtaining a PhD we term being an early career researcher (or ECR). You are at the beginning of your independent research career. This sounds high-handed and dreadfully snobbish of me I know, but that is the system. It was also my lived experience that until this point the Dean of Arts and Humanities had been a senior academic in their own right who had then gone into leadership.

Breaking that pattern was clearly a managerial choice, and a typically Shellardian appointment. Only the elevation of James Gardner to Dean of International was more mystifying. Dean of International what? We never did find out. But Gardner was reported in the public domain to be paid upwards of £170,000 per annum for having a BA, so the syntactical mystery of the second half of his job title probably did not concern him overmuch.

Personally, I found Barbara a polite and jolly person to be around, although she once took time out of her busy day to call me on the phone to tell me she had found me petulant in the Senior Management Meeting earlier that morning. The main business of that meeting was another wave of redundancies. Given Shellard's salary increases, that was not something I as an educationalist could ever support, especially seeing so many fantastic colleagues lose their jobs. So, we clashed. The cuts affected co-workers whom I respected deeply and the mental health consequences were, in some cases, dire. I was not going to be complicit to those decisions in silence.

Barbara did not understand Distance Learning, and thought that our 18–22 MA Sport History annual student intake would be easy to teach, given that most of the materials were written. This conveniently forgot the amount of individual input each student required, whether on a part-time or full-time pathway, to navigate the course on their own. Factor in that this was usually study in a spare bedroom, after work, and in between family life. How isolating a learning experience! So the responsiveness of the teaching team was vital, and I spent hours on the phone. It would actually have been easier to round everyone up and say something once, but distance learning doesn't work like that.

About half of the annual intake were studying part-time as well as working, so we actually dealt with about 30 students per annum, which is very healthy for a Humanities MA degree. The fact that we retained our graduates, and so many progressed to PhD study, was also a good news story.

As an aside, many universities worked out during the COVID-19 pandemic that distance learning is resource-intensive, when most teaching went online, but all that was seven years later. Being ahead of our time, given the evident success of the course, meant that we were often under-valued, and MA teaching time was continually cut to allow more time to teach elsewhere. If there had been a more entrepreneurial approach, other MA provision in the Faculty could have followed the distance learning model. Cuts, and remodelling to reduce timetabled teaching hours, to a large degree explained why I was working 60–70 hours a week to maintain provision. It was unsustainable from a health point of view.

Matthews also viewed the FIFA MA as too expensive to run, in spite of its wider reputation, and cut staff time on the course to a minimum, hence moving the emphasis from a planned curriculum to a series of visiting speakers and trips. Clearly teaching quality mattered less than saving costs, although I have no idea how students make sense of the course.

The managerialism I've described above is now everywhere in higher education, and to the detriment of the sector. There are a lot of people who want to become an academic by proxy, without doing the actual work of research, teaching, and creating new knowledge.

By now I had the maximum quota of 10 PhD students, full and part time, most of whom were directly self-funded from the MA Sport History. The 'grow our own' postgraduate community was a direct benefit of individualised learning, and by introducing the new specialised modules on sport and literature, football and rugby, we had been able to help students develop a 15,000-word MA thesis which often became the basis of their PhD study proposal.

I was particularly proud of the diversity element on the MA with a student from South Korea, who worked on his English in a pre-sessional course before completing. Jason Lee from South Korea also did the MA and went on to write a PhD thesis with us on football in North and South Korea, then becoming an academic. Local students like Dave Dee followed the MA/ PhD route and he is now a well-respected senior member of staff in History.

There were lots of very strong women students on the MA, although it would be too list-like to name them all, and I wouldn't want to leave anyone out! I began working with Mountain history specialist Tom Barcham on the MA as a single man, and by the time he graduated his PhD he had a family of young children and a very demanding job. People often think supervisions are done over a glass of sherry in a hushed wood-panelled room. However, I used to meet Tom and his wife when their first child was a baby in a motorway service station just outside Tamworth and talk about his thesis over very brown stewed tea!

In terms of disability, Michael Cockayne, who was on dialysis three times a week, was able to complete his MA due to the Distance Learning mode of delivery. An occupational health adviser at the hospital had encouraged him to use the long hours of dialysis to study, and I had been up to Manchester once to meet him in person. Sadly, he graduated posthumously and we established the Michael Cockayne Dissertation Prize for the best thesis in 2012/13 in his memory. Our eldest student completed aged 86, having begun the course after the death of his wife, and having had a professional career pioneering the use of physiotherapy at Leicester Tigers, and with the NHS in Leicester. Sadly, he also graduated posthumously, another emotional experience. Their excellent academic work was testament to their absolute dedication.

The students with whom I worked were inspirational. Danielle Griffin wrote beautifully on Canadian anti-apartheid sport policy and the Montreal Olympic Games for her PhD thesis. Kevin Martson defended his viva on youth sport in France in 2013, the same year as Paul Campbell and Conor Curran (who I didn't supervise). Madie Armstrong wrote on 19th Century mountaineer, Lizzie Le Blond. Steve Crewe on works' sport and, like Catherine Budd, went on to teach at undergraduate level. Graham Greensit was already working at a university when he studied with us; Keith Myerscough had retired from teaching to write, and his work on basketball and swimming showed that was a wise choice. Journalist Jo Halpin's work on women's hockey at MA and PhD level connected with the establishment of the hockey museum in Woking, and with special collections at Bath University. I could go on, and on and on.

I particularly enjoyed working with what are called non-traditional students. The term usually means someone who hasn't worked through an A level, BA, MA, PhD progression.

Amanda Callan-Spenn came to a seminar and presented her work on actress Sarah Mayer, the first non-Japanese woman to obtain a Judo black belt in Japan in the 1930s. As a former professional Latin American ballroom dancer, Amanda didn't have qualifications usual to begin a PhD. But she had written 12,000 very detailed words in pursuit of Sarah Mayer's life. So, we managed to persuade the university systems that it would be a good idea for her to write a PhD. Like Jo Halpin who transferred with me to Wolverhampton in 2016 when I left De Montfort, it was an absolute pleasure to work with Amanda and her brother Mike on the history of Judo, and both have made international contributions to the history of martial arts. Amanda has since gone on to teach at De Montfort, which is a nice synchronicity.

But my efforts on the biographical and literary aspects of sport were not always appreciated. One particular student on the MA came to my office very offended about something which Jeff Hill had written. The student had so over-identified with *Fever Pitch*, the autobiographical piece written by author Nick Hornby about his love of Arsenal, that he found Jeff's assertion in *Sport and the Literary Imagination* that all memoirs are to some extent constructed, and a *version* of the truth rather than 'The Truth', unthinkable. I did try and give some perspective on this, contextualising that people write autobiographies, and biographies for all kinds of reasons—not least to make money. I also pointed out that it is impossible to write a life in full, so biography is necessarily selective, but he wouldn't have it.

The outraged student returned a week later clutching an email from Nick Hornby, no less, which stated that the book was a memoir of his early life, which is not the point we were discussing. I was however, very impressed by the student's determination. When I could not be persuaded that the book was *true* rather than a construction of events, the student declared that I would not be the best person to supervise his intended PhD on the topic. On that, at least, we could both agree!

In 2013 there was at least a Faculty-led process to recruit an interim Director, but it had much the same result as the old boy network. Myself, Matt Taylor and Neil Carter were up for interview. I knew before I applied that Matt, already a professor, would get it, but thought it was important not to accept without making my own case. Two members of the ICSHC group were on successive fixed term contracts. At interview I said I would make them both permanent, to be told that had been arranged earlier in the week. I shared an office with one of these chaps at the time and had listened to him moan about being on a fixed term contract for two years. When I asked why he had not told me about the permanent contract, he replied that he didn't want me to get the job. I arranged for an office move. The feedback from the interview panel was that Matt was considered a 'safe pair of hands.'

From that point Matt led the validation of the unwanted BA courses: he couldn't not. The four of us left working full time in the Centre (myself, Neil Carter, Matt, and Rob Colls) wrote the validation documents. In this way I was vindicated not to have led on the validation of the BA, as I would have volunteered my time from my existing role, whereas by acting as Interim Head of Centre, Matt was paid.

There just wasn't the dynamism of the Centre that I joined in 2006, and I could see that in a vocational university with financial issues, research was being downgraded. So it was with regret, but no nostalgia, that I began to invest in my exit strategy.

Our research and enthusiasms take us on different intellectual paths and mine was following object-based cultural studies. Museum and heritage work was particularly interesting, and public history work especially so.

Having begun to serve as a Non-Executive Director at Silverstone where there were plans for a museum on the circuit, I also led the validation of an MA in Motor Sport at De Montfort that summer. It was part of a chance to develop my board-level leadership skills outside of academia. Led by Sally Reynolds, the Silverstone Museum would eventually open in March 2020, just days before the pandemic lockdown due to COVID-19. It was the UK's largest visitor attraction to open in 2020, at around £20 million. I had hugely enjoyed working with archivist, and now Head of Collections and Research, Steph Sykes-Dugmore, and the collections of the British Racing Driver's Club. Working at Silverstone became something of a sanctuary of intelligent and able women, pioneering a new sporting museum.

I had also been able to secure paid six-month internships at the Adidas Headquarters in Germany, specifically for the MA Sport History students, of whom two or three a year would go over and enjoy applying some of the research techniques we developed on the MA. It was particularly rewarding to see teachers who studied the MA part-time seeking a career change to work in the archives, and those who had progressed straight from their undergraduate studies to combine work and study at Master's level. Several wrote related dissertations on the subject, helping both Adidas and their careers. Pia Wild worked in Germany after the internship ended, and is now with Warner Brothers Studios.

When Silverstone was fully established, David Freestone whom I had worked with as a History undergraduate and on the MA, went on to work in the archives there, helping also on F1 race days and he has subsequently gone on to work in the archives at Lola. The internships are a vocational initiative of which I remain proud.

My UEFA-funded research was published in 2013 as *Globalising Women's Football* with Peter Lang, a first look at the professionalisation of women's football, its terms and conditions as an industry. In July 2013, I had was bound for the women's Euros final in Stockholm, having been invited to put together the first academic panel hosted by a UEFA conference on women's football. The conference was entitled UEFA's Knowledge and Information-Sharing Scenario (or KISS) programme which had been in place since 2005. Honestly, for a conference on women's football to have the acronym KISS! I had been to so many similar UEFA, Olympic and FIFA events, so I knew stoicism was required.

The panel included Stacey Pope, and Sine Agergaard of Aalborg University, Denmark, head of the International Network for Research in Sport and Migration Issues. Sine had teamed up with Nina Clara Tiesler of Lisbon for an event *Women, Soccer and Transnational Migration* we held in Copenhagen in 2012. Kevin Tallec Marston also presented on his research on youth football, and Natalie Smith on sport management.

The whole panel was very well received, including by Michel D'Hooge, who headed up the women's football committee for a time and was a medical specialist, who had been President of the Belgian FA. But the tone of the conference was typified by overconfident UEFA marketing guy, Noel Mooney, who suggested that women should perhaps make themselves more attractive to encourage more sponsors. The groan in the room was loud, as most of us had heard this nonsense for several years. Mooney apparently genuinely thought he'd had an epiphany that was not available to lesser mortals. The considerable influence of Steffi Jones soon shut him down. Mooney is now CEO of the Welsh FA. Australian Moya Dodd told me later that she felt she could not challenge, because as a co-opted member of the FIFA Executive Committee from 2013, she could soon be deselected and she wanted to stay in her position. This did happen in 2017 when she was outvoted as the Asian female seat member in favour of Mahfuza Akhter Kiron of Bangladesh.

I had originally been informed that while our flights and accommodation in Stockholm would be funded by UEFA, along with a complimentary 15 euro ticket to the 2013 final, we should expect to provide our own food and drink, apart from sustenance at the conference itself. Stockholm was eye-wateringly expensive. In the end though we need not have worried. There were so many young UEFA employees with company credit cards, buying rounds of strawberry daiquiri, that we were easily accommodated. We were also asked to a swanky restaurant one evening to celebrate the women's conference, travelling by white cruiser along the Stockholm waterways, with a glass of champagne, to our destination. This was quite a turnaround in our expectations. The restaurant and champagne bar were booked out solely for UEFA staff and delegates.

We were then somewhat embarrassed when, for the 2013 final itself, we had to wait for Michel Platini to have his Presidential police escorted motorcade, when actually this was a kerfuffle entirely of his own making. We walked a red carpet separated from ordinary family fans by a red velvet rope to hospitality at the stadium. It was honestly not necessary when most spectators had paid a few euros for their seats.

A Germany victory for Sylvia Neid, 1–0 over Norway with a young squad in transition, saw her retain the title she had won as head coach in 2009. Neid stood down in 2016 ahead of Steffi Jones taking charge of the women's team, but as we know in 2017 Sarina Wiegman had other ideas, as hosts The Netherlands took the UEFA trophy. I had some time to look around the Olympic stadium and city itself in Stockholm, which was quite beautiful.

Ironically the literature on women's football (fans, professionalism, migration, player rights, medical topics, and so on) as an explicit topic in its own right has grown exponentially since 2013. Women's football is one of the considerable growth areas in academic study internationally, from sociological, anthropological, historical and medical disciplines. But UEFA has increasingly gone down the marketing and insight route, and less so the academically rigorous one. It is to the detriment of their findings.

As a recent example, I was invited in 2021/22 to endorse a UEFA report in which market research consultancies Oliver & Ohlbaum Associates, Fly Research and Portas Consulting pulled together the original data. The report was written by young marketing men, and a female Oxford graduate who had played football but was not aware of the rapidly expanding academic literature, though she declared herself to be 'very invested' in the topic. I was appalled by the lack of rigour in the methodology, the framing of the research questions, and in the final assessments. This should never have been commissioned as it was. It was so woeful that had a BA student of mine produced the report I would have been disappointed. A MA student would not even have countenanced such a poor effort.

I was initially included in a group of academics, most of whom had not published at all on women and football, (or had not published much of note), who were asked to endorse these findings. I have not listed their names here, as no further oxygen is needed for this kind of behaviour. I am sure if you are curious, you can find the document online. I asked UEFA staff what seemed to me to be an obvious question—which is why the academics were not pulled in at the outset to help define the methodology and so forth based on what we knew from the extant literature. No one could answer that question. Now, with what had been collated we were basically being asked to nod through what had already been done. While the marketeers had been paid, it was assumed academics would back the document for the benefit of being associated with UEFA. I withdrew.

Rather than Defining the Business Case for Women's Football, and Defining the Case for Women's Club Football in Europe, the report reads the future through a series of propositions, such as, 'The number of fans could double.' I do not currently own a crystal ball, a magic lamp or any other way of anticipating the future, but I could have provided much the same information in about five minutes for the price of a cup of coffee. As a waste of resource, it reflects UEFA's arrogance. There are many and varied studies of fan groups, migration, professionalisation, medical conditions and economics in women's football across the globe making key original contributions to knowledge. None of the academics that I admire who have written on these topics were used either in the preparation of the report or the UEFA women's football module. Funny that. The assumption that the subject does not require intellectual rigour, and there is not a literature upon which to draw, is quite baffling.

Instead, the UEFA report is full of get out clauses, as in: 'This report contains forward-looking statements based upon current expectations and assumptions regarding anticipated developments and other factors. They are not facts, nor are they guarantees of future performance since they are subject to numerous assumptions, risks and uncertainties, which change over time. Forward-looking statements speak only as of the date they are made, and various factors could cause actual performance to differ materially from that expressed or implied by these forward-looking statements.'

Quite why academics, especially those who have reached senior positions as professors, would put their name to such a document is beyond my understanding. That they continue to present such nonsense at conferences to the present day as their own original research on women's football is not to the glory of the academic profession.

The Opening Ceremony of the 1999 FIFA Women's World Cup in Los Angeles. Held at the Rose Bowl, the crowd was over 90,000, a record for a women's tournament at that time. Rockets and glitter cannons fired, there was a flyover from the US Air Force, and plenty of Hollywood glamour.

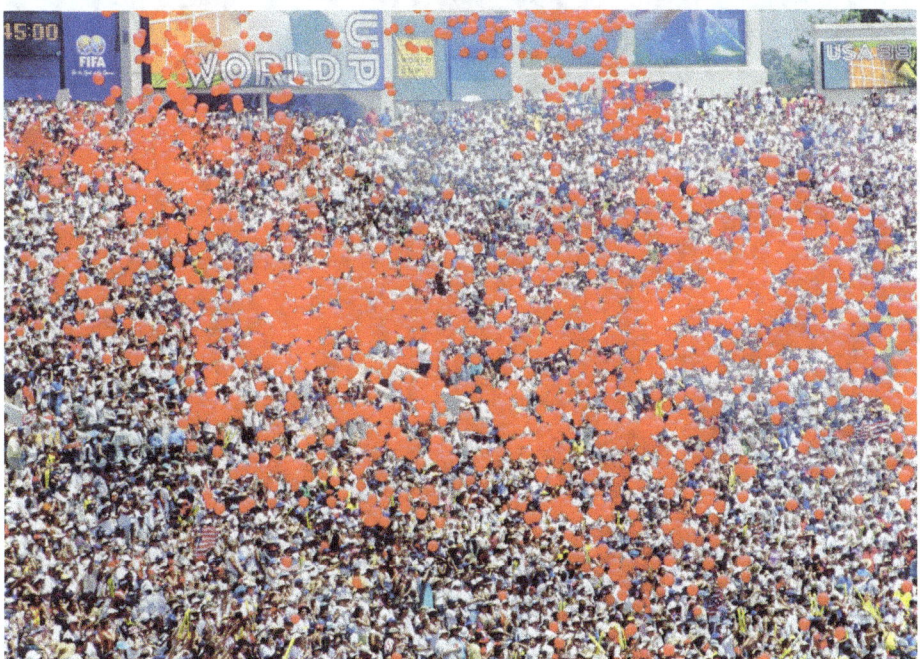

The red balloons disappeared into a perfect azure sky that David Hockney could have painted. The packed stadium was treated to musical acts by Jennifer Lopez, Billie, and Hanson.

USA in 1999 was the first FIFA tournament for women to feature sixteen teams. President Bill Clinton claimed, 'It was the most exciting sports event I have ever seen.'

Nutmeg the mascot, a fox, was much in evidence in 1999 merchandise. The first Women's World Cup mascot in 1991 was a Phoenix, named Ling Ling by the Chinese hosts. The second was a diminutive Viking with pigtails named Fiffi by the Swedish hosts.

The final and third-place play-off were held as a double-header on the same day. Brazil defeated Norway on penalties to take the bronze medal, after a scoreless full time and, due to television scheduling, no time for a golden goal. The US-China final was also scoreless after extra time, with the US winning by the narrowest of margins, 5-4 on penalties.

Not everyone was there for the football. FIFA hired out the Paramount Lot for one party during the week of the Executive Committee meeting. Professional dancers offered guests the chance to samba, jive or cha cha cha. The party cost $1 million.

In LA for England's 2006 World Cup bid, Sir Bobby Charlton was approached by Jean, who, after startling him in a coffee shop, composed herself to chat with him and wife Norma.

1999 Soccer Barbies and Christies, endorsed by Mia Hamm, symbolised USA's commercialised sports merchandise boom.

This contrasts with the tickets to the 1st FIFA Women's World Championship for the M&M's Cup in China, which was not even given a World Cup title. The ticket stubs feature the phoenix mascot Ling Ling, and a goat with breasts, the identity of whom remains a mystery.

In 2011, the slogan for the Women's World Cup in Germany was 'On the ball with the beautiful game'. It seemed irrelevant to the organisers that the hosts were the reigning champions, having won the 2007 edition in China. They were eliminated in the quarter-finals by eventual winners Japan. The mascot was Karla Kick, a football-loving kitten.

At the FIFA Executive Committee meeting, being of short stature, Jean borrowed Sepp Blatter's Presidential box on which to stand to deliver her presentation. Here she conveys her gratitude to its owner, who is relieved to have it back.

The 'French-Welsh male professor' Jean Williams at the entrance to the Paramount Studios party with moustachioed partner 'Simone'. A striking couple.

Hollywood glamour met football in a PR dream for FIFA, as a weary Charlie Chaplin welcomes delegates to yet another Congress dinner with his signature charm and quiet resignation.

Prince Harry, Royal Patron of the Silverstone Museum, was on hand in March 2018 to mark the start of the build. The Museum opened in March 2020, becoming the UK's largest new visitor attraction that year.

Queues at the 2019 Women's World Cup opener in Paris. FIFA's decision to reissue printed tickets the day before kick-off, left early arrivals who had printed tickets missing the ceremony and first ten minutes despite arriving an hour early.

With Hispanicist David Wood (rear left) and Alex Jackson (far right), Jean welcomed Silvana Goellner (rear centre), and Verónica Moreira (front left of image) from Brazil and Argentina, respectively, to the Hidden Histories project in 2018.

At the 2013 Women's Euros Final in Stockholm Sweden, Jean with colleagues (L-R): Stacey Pope, Sine Agergaard and Natalie Smith at a UEFA Women's Football Conference. Kevin Tallec-Marston also worked on the project.

In freelancer life, Jean has had several lovely invitations to present, here at Ticketmaster Legends of Sport 2023 edition focussing on women's sport.

At the Premiere of Copa 71 at the Toronto International Film Festival in September 2023. Jean has since gone on to be executive producer of the short film Back of the Net, written by and starring Ella Dorman-Gajic and is a historical consultant on The Corinthians: We Were The Champions.

CHAPTER V
THE ARTIFICIAL WORLD CUP, 2015
Jacqui and the Chocolate Factory

I simply had not thought it through. As I listened to the sound of what seemed like multiple rowdy rodents on the dirt floor of the cellar below me, I wished I had planned my three-week research trip to the US with more care.

Off the back of an extraordinarily busy 2012, an Olympic year in which I had tried, (and failed), to buy the auctioned gold medal of Leicester swimmer, Jennie Fletcher, I had won an international scholarship to the National Sporting Library and Museum, (NSLM) Middleburg, Virginia USA, for February 2013. I landed on 4 February for one night in Washington.

I had first visited Washington in 2008 for a conference at the German Historical Institute on German-American sports history. It was very convivial and a fantastic event. When I was in Washington the first time, a TV crew had heard my accent and asked me, as a Brit, what I thought of Presidential candidate Barack Obama's use of social media to connect with a wide general public. Many of these services didn't exist for a broad public before Obama took office in 2009, and his mastery of new forms of communication technology have led to claims of him being the, 'First social media President' (which others have contested).

Now, four years later, I was returning to Washington just after Obama had been inaugurated, for a second term. After a one night stay at the InterContinental, The Willard I was transferring to Middleburg for a three-week research trip on an international scholarship. The project was to look at female equestrian experts—from breeding, to carriage-driving, to equine health specialists to well-known competitors.

I had been told to expect free, cosy lodgings courtesy of the Museum, in quite a small town with a walkable daily commute to the archive, so I hadn't bothered to hire a car. Big mistake. The hotel hailed me a taxi, the driver had a cracked iPhone screen as his sat nav, and had never heard of Middleburg. *Uh, ho.* I was not sure he was a proper taxi service, but there was insignia and what looked like licensing in the cab. My driver looked distinctly nervous.

The nation's Horse and Hunt capital, Middleburg even had a hairdressers called The Painted Mane. My taxi driver was black and he looked relieved to deposit me at the Museum, and get back to Washington as soon as possible. Middleburg, I would find out, is approximately 80% white. An anglophile enclave, the town had a postcolonial fascination with the British, while also wanting to outdo them at every turn. So, I was welcomed warmly, but at a distance. I duly waited for the lift to my accommodation, which turned out to be a little wooden shack.

As I tried to unpack upstairs the bedding was damp, everything was dank, and with only a phone number to call, outside it began to drizzle, then pour. There was no wifi provided so I couldn't find alternative accommodation. *Tough it out,* I thought, *it's only one night.* As I tried to make myself comfortable on the sofa rather than the clammy bed for some sleep, the rain intensified and the scratching below in the cellar grew louder.

One hour. Two hours. Three hours later. No one from the museum answering the phone when I called. In the end I disturbed Simon (who else?) back in the UK where it was the early hours. He booked me into a B&B he found online, I repacked my case, walked across town in the downpour and into a nice warm, quiet room at about 5am. *Phew.*

I had relied upon the hospitality of my hosts, only to find major changes at the Museum were in process which meant that they were not inclined to put themselves out on my account. A new Executive Director was moving into post and the museum was now in flux. Restructuring was in process, and people not sure of their employment status were not overly enthusiastic about my presence.

I was blissfully content in the little B&B I had found, quite willing to pay out of my own salary rather than go back to the wooden hut, but I had been given the last room. My haven was normally hired out as a romantic retreat, having a jacuzzi corner bath and a four-poster bed. The problem was that Valentine's night was approaching, and it was booked out for at least ten days. Understandably I was asked to vacate, and this posed a problem for the Museum. I made it clear a mildewed wooden hut with resident furry guests was simply not for me. The Museum's solution was to transport me to Mimi's, from the ridiculous to the sublime!

How to describe Mimi's place? Well, think not so much of a petite older woman's house, but a huge party barn for guests on a vast ranch that Mimi owned. Turned out, there was nothing diminutive about Mimi. The woman herself was in Florida, a snowbird leaving the sub-zero conditions of Middleburg for a winter of warmth. Mimi had done very nicely for herself, hats off! Chapeau Mimi, I thought on my dawn runs three miles along the dirt track into town to the Museum, and back again to the barn for coffee.

On my morning runs, I would pass Mimi's horse racetrack on the left, complete with stands and announcer system, and her helipad on the right. As I did so I was accompanied only by Northern Cardinal birds in the hedgerows, their scarlet plumage in stark bloody relief to the surrounding white hoar of frost and snow on the black branches of the verges.

So, it was quite a lonely three weeks, with the light lost about four in the afternoon, and then a very long evening watching PBS television or spent working, until the company of birdsong at 5am.

I could have just hired a car of course, and spent my time in Washington. But, choosing instead to test my resilience in a millionaire's party barn, I found Middleburg itself quite fascinating, even while many of the plantation houses had their origins in wealth from slavery, in division, and the exploitation of black labour. Nearby is the famous 400-acre Glen Ora estate on the Loudoun and Fauquier county line. Best remembered as the country retreat of Jackie and John F. Kennedy from 1961 to 1963, Glen Ora was also the house where Wallis Simpson, aged 17, met Lloyd Nolan Tabb, from whom she learned about football so that they might have something in common. Knowing Simpson's future politics as the Duchess of Windsor, it was safe to say the layers of historical context were very complicated, then and now.

Glen Ora became legendary when Jackie tutored her children to ride there, away from the intense political pressures of Washington. As supporters of civil rights, the Kennedys would also have been aware of the growing number of black businesses in the area and the previously segregated drug store lunch counters gradually became integrated in 1961. Walking around, it was humbling to think that in something as mundane as the drug stores I was passing, that their lunch counters could be such an important site of victory for civil rights.

At the same time of course, the everyday nature of segregation, its lived ordinariness, was exemplified by who was allowed to lunch where, and with whom. To make exactly this point, the Loudon County leader of the National Association for the Advancement of Colored People (NAACP) William McKinley Jackson had sat with the town's black physician, Maurice Edmead, and other friends at the Red Fox Tavern. Jackson led many initiatives to desegregate facilities in the county—from schools, to swimming pools. This integration was wrought by conscious acts of friendship and defiance. I wished I had time to learn more, but did some basic research on the issues but cannot do the complications of the topic justice and keep on track.

Although Jackie's offer to buy Glen Ora was declined in 1962, she purchased Wexford and 166 acres nearby, named after the Kennedy family home in Wexford, Ireland. Both John F. Kennedy Jr. and Caroline learned to ride there, although the President visited only three times before his assassination, and was not a fan. So, there was a complex local history for me to explore, let alone the Museum itself, which was a stunningly beautiful resource.

My absent host, Mimi Abel Smith, was the previous owner of Hickory Tree Farm, a

300-acre Thoroughbred breeding, training and horseracing facility of rolling pastures, with spectacular views of the Blue Ridge Mountains. She had sold Hickory Tree Farm and downsized herself by now to a smaller house nearby, but had kept the party barn. There was a doghouse close to the party barn which was a mock-Palladian villa—complete with an eight-sided lantern in the roof, and a sign on the gate that read, *Thimble Hall*. A pampered pooch, or four, had obviously called *Thimble Hall* home. No one, and I mean not a soul apart from I, went dogless in Middleburg. Not having a canine companion was much like leaving the house without wearing your trousers. Dogs, like horses, were intensely political, nationalistic symbols of a post-colonial past that wasn't quite ready to be a distant country.

I am definitely a friend of the fox, the horse, and the hound. Hunters, not so much. Well, the Middleburg Hunt had its origins in what was billed as 'the great international foxhunting match' between Alexander Henry Higginson's Middlesex English hounds and Harry Worcester Smith's Grafton hounds in 1905. The gentlemen had a dispute about the relative superiority of their respective English and American packs of hounds. Mr. Smith's American Grafton hounds decisively won the match. The carnage of the match lasted over two weeks, and was widely reported, establishing Middleburg as the axis of the Hunt Country of America. So, I was never going to be entirely comfortable in the place, even in some luxury. There was not a lot of tofu on the menu, and jackfruit had not yet become the Kim Kardashian of vegan cookery in 2013; let's leave it at that.

Worse, I had never watched *Downton Abbey*. An unforgiveable faux pas. The annual fundraiser for the Museum had been organised by the Vice Chair, Jacqueline B. Mars who had followed the period drama and was rather taken with Dan Stevens, the actor who played Matthew Crawley. I offered the opinion that no one under 60 in the UK watched *Downton Abbey*. It was not a popular view. It was also an incorrect perspective, which I later revised. Lots of young folk watched *Downton*! During lockdown 2020, I binged the whole series—it was fantastic!

Spoiler alert: Matthew Crawley is the solicitor who has inherited the Downton estate and eventually marries Lady Mary, before dying soon after the birth of their son and heir. Dan Stevens would be the star guest at the Middleburg charity event at which the goody bags were full of items of traditionally British food and drink, now owned by Mars, the multinational manufacturer of foodstuffs. So, I was greeted by a bottle of brown sauce, a well-known salad dressing, tea from a famous English brand in a caddy, savoury pickles, chocolate, and all manner of items which embodied British tastes—or a Mars interpretation of them anyway. Although from humble origins, I am pleased to report I had never before had condiments as a present. But, of course these seemingly quotidian candies, table sauces and pickles were elevated by the host. I'd certainly never been gifted ketchup by a billionaire before!

The event itself was straight out of Downton, with a lavish garden party feel. I did wonder why Jacqueline B. Mars, the one-third owner of the largest chocolate output in the world, and an estimated private fortune of $45.8 billion in 2024, according to Bloomberg, had bothered with a fundraiser at all. But then I looked up Dan Stevens: a born leading man, and British to boot. Jacqueline had been shrewd enough to grade tickets based on those who would get to be in a room with Dan to gaze at a distance, those who would actually meet him and the very few who would be on the same table. Eyewatering prices for a chance to ask a transfixing actor to pass the (Mars-owned) salt. Jacqueline was 74 in 2013 when I was in Middleburg, and had retired from Mars to run Stonehall Farm, The Plains, Virginia, a 400-acre working farm that specialized in organic farming, horse training and horse breeding. Having trained horses ridden by Olympians, she is still a trustee of the US equestrian team, as well as her ongoing board connections with the National Sporting Library and Museum.

Finally, the research at the museum and archives was worth any amount of small personal discomfort. There were beautifully illustrated tracts on the history of equestrianism, letter and diaries from the Anglo-Irish cousins, Edith Somerville and Violet Florence Martin, (writing under the name Martin Ross) and all kinds of fantastic photographic sources. The art collections at the NSLM were stunning. These included sculptures of Nic Fiddian-Green and Tessa Pullan, oil paintings of Alfred Munnings, John Boultbee, John Frederick Herring Jr, and others. Notwithstanding my own antipathy to blood sports, and what are sometimes called 'field sports' (a polite term for choosing to shoot things when there are fully stocked supermarkets nearby), it was a world-class facility and a great honour to have been able to spend time there.

I then spent most of March and April 2013, when not teaching, camped out in the Farmhouse at Silverstone circuit. This was to be a life changing decision in a number of ways. Working at Silverstone with Steph Sykes-Dugmore the archivist, was huge fun, and she fuelled me with endless cups of tea. Steph introduced me to Sally Reynolds who was leading the project to establish a museum on site, and were looking for a subject specialist to advise on the historical content. Since I'd worked in the collections extensively, and at Brooklands, I was pleased to accept their invitation to become a Non-Executive Director as historical specialist.

I had recently published with Kevin Moore, Jeff Hill and Jason Woods on the use of a Museum at the Indianapolis Motor Sport Speedway circuit, and how history is part of the experience of the Indianapolis 500, through acts of commemoration and memorialisation, such as the countdown to the race itself. We debated, as academics and practitioners, the museum-academic relationship which provided areas for growth and professional development on both sides.

Simon and I had been to Indy for our 10th wedding anniversary, and had attended a number of other iconic events such as the Le Man 24 hours. Sally explained her aim to establish the museum and since it was a good opportunity to develop my board-level knowledge, as well as my motor sport contacts, I agreed to volunteer. Though as Sally would later joke, the project was often declared lifeless; she managed to resuscitate it several times along with Stuart Pringle who was motor sport director of the circuit, and then took over in entirety. As a female-led project, Sally became the museum's first CEO, supported by Steph, before a range of difficulties—not least the pandemic—saw a change of leadership.

I learned a lot about how the heritage-themed visitor attraction industry worked. We were invited to a very exciting Grand Prix at Silverstone in July, as the museum project progressed, and were effectively ambassadors for the idea of a historic facility at the circuit. To give an example of our board-level conversations, the water towers became a perennial favourite.

You may remember that in 2012, due to the Olympic Games, Glastonbury could not go ahead due to the shortage of portable toilets? Logistically at Silverstone, for the hundreds of plumbed toilets to flush, and people to wash their hands, the two huge water towers were vital during a Grand Prix. But they were situated in the approach to the circuit. We needed them moving to the outer field, so that the museum building stood alone, but the timing of that transfer was vital. As to the portable toilet provision which supplements these permanent facilities, there are luxury and standard models depending upon the level of hospitality: some opulent models even piped Handel's 'Water Music' through integrated loudspeakers. With 140,000 spectators, let alone staff and volunteers onsite, and toilets flushing approximately every 10-20 seconds, everything needed to run immaculately.

Having written about how large events were run, my interest by now ran beyond the academic. I was by now writing *A Contemporary History of Women's Sport 1850–1960*, trying to cover relatively neglected sports codes (tennis, cycling, cricket, golf, archery, field hockey, motor racing, swimming) and developing my Olympic writing. The book came out in 2014 as Part One, because I had so much material.

I haven't yet got around to writing Part Two, from 1960 to the present day. I was also interested in women writing about sport in various ways, and making a living as entrepreneurs. So, I also researched at Brooklands in Surrey, home of the first purpose-built racing circuit. Ethel Locke King DBE, the co-owner of Brooklands with her husband Hugh, led a motor racing revolution and Brooklands had more women involved from 1920–1938 than later all-male clubs.

I had an early insight into the world of amateur male historians of motor sport when an archive volunteer at Brooklands gave me race timings, and told me that the really interesting data was to be found there. For statisticians, yes. But it took a full day of working around this guy to get to the economic, social and cultural history of the women that I was actually writing about. No longer in use as a circuit, Brooklands had a fantastic hotel on site, and the themed décor would also come into use as an exemplar

THE ARTIFICIAL WORLD CUP, 2015

in the later public history work I did at both St George's Park and Wembley.

In June 2013 I spent a couple of weeks at the Adidas HQ in Germany. One of my MA students was completing his paid internship, and he showed me around what felt like more of a university campus than an industrial complex, as there were several very nice food and beverage facilities, sports infrastructure for casual games such as volleyball, and table tennis, and lots of greenery.

You probably already know the story, but bear with me for those who don't. Brothers Adolf and Rudolf Dassler grew up in the Bavarian town of Herzogenaurach, now home to both Adidas and Puma. Their father was a shoemaker and their mother ran a small laundry. Adi loved all sports, mainly athletics, football, boxing, ice hockey and skiing. His genius was to produce increasingly specialised footwear for each discipline, using materials like military cloth and rubber, recycled after World War One. Rudy joined the enterprise, and production grew. At the Summer Olympics of 1928 German Lina Radke won the inaugural women's 800 metre race wearing a pair of specially fashioned spikes. But it wasn't immediately clear who the manufacturer was. An identifying mark was needed. By the Los Angeles Olympics of 1932 more international athletes were wearing their shoes, including Jessie Owens but again the visual identification problem remained.

However, when Hitler came to power in 1933, the Dassler brothers, like many other young men, joined the Hitler Youth. By 1938 the Dasslers employed around 120 people making 1000 pairs of shoes a day, and with the outbreak of war they were told to dedicate their efforts to military footwear, 10,000 pairs a day. Adi and Rudy quarrelled and never reconciled, forming Adidas and Puma respectively. The three stripes of Adidas were visually designed to be quickly and easily recognisable in photographs and on film. The Puma of Rudy's brand was a similar device. Shortly after Adi won the contract to supply the West German team, using new technology of the time, he developed screw in studs of different lengths. In the 'Miracle of Bern' the Germans won the 1954 World Cup, beating the heavily favoured Hungarians 3–2 in Switzerland.

Until the advent of Nike in the US, Adidas and Puma developed into global sportswear giants and later in the 1970s Adi's son, Horst, became a noted sports marketer, persuading Coca Cola to become a sponsor, before adding McDonald's and Levi Strauss. As head of International Sport and Leisure (ISL) which packaged global television rights for FIFA, and then the International Olympic Committee for its own rights, Horst created mega events especially in the newly professional Olympic era. Years after his death in 1987, ISL collapsed with huge debts, and by then Adidas had broken up as a family firm, which has huge implications for the archival holdings, and for historians.

Having researched at the National Sports Shoe Collection in Northamptonshire, I knew that innovation drove the growth of the business. There was a Hall of Fame building to house the hall of fame, where product launches also took place. Within that, there were historical installations in a Walk of Fame in which each of the MA students had made contributions, leading to a replica of Adi's original office from 1949. Here sports stars who were signing on as Adidas athletes would be made aware of their predecessors and the historical legacy of the brand. It was a technique that famously didn't impress Michael Jordan, who instead chose relative newcomer, Nike, who told him he would be a main name, and hence Air Jordans were developed.

There were also some fantastic bespoke items, including a cat-like hooded shrug with small ears and claws, made for Rhianna. It was also noticeable that singers, like Missy Elliott, were as much evident as sportswomen, blurring the link between leisurewear, fashion and performance clothing. Having seen a huge collection of Manfield football boots in Northamptonshire, I saw that Adi Dassler had amassed a huge collection himself, and had literally taken them apart in his search for how to improve their design with his own innovations. Official World Cup-endorsed balls, like the 1974 Telstar model, featuring licensed Durlast polyurethane technology were further examples of this. There were lots of endorsements from the likes of Uwe Seeler, the Kaiser, Franz Beckenbauer, and his family.

My specific interest was how the training shoe came to be such a ubiquitous item of footwear. Originally sold as a shoe specifically for hard flooring, snow and icy conditions, with a moulded rubber sole with multiple points of grip, almost providing suction, the training shoe quickly became an item worn in the street in fashionable colour combinations. A variety of styles followed such as the Samba, launched in the approach to the first World Cup after the Second World War, Brazil 1950. From my work at the Sneaker conference at Northamptonshire Museum, where there is a nationally designated shoe collection rich in sports shoes, I had met and heard from a number of highly specialist collectors who particularly looked for rare Adidas models, such as those made in Yugoslavia and Czechoslovakia. So, it was hugely rewarding to spend the time charting this history—getting to work with academics from other disciplines. Publishing on both football boot and shirt history, *Kit: Fashioning the Body For Sport*, came out as an edited book in 2015, and we had a great one day conference in Leicester to develop the papers for publication.

It is probably worth also saying that I had good fortune to get into difficult to access archives later in the year through relationship-building with major sporting museums. This is a particular skill if you are new to the field, and takes some time to build trust.

The first success was to look at the Dod collections at the Wimbledon Lawn tennis archives. Charlotte 'Lottie' Dod was the first great female all-rounder. Winning Wimbledon five times in all, including three times consecutively, 'The Little Wonder', as she was known also went on to hiking and climbing tours, cycling in Europe, sailing, hockey, and Winter sports including curling, skiing, skating and tobogganing. Still today Wimbledon's youngest ever women's singles winner, aged just 15, she also took the 1904 British Ladies Amateur golf championship, to become the only woman to hold both tennis and golf elite titles.

In 1908, she won a silver medal at the London Olympic Games in archery, the same sport in which her brother, Willy, won a gold medal. She was a legend at Wimbledon; therefore I was eventually given access to the Dod collection of her life, with many photographs taken by her brother as a hobbyist, including of the family cat, Aladdin. Much of this research was written up in *A Contemporary History of Women's Sport, Part One, Sporting Women, 1850–1960* published in 2014.

I should add that teaching distance learning, and mainly on PhD supervision was flexible enough to meet the needs of students while also completing the research. Quite a few students graduated the MA Sport History and moved onto study with me on a PhD at this time. It modelled good practice to have a research-led curriculum, with museum and public history outputs, such as the exhibition I was approached to design for the Supreme Court, on Sport and the Law.

My second big archival success was getting into the Dame Mary Glen-Haig files at the Olympic Museum in Lausanne. A really important person in Britain's Olympic history, Glen-Haig was born 10 years after Lottie Dod won her silver medal in the Olympics. Glen-Haig competed in four Olympic games: in 1948, 1952, 1956 and 1960, in the Foil discipline. Her father, William James, had fenced at the 1908 London Olympics and had instilled in her what an honour it was. A hospital administrator by profession, in the 1970s Glen-Haig Chaired the Central Council for Physical Recreation, an important body for funding amateur British sport at a time when the government did not directly support Olympic athletes. It would not be until the advent of the National Lottery in 1994 introduced by cricket-mad Prime Minister John Major, that British Olympic athletes could become fully professional, as the Games themselves became Open (meaning open to professionals) in 1988. After a disastrous Atlanta Games in 1996, Lottery funding for Olympic athletes began in 1997, British-funded athletes returned 28 medals, 11 of which were gold, at the Sydney Olympic Games in 2000. British Para athletes also saw a dramatic rise in funding and returned 131 medals, of which 41 were gold, to finish second behind hosts Australia.

What really set Mary Glen-Haig apart however, was the pivotal role she played in international sports governance, becoming only the third woman to join the International Olympic Committee as a member in 1982, after Flor Isava-Fonseca was made an IOC member in 1981, along with Pirjo Häggman. Fonseca served on the Executive Board from 1990 to 1994, becoming the first woman to do so. Later, Mary Glen-Haig was joined by the Princess Royal as a member of the IOC, and the close link between the Royal family and the Olympian was made clear by a personal recommendation to the IOC President, Juan Antonio Samaranch in the file handwritten by Prince Philip.

Both the Queen and Prince Philip were huge fans of the Olympic Games, and then the Olympic and Paralympic Games. For instance, in 1956, they attended the equestrian events in Stockholm aboard the Royal yacht, and extended their stay afterwards. When the Games returned to London again in 2012, Glen-Haig was an ambassador, and died aged 96 in 2014. So, she had witnessed a huge change in the status and scope of the Olympic movement, and had been part of that wider change.

After a 30-year embargo common in Olympic archives, it was a professional pleasure to access the files and to be able to write about her career in *Britain's Olympic Women: a History* in 2021. The gap in publication dates (2014 and 2021) reflects some big personal changes that this chapter will now detail.

Not Staying in My Lane

The beginning of the end was clearly approaching at De Montfort. Paradoxically, one thing that accelerated the process was a funding success in the 2013/14 academic year. I had always been interested in the work of Stuart Hall, a Jamaican-born British Marxist sociologist, cultural theorist, and political activist. I had read a lot of Michel Foucault during my Master's in Modern Literary Theory and Practice at the University of Leicester, and Hall developed Foucault's work in expanding the field of cultural studies in the UK. By treating popular culture in a very rigorous way, Hall's work allowed the symbolic significance of an object to be decoded. I had been told so often that the theoretical aspects of my work made for sport *studies* rather than sports *history*, that I gave up trying to appease the critics. In the end, I didn't actually care whether I was a historian of sport, or a sport historian, or a sports historian, all of which were actual topics of debate over lunch!

Which is a long-winded way of saying I gave myself permission to follow my intellectual interest in the history of the Men's World Cup posters, the artists and their designs and won £30,000 Higher Education Investment Funding (HEIF) for a project on the topic to culminate in an exhibition at the National Football Museum Manchester, for the Brazil World Cup in 2014.

The National Football Museum was then the world's leading museum of football and had just been recognised as part of a Designated Collection by Arts Council England. It housed the FIFA-Langton collection, including Harry Langton's collection of over 40,000 items relevant to several football codes. First at Preston, then in Manchester, the football museum also had several key pieces of artwork, and a fantastic collection of World Cup posters among them. When the Museum of Rugby opened, (now the World Rugby Museum), Harry Langton's work was also core to its success.

THE ARTIFICIAL WORLD CUP, 2015

In this football–art history research I was helped by Kevin Tallec Marston who was close to completing his PhD study with me as second supervisor. Kevin in turn was in contact with the lawyer that FIFA had used to analyse the copyright and licensing complexities of the posters, and their artists. It was a great example of combining in-depth FIFA industry knowledge, cutting-edge academic research, and public impact with the museums and archives sector in both Brazil and the UK. The lawyer had been asked to get permission from the artists, where known, for FIFA to copyright the poster images. This was particularly difficult where big names, like Spanish painter and sculptor, Joan Miró, was commissioned to produce the 1982 poster. I found the work the lawyer had done fascinating, and it was very kind of him to help me, as it was Kevin.

As well as an existing contact with Dr Kevin Moore the Director at the National Football Museum, I wanted to connect with what was happening in Brazil. André Megale, a graduate of the FIFA MA, and two Brazilian researchers, José Renato Santiago and Marcelo Unti, had launched the Brazilian Institute of the History of Sports (IBHME). A lawyer with extensive business contacts, André also had connections at the Museum of Football in São Paolo. However, when I asked for André's email to write and invite him to participate in the project bid, the male member of professional services staff would not share it, citing data protection. Given that I had taught André a few years back this was plainly silly. When I complained to academic colleagues, they replied that André was a personal friend so the contact was not something they could pass on. Hmmm.

My workaround was to reach out through the FIFA Masters alumni, who gave the email by return the same day, and their good wishes. André soon replied that he was delighted to be personally involved. His clients included the Brazil Stock Exchange and he was already in contact with the Vice Chancellor, Dominic Shellard, at De Montfort, who had asked for two internship opportunities. Shellard had launched DMU Global in which he had committed to give 50% of students some sort of international work experience as part of their degree. André later went on to work as Director of Governance and Compliance at the Brazilian Football Association; so much more else could have been done to connect with him from De Montfort.

Vice Chancellor Shellard was planning to hold an exhibition on football during the 2014 World Cup in Brazil, at the British Consulate in São Paulo. I don't know that he had ever written exhibition material before or knew anything about Brazilian football. But this was part of the VCs plan to be at the world cup for most of the tournament. However, it was pointed out to him that making another large swathe of staff at the university redundant while spending a month in Brazil might not be a good look. He was clearly piqued.

I had budgeted in the £30,000 bid to go out to Brazil myself for two weeks and conduct research (as well as take in some matches, I hoped), and also offered David

Goldblatt help with his flights if he co-curated an exhibition with me at the National Football Museum. I knew David was intending to write his own book on Brazil.

I'd also reached out to Alex Bellos who had written a brilliant book about Brazilian football, especially male player migration and globalisation. Almost 10 years later, Alex and I nearly wrote a book on women's football, as part of his *Football School* series, with illustrator Ben Lyttleton. But the publishers were not convinced of the market for such a book amongst 7–13-year-olds, even with a big name like Alex's on the cover. Women's football, even in 2021, was not big business we were told, and boys in particular would not read about women's and girls' football. Furthermore, the publishers wanted us to bring in a sponsor to offset costs. So, the book never got written.

Back in Leicester, it was put to me that if the VC could not go for a month, I should not be going to Brazil either. As mine was two weeks of a research project, which the university had funded, the logic of this conclusion was hazy at best. But by the time I was looking to book tickets my dad's health was beginning to concern the family.

At this stage I had done the most work on World Cup history for 2014 in preparing the bid, and had developed other links in South American academia that could provide further collaborations for funding bids, especially in Brazil and Argentina. But the task of writing the exhibition content was given to one of the guys in the centre who had shown no previous interest in researching the subject. That showed in the final product. The panels were entitled, *They Can Play*. This quotation was a withering understatement by Alf Ramsey, when asked how good South American players were. The exhibition itself had way too many words on each panel, in English only, seeking to explain Brazil's relationship to European football by outlining the careers of Ronaldo, Roberto Carlos, Pelé etc. In the most football obsessed country in the world, each panel also provided a picture of Ronaldo, Roberto Carlos, Pelé etc just in case visitors to the British Consulate in Brazil did not recognise them.

Furthermore, the two academics the university sent over to Brazil during the world cup were footwear and contour fashion lecturers. I don't know how much business the university picked up in terms of contour fashion and footwear, but not to send over football specialists in a World Cup year in Brazil, when an influential De Montfort alumni was setting up a sport history centre in the same city as the British Consulate? Unfathomable.

The whole atmosphere at work became Baltic. Winning the funding for a £30,000 project on men's football in the run up to a World Cup was not popular, and it was even said to me that if I bid less in future for funding, it would be better for the centre as a whole, as I could teach more on undergraduate History courses. No one else had thought to bid, evidently.

What made all that insularity particularly illogical was that away from Leicester, it was a great success. As well as several World Cup conference Keynotes, I spoke at the

THE ARTIFICIAL WORLD CUP, 2015

University of Oxford, and we held an event at the British Library, plus there were several high-profile media calls.

Most disappointing of all, when André Megale came over to Leicester ahead of us travelling up to Manchester for one of the National Football Museum public drop-ins, he was surprised to receive a rather frosty welcome. For instance, the VC agreed to meet him one evening to discuss the two internship opportunities. We waited outside his office but the VC was half an hour late, and kept the meeting with André to 15 minutes. I was not invited in. The VC then gave André, an alumni who had travelled over from Brazil (where it was 35 degrees), a Leicester Tigers ticket on a below zero evening in February. There was no offer to accompany André, and no ticket for me. André confessed as we travelled to Manchester the next day he had given up at half time and gone to warm up in his hotel. It was one thing to be cold to me as a member of staff, but not to greet an alumni guest courteously, especially one who was providing two internship opportunities in Brazil, was just rude, and bad business.

Gary Lineker was making a documentary ahead of 2014, and a researcher had seen that André was over from my social media feed, so interviewed him at the museum in Manchester for a BBC documentary about his work setting up the Brazilian Institute of the History of Sports and the general public mood ahead of the World Cup. Anchored by Lineker, and going out on prime time in the build up to the tournament, it had great public impact. I waived André off and was glad to see his time in the UK had been well spent. But I considered that colleagues had behaved poorly.

In April 2014, Brenda Elsey invited me as the Women's Studies scholar to the Hofstra International Conference, 'Soccer As The Beautiful Game' where there were over 100 academics, journalists, players and coaches, but no one else from De Montfort where there were supposed to be a concentration of football history specialists. I presented the world cup poster research, and witnessed Pelé being awarded an honorary degree to celebrate his career as a player, coach, and entrepreneur. Grant Wahl presented, as did Brenda and Stanislao Pugliese who co-directed the conference. By attending such an imaginatively curated schedule in New York, I could see how things could be done differently than the small-mindedness at my own institution. With Daniel Haxall as Editor I published the poster research in *Picturing The Beautiful Game: a History of Soccer in Visual Culture and Art* with Bloomsbury in 2018. (I am still doing that work in follow up pieces, as you will read in my analysis of the gendered nature of world cup mascots later.)

Back in the UK, between April and July 2014, there was a schedule of events held up in Manchester at the NFM to celebrate the World Cup in Brazil. Not everything went smoothly on such a large project. The only downside in working with the museum was that two senior male members of staff assumed that the project was being led by David Goldblatt. He was the bigger name, obviously, but I had made it clear to them I was the

Principal Investigator and therefore held the budget. When it came time to record a quick film talking about a history of the World Cup in 24 objects, they recorded David talking about them all—even the posters. I had sensed the two men pre-planned to do this, as we had all met up at the museum that day as a group, before they asked David to hang back and make the recordings. I had already reached the train station by the time David called me to say he wasn't entirely comfortable with the position that he had been placed in by the museum staff. I told him it was fine. Why give the chaps at the museum my time, if their assumptions about women's ability to lead a Men's World Cup project were so misogynistic? I knew well enough by then to pick my battles, got on my train and left them to it.

Completing the 2014 World Cup project also added to the contemporary collections of the National Football Museum in a very creative way. We co-created a process whereby members of the public could drop into brief lunchtime talks led by academics about their research. We also worked with local art group, Soup Dragon Collective, in sessions where people could drop in with items they had linked with memories of previous World Cups. We then interviewed the member of public on camera, talking about the significance of the object. The film was animated by Soup Dragon Collective, and we also scanned the object in a 3D printer.

During the exhibition, *A History of the World Cup in 24 Objects*, we displayed the public objects in an interactive lightbox, and by pressing on the image of the piece, the story behind it would be played as an animation. As an example, one of my graduate students dropped in with a ticket from the 1966 Final match. Tickets were sold by mail order, often in multiples well ahead of matches. My student had sent off for his at the same time as his older brothers, but he was aged only 14 and his Mum did not want him to travel from the North to Wembley Stadium, so he didn't get to go, while his older siblings did. He watched at home on the television with his Mum. I think by 2014 he had just about forgiven her!

As well as releasing new objects and stories in the public domain, given that some items were permanently donated, at the conclusion of the project the interviews were archived at the museum. Meanwhile people could keep the 3D printed item for their memories. It was great fun and we did a number of new things for the museum as well as in academia.

Three big things happened in quite quick succession after the 2014 World Cup concluded in July. The first was that I was declined my application for a personal Chair, or Professorship, by the Pro Vice-Chancellor for Research and Innovation, Andy Collop. I had previously met him to say I would be applying and to ask for any guidance/feedback. Just to clarify the process, in the UK if there is an application for promotion to a personal Chair, the individual has to identify to the university eight Professors of international standing who value the work of the applicant. Three or four from that list would be contacted to provide a reference to reinforce the quality and quantity of work. Then a promotions panel considers all the evidence. I had duly provided eight names, and four had provided references. It was not the testimonials that were the problem.

With a background in Mechanical/Civil Engineering Collop had spent exactly eight of our 30 minutes in that first meeting looking at me, and the rest of the time directed his attention to his computer screen. This had meant I had spent 22 minutes looking, not at him, but the winsome smiles of two little girls in a photograph behind him, with a child's painting underneath comprised of the words, 'We Love You Daddy.' I had 22 minutes to ask myself, *What is it about fathers of loving girls who treat women at work as second-class citizens?*

At our second meeting for feedback as to why my application for a Professorship had been rejected, Collop was even less able to make eye contact. In his discipline, he explained, high ranking h-index journals and citations were the key to building a career, with metrics the principal marker of distinction. 'Monographs', Collop informed me, 'don't matter.' Monographs, by the way are book length projects backed by original research and with extensive references, footnotes or endnotes. I pointed out that monographs were very important in the Humanities, and I had written four which had been reviewed as foundational texts. Two of the four were funded by FIFA and UEFA respectively, so internationally focussed and widely reviewed overseas.

Helpfully, the Institute of Historical Research had recently completed a study on exactly that point, in an article headed, 'Why Monographs Matter in the Humanities', which I evidenced. Fifteen minutes into a half-hour meeting, involving the same wan photographic smiles of the little girls above the 'We Love You Daddy' child's graffiti, Collop offered that I could apply again next year and explain why monographs were to be taken seriously. How kind! It hardly mattered to him that he was Pro VC for the whole university, not just his discipline. I now had a double burden of reapplying, and specifically to educate someone whose job it was to develop a research workforce about disciplines other than his own. I really, really didn't love this guy.

The second thing was that my dad, whose health had been gradually declining for some time, was taken into hospital on the 7 August. He had a fall, and we weren't sure whether a minor stroke had occasioned it, or whether it was the other way around. I'd taken him for a private referral, but his health deteriorated pretty rapidly. August was a horrendous month, and during the Bank Holiday, on 31 August, he died, almost 90 years old.

The third thing was that the interim basis upon which Matt Taylor had led the Centre came to a conclusion when the post was advertised externally for a permanent Professorial appointment. I applied, and went along to the interview for the Director of the International Centre for Sports History and Culture as an internal candidate. The Dean, Barbara Matthews, Chaired the panel.

Martin Polley, a Senior Lecturer in Sport at Southampton had been made redundant, moving to Winchester to teach on various courses. Having completed a PhD in sport and diplomacy in 1991, Martin was very well known and respected in the field. He is a nice guy. However, I felt he didn't have the depth of academic monographs, transnational profile or international funding awards to match my application. I could evidence pedagogic income from leading the MA for eight years, and my part in successive RAE/REF research returns for History which had bought in what is called QR funding. This included a double weighted 140,000 monograph for 2014, which was twice the length of a normal academic book. So monographs really do matter. I'd won individual funding internationally, had a large number of PhD completions, and external NED leadership, as well as sitting on the Faculty Senior Management Team. So, on paper and in terms of delivery at De Montfort, I felt I was the stronger candidate.

I made this case in the interview with a five-year plan, including a business plan of how to grow the Centre through links with museums, like the National Football Museum and Silverstone, and a parallel development plan for a new separate BA Sports Studies degree based in the Queen Elizabeth Leisure Centre. We could have established a Sport Science provision and had applied elements that would enable us to bid for laboratories and industry work which is where the sector investment was going. The internal candidates were also each invited to a pre-interview meeting with the Dean. It was clear Martin would apply. So, I made my case. Then I gave an argument that if it were not to be me, it should be Martin. It was testament to the state of HE that someone so talented should have been looking for permanent work.

Sure enough, Martin took the job in early September as Professor of History. I was very pleased for Martin, and ten years on, I still remain so. I just regretted that the recruitment process came to a predictable outcome. Colleagues can be both very nice individuals and paid up members of a boys' club. Had Martin's name been at the top of my CV, and my name at the top of Martin's CV, would the outcome have been the same?

Martin Polley was wise enough to make me deputy head of centre, but there was nowhere at De Monfort left to go. I could maybe have tried to move into sport business and this was suggested to me. But the Leicester Castle Business School at DMU was itself a new initiative, housing the ailing BA courses we had validated. Although Dana Brown took over as director in 2016 with a determination to succeed, she had left Castle Business School, somewhat thwarted, by July 2019. Besides, when I joined the centre there was still ambition to be international in scope. I felt I'd outgrown what had become an increasingly insular group. I decided then to get the Professorship in 2015 and take redundancy the next year. I went on holiday for a week to recuperate, mourn my dad, and reflect on the beginning of a new academic year.

Then term began again for the 2015/16 academic year. I went out to Miami in May to the North American Society for Sport History conference with the money I had not spent in Brazil. While out in Miami, I knew I wasn't mentally in a place to go out to Canada for the third Women's World Cup in North America, and physically my ankle was badly injured from a fall so I couldn't put any weight on it. There was no way I could travel from fixture to fixture at a World Cup

I did eventually get my Chair in August 2015 after the Women's World Cup tournament concluded. I was awarded a £2,000 pay rise. Since I stood down as Faculty Head of Postgraduate students, for which the allowance was, you guessed it, £2,000, it wasn't exactly a hearty congratulation. I was annoyed to find the guy who had massaged my shoulders so enthusiastically at the dinner after our Oxford Women and Sport conference had been sent my application for his opinion. He was not one of my eight nominated academics, first or second time around. The whole thing felt more than a little off. So, De Montfort got its first female Chair in Sport History in a grudging and mean fashion.

Another swathe of redundancies was announced, and in the 2016 academic year, I had almost 20 years in the bank. I took the redundancy, got another job, and on 31 October 2016, frightfully pleased, exited stage left, taking two of my PhD students with me, while some of my other Doctoral students left De Montfort all together. I made the case to the Dean and the HR department as to why I was leaving after 19 years of service, citing the repeated hostility, which the grievances I had been required to take out evidenced. One does not have to be a Critical Higher Education analyst to see how the situation could have been handled differently.

The situation had been badly managed by the Faculty and the University in terms of gender equity. I had loved my job in 2006, and couldn't wait to leave in 2016. Where's the career progression in that, for all the management speak that was going around Higher Education? But the good news is I've since gone on to do more interesting work as an individual and with my small team than I did in those last five years at De Montfort when things declined. When my energy wasn't so diverted into survival mode, there was much more drive to put into my work. And far fewer committees and working parties on which to sit.

Redundancy provided extra resources and inspiration. As well as paying off a chunk of the mortgage, a George Best-sized portion of the redundancy money went on a holiday in the penthouse of a rather swanky hotel near Marbella. I had by now lost about 8 kilos (or about 18 lbs in old money) and regained my fitness so was swimming around the kidney shaped pool in Spain in some lovely designer outfits bought for me by Simon. It was while on the sunbed in Spain, with something refreshing in hand, I had the epiphany to set up my own consultancy and so *jjheritage* was formed.

On my return, I hired a personal trainer, got super healthy and got back to myself. Groovy. Open water swimming included the Serpentine and the Great North Swim, a mile in Windermere. Triathlons followed. Eight years later I play tennis—sometimes three or so hours at a time, to a decent standard, and I carry on and do the gardening.

I feel slightly sorry for the broken 2016 self that took the redundancy to get away from a toxic situation. I hardly recognise her as I serve and volley in the sunshine in lovely surroundings. But I know she stuck in there to make a point. I hope if you are in a chronic work situation you at least know why you are there, and have a plan to get out. Universities should be providing career progression for committed, ambitious women, not exhausting and obfuscating their female talent, while average male staff remain in post doing the same thing year after year. Or a bit less.

But back at the football, why have I called Canada 2015 the Artificial World Cup?

Grass is a Gas in Canada 2015

At the 2015 Women's World Cup in Canada, FIFA gaslit on grass. One of the ways that world-class elite female players were demeaned, ridiculed and sold short in 2015, was an illogical determination by FIFA that the tournament would be played entirely on artificial pitches. The governing body commissioned statistics from athletic analysis tool, Prozone, and asked UEFA medics to evidence that an artificial surface was no more dangerous than grass, nor had it any impact on the way football was played. This fiction was decided before a ball was kicked. As is their wont, FIFA concocted an elaborate narrative in which there was nothing to see here. The players were depicted as somewhat hysterical for having concerns about their own welfare, and the full FIFA PR machine denied there was a problem, but provided no supporting scientific evidence as to why artificial pitches had been mandated. As the FIFA head of Women's Football said at the time, 'There is no plan B.'

So, how important is grass? Many people rate cut grass as one of their all-time favourite smells. It is in part a nostalgic smell, of summer, and the village green around which historically many people have gathered to socialise and celebrate. If you walk on to a football pitch that has recently been trimmed, it is a heady vibrant smell of a living plant which the sun makes more intense in scent. It is also the surface on which every elite senior football tournament since 1930 has been played. More recently, the men's Qatar World Cup 2022 had grassing updates three years before a ball was kicked. Had no one in Canada prior to 2015 really seen football played on blades of grass?

Although ubiquitous, we take grass for granted at our peril. Grasses commonly have one embryonic leaf, or cotyledon. Now, your common or garden lawn may contain new worlds for you to examine. Is yours mainly comprised of strong creeping red fescue, or slender creeping red fescue? Is your meadow grass smooth or rough-stalked? The majority of Northern UK lawns have a combination of ryegrass, bluegrass and some

THE ARTIFICIAL WORLD CUP, 2015

kind of fescue. While sheep's fescue may be used for turf in very dry or infertile conditions, it can tend to grow in different directions and does not produce a uniform sward. That would not do for the Wimbledon Lawn Tennis Championships. But football is not like tennis, because in the latter the elite players have to be prepared to compete on clay, hard courts and grass. Similarly, hockey players tend to specialise in field or ice surfaces for their sport. But football, for almost 100 years at the time of writing, has always held senior World Cups on grass.

By way of balance, as I've been a bit general in my comments about grass and artificial turf. There are of course pros and cons. Some say real grass is more labour-intensive and resource-heavy in watering, mowing and so forth. On the other hand, synthetic polypropylene or nylon fragments from artificial turf eventually make their way into soil as microplastic pollution. The long-term effects are yet to be better understood. Artificial turf can last between 10-20 years and most is difficult to recycle, although some is already recycled. Animals also dislike it. In Canada many elite pitches went over to artificial turf due to the cold months, the multi-use functionality, whereby concerts and other events do not harm the grass, and some consider the sustainability to be more favourable with fewer resources. Three venues Edmonton, Vancouver and Victoria had been used in 2002 when FIFA inaugurated the Under 19 Women's World Championship in Canada, so there were some precedents in youth tournaments.

Although used widely in elite football, there is no poetry in playing on artificial turf. The UEFA Champions League final and other men's elite competitions stipulate a natural surface as part of their regulations. So, grass, and the cultivation of sports-specific live plant surfaces, is of the utmost importance. Grass is not to be taken for granted. Especially if you are a woman football player.

Not only was the FIFA decision to hold 2015 entirely on artificial surfaces an illogical ruling, it was highly symbolic. Artificial turf by its nature is not alive—it's dead. It was not that the Local Organising Committee in Canada lacked the logistical ability to seed, water and mow some grass. It mattered more that women players would be forced to play under the regulations of the tournament or withdraw their labour, as male professional, Thierry Henry, had chosen to do on the MLS artificial pitches due to his concerns about injury.

It was clear that FIFA was trialling artificial surfaces as possible technologies for future World Cups but would not use a men's tournament to do so. As such, the female players of 2015 were forced to compete in unscientific working conditions not proven before at this level, or to withdraw from the tournament. It was not a financial decision, or a scientifically evidenced decision. It was about power. I'll come back to this when considering the amount of money Chuck Blazer, the General Secretary of the Confederation responsible for winning the bid to host the 2015 Women's World Cup, spent on renting a Manhattan flat… for his cats. Bear with me.

RADICALISED BY FIFA

At the Canada Women's World Cup of 2015, Australian striker Michelle Heyman described the conditions of the playing field at Edmonton where the synthetic turf was absorbing heat at a rapid rate due to the rubber and other materials as 'like walking on hot coals.' Blisters, white dehydrated skin, and abrasions to the feet were not the only changes in playing conditions. If you've ever gone over on astroturf at speed, you will know you leave the pitch with quite a lot less skin that when you arrived. That skin does not grow back soon. The stadium at Edmonton provided no shade for the players and the heat of the playing surface was often disregarded because the air temperature was 23 degrees. For a match scheduled to kick off at 2pm, the air temperature would eventually rise to over 31 degrees. The retention of heat was a key factor affecting working conditions at pitch level and for player welfare on the field of play.

FIFA has always sought to undercut, and 'other' women's football, at the same time as *appearing* to promote it. One enduring pattern of behaviour is to trial new forms of technology at a Women's World Cup that players would not necessarily be experienced in using in their club or national football. VAR technology would be one such innovation for France 2019, but in 2015 all of the tournament's venues had fields composed of artificial turf which had never before been done in any senior World Cup. Why not choose different stadia that could be turfed with the playing surface on which most women played?

Furthermore, there was no consistency on the type of artificial turf in the selected venues, with different brands including FieldTurf, FieldTurf Duraspine, FieldTurf Revolution, Xtreme Turf, and Polytan LigaTurf. There was also the first use of Hawk-Eye goal line technology at a Women's World Cup, after a similar system, GoalControl was inaugurated at the Men's World Cup in 2014.

Players believed artificial turf resulted in a higher risk of injuries and here the official FIFA report differs from player autobiographies. While the official report does not comment on injuries during the tournament, player autobiographies, including Megan Rapinoe's memoir, show that she suffered her third anterior cruciate ligament (ACL) injury in December 2015, during Women's National Team training in Hawaii. Of course, such an injury is not directly attributable to the situation in Canada in June and July of that year, although turf temperatures were registered as 66 degrees Celsius, or 150 degrees Fahrenheit. But we could explore how many others were injured in the next three to six months after the tournament.

I am not aware of any study that has gathered the evidence from the player autobiographies looking at ACL injuries, and am just beginning to do that work now. If we found a rise in ACL incidence up to six months after the World Cup it would further evidence the emerging autobiographical view of elite professionals that the playing surface was at least a contributory factor in their incidence of injury. It is worth exploring as part of an holistic look at overall working conditions, and injury patterns.

THE ARTIFICIAL WORLD CUP, 2015

More than 50 players protested the use of artificial turf instead of grass on the basis of gender discrimination. They filed a lawsuit challenging FIFA's decision to play on artificial turf, claiming FIFA would never allow the Men's World Cup to be played on artificial turf and thus the organizers had violated the Canadian Human Rights Act. On 1 October 2014 a case with the Ontario Human Rights Tribunal was filed by a group of women's international soccer players against FIFA and the Canadian Soccer Association. It noted that, in 1994, FIFA spent $2 million to plant natural grass over artificial turf in New Jersey and Detroit for the Men's World Cup in the US.

Celebrities and prominent players showed their support for the women soccer players in defence of their lawsuit, including United States men's team goalkeeper, Tim Howard. There were threatened boycotts, but ultimately in January 2015, the lawsuit was withdrawn. Perhaps mindful of the potential of injuries though, FIFA increased the size of squads from the 2011 edition, which had 21 players, to 23 competitors, three of whom had to be goalkeepers. Both Formiga of Brazil and Homare Sawa of Japan attended their sixth World Cup, a record for men or women.

Instead of dealing with the changed playing conditions, FIFA heralded the largest Women's World Cup to date, having expanded from 16 to 24 teams. Back in December 2010 there had been only two bids for this edition of the World Cup, and Zimbabwe was considered a long shot, withdrawing its proposal in March the following year. One wonders what FIFA would have done turf-wise had the tournament gone to Africa. Alternatively, Canada had been building its hosting reputation with FIFA including the 1987 FIFA U–16 World Championship, 2002; the U–19 Women's World Championship; the 2007 U–20 World Cup, which set an attendance record for that tournament, and the 2014 FIFA U–20 Women's World Cup (incidentally all on grass). So, the expanded schedule in 2015 of 52 rather than 32 matches for 24 teams looked to be in good hands. However, the seeding of teams drew some criticism, as did allocation of some nations to the six groups.

All of this politicised the Canadian Women's World Cup to an unprecedented degree. Most of the public were not aware of the situation around how Germany had come to be hosts of Women's World Cup in 2011, and very few UK journalists cared to comment on the artificial turf issue. By now, I had been invited to give a keynote at Duke University in June 2015 by Professor Laurent Dubois, who ran a really innovative soccer course, combined with modern foreign language elements. Laurent was Director of Forum for Scholars & Publics at Duke University, and also invited academics Brenda Elsey, Jennifer Doyle, and Josh Nadal along in 2015. I think Lindsay Sarah Krasnoff was there too. Certainly Grant Wahl attended. Using core football content, students would discuss their thoughts on the issues in the language that they were studying. It was a brilliantly engaged process of learning.

Other speakers at Duke included Carla Overbeck, former Captain of US National

Team, and her teammate Cindy Parlow Cone who helped to win the World Cup in 1999. Media analysts included Shireen Ahmed of Canada; Sarah Gehrke, the Media Relations Manager for Washington Spirit and former Mexican national captain from 2003 to 2007, Mónica González, who went on to a broadcasting and coaching career. González had also had a professional career with the short-lived Boston Breakers in Women's United Soccer Association between 2002 to 2003. Attempting to get back into the team once more for the World Cup in Germany 2011, she sold her car to train full time, but was cut from the squad before the kick-off. González explained what it was like playing for the Mexican FA, and I was not surprised that they had declined to help my research when I was out there in 2004-5 season.

Not only did players like Carla, Cindy and Mónica educate us about the working conditions of players across various cultural contexts, we were helped by Grant Wahl who was at the time writing world class journalism at *Sports Illustrated*. I think it was Josh Nadal and Grant, in conjunction with Laurent, who suggested we get together, and with a varied set of language skills and cultural perspectives across the team, write popular journalism based on our academic research. I was only too delighted to collaborate on *Upfront and Onside: Dispatches from Women's World Cup 2015*.

It is a testament to the generosity of Grant Wahl that he should have provided us with a platform for this kind of critically engaged writing at *Sports Illustrated*, and some of the writing was picked up by Fox Sports. The publication perhaps best known for its 'swimsuit issue', and one of the most conservative media outlets in the US, was discussing serious issues like Shireen's writing on the hijab ban in France. And everyone, but *everyone*, who met him has a similar Grant Wahl story. He was a feminist, and had inherited his mother's love of the US women's national team.

There was no comparable serious journalism on these issues in the mainstream media, apart maybe from some of the work that Jeré Longman, Jeff Kassouf, and a few other US reporters were doing. I remain very proud of the writing of the group, and it's a shame not all of the articles are still available. There's a brilliant line by Laurent in his summary of the turf issue where he says, imagining that FIFA would pay for grass pitches, the surface it had used for the 2015 men's U-20 World Cup in empty stadiums in New Zealand, was 'a bit like imagining that Sepp Blatter is actually Gloria Steinem.' I wish I had written that Laurent!

By now Jen Doyle had retired *From a Left Wing*, a blog which she had written from December 2007 to July 2013, in favour of her new project *The Sport Spectacle* and I cannot recommend the writing highly enough. I also met Gwendolyn Oxenham at Duke and adored her as an essayist in *Under the Lights and in the Dark: Untold Stories of Women's Soccer*, as a filmmaker in *Pelada* and as a historian in *Pride of a Nation*.

Josh Nadel's brilliant analysis showed how the stifling tactics of Mexico's long-time coach Leonardo Cuellar, in post since 1998, had not kept pace with the development of the players' skill level in those 17 years. Such longevity is often widespread in coaching women's soccer worldwide. We were right on cue: as academics we collided with a particular moment in FIFA history.

On 27 May 2015, the Office of Public Affairs in the US Department of Justice issued a Press Release in which it detailed that nine FIFA Officials and five Corporate Executives had been indicted for racketeering, conspiracy and corruption. According to FIFA's own accounts, 70% of its $5.7 billion in total revenues between 2011 and 2014 was attributable to the sale of TV and marketing rights to the 2014 Men's World Cup in Brazil. And they couldn't afford a few bags of grass seed for a Women's World Cup in Canada?

For historians of FIFA, the 2015 scandals were to football what really bad soap operas are to television; so outrageous, it is impossible to look away. Think *Dallas or Dynasty*. Or for British readers, *Triangle* starring Kate O'Mara. Big hair, shoulder pads, betrayal... and lots of greed. We learned Chuck Blazer's eight storage lockers in New Jersey held his personal effects including wire taps and notes of transactions that he had recorded after becoming an FBI informant in 2011. The most senior American in world football at the time, Blazer was Executive Vice-President of the United States Soccer Federation (USSF, or US Soccer). By 2011 he had stood down as General Secretary of CONCACAF (The Confederation of North, Central America and Caribbean Association Football) where he had been since 1990, along with President Jack Warner, but remained on FIFA's ExCo from 1996 to 2013.

Although FIFA, CONCACAF as hosting confederation and Canadian Soccer would not pay for natural turf for a Women's World Cup, we discovered that one of the two apartments Blazer rented in Trump Tower paid for by the confederation was just for his cats!

Now I am not against felines in New York duplexes per se. But I do draw a line that the main business of football organisations ought to be, you know, the football and not principally providing luxury accommodation in Manhattan penthouses for pets. I do not know why Chuck Blazer did not want to live with his cats. Some said the moggies in the connecting condo were considered unruly. By whose moral compass? Whatever the answer to that particular mystery, there were many more to come.

On 2 June, ramping up the jeopardy, Sepp Blatter, who had been re-elected with an overwhelming majority of 133 votes to Prince Ali bin Al Hussein of Jordan's 73 in the FIFA Congress days earlier in May, declared he would step down in about six months as a result of the scandal after 17 years in the role. He was not personally implicated at that point, but maybe anticipated further indictments.

There were scenes of FIFA officials being sheltered from the waiting media by hotel staff, holding up crisp white bedsheets as they left the luxury hotel Baur au Lac in Zurich under the guard of Swiss police officers. The indictment alleged trails of bribes, backhanders and inappropriate deals, and the world governing body seemed to implode in a mire of corruption.

At this stage I quite wanted Sue Ellen Ewing of *Dallas* to saunter into Sepp's expensively furnished office at the FIFA HQ in Zurich wearing an '80s power suit in neon pink, throw down a cut glass tumbler of Scotch, say something pithy, and take over as FIFA President the same afternoon. I mean, who wouldn't want that? Sadly, this was not soap opera-land and I was not writing that particular script.

Back to the football.

Kicking off on 6 June 2015, the Women's World Cup was completely overshadowed by the FIFA scandals. And it is clear that the style of football played in 2015 was changed by the artificial turf—as is conceded by the Technical Study Group document edited by Dawn Scott and Vanessa Martinez Lagunas in which, interestingly there is no recorded mention of injuries.

The actual length of play was conceded to have been changed by the playing surface, with the ball actually in play for 26.53 minutes on average in the first half, and 26.23 in the second. The ball was described as bouncing in unpredictable ways on the harder artificial surface. The overall distances covered by most positions, and the number of player runs were also significantly down on 2011, when records were first taken by the Technical Study Group. Just pause for a moment. The first technical study group was convened twenty years after the first Women's World Cup. Onwards.

This shorter distances may have been due to the heat. However, since many of the records from Germany had to be recalculated in 2015 due to imperfect equipment, it is hard to make direct comparisons. But the strikers covered significantly more distance than in 2011, and at higher speeds, so we must be mindful of that when we look at the incidence of ACL injuries in player autobiographies.

There were 22 penalties, 23 headed goals, and more goals from set play, like the 28 corners that provided assists. Set plays were more important than 2011, as was the bravery of goalkeepers in defending on hard surfaces, with significant abrasive risks. The number of shots per match was 1.5 less than in 2011, on average at 13.2 across the tournament, and more shots were taken outside the penalty area. When we look at the number of goals scored and conceded, it was dramatically more than 2011 at 146, compared previously with 86, but exactly the same as France 2019, which was played on grass.

The artifical world cup was an unhappy experiment, not widely replicated. And of course, these results could be down to a range of factors in player fitness, position-specific training, overall preparedness like jet lag, and so on. The technical study does not give much detail on injuries and other factors that might help to examine the actual effects of artificial surfaces, but we would also have to factor in that many players also train on these surfaces. So, the effect of the playing surface overall is a complex issue.

THE ARTIFICIAL WORLD CUP, 2015

In Canada, teams played in six cities (Edmonton, Moncton, Montreal, Ottawa, Vancouver, Winnipeg) in five time zones. This caused a lot of jet lag amongst players and teams. There was a gradual rise in the television audiences at Fox Sports, Telemundo and the BBC across various platforms but the time zones made matches hard to watch. The venues were oddly chosen too. Moncton, a city then of only 71,000 people, had only a stadium capacity of 13,000, while BC Place in Vancouver could take 54,000 spectators; the Olympic Stadium in Montreal and the Commonwealth Stadium both held up to 56,000 fans. Toronto was noticeably absent as Canada's largest city, but was hosting the Pan-American Games.

National sponsors were Bell Canada telecommunications, Budweiser for Labatt Brewing Company, and Trend Micro, a cyber security multinational. Adidas, Coca Cola, Hyundai-Kia, and Visa were main sponsors, as was Russian energy giant, Gazprom, although the Canadian government issued sanctions for the invasion of Crimea in the last week of the tournament. The expanded tournament created new opportunities for eight teams, which, in turn, expanded the international media interest in the Women's World Cup.

The new European teams were Spain, Switzerland and the Netherlands. From Africa, Cameroon and Côte d'Ivoire joined, with Cameroon previously having appeared in a FIFA competition at the 2012 Olympics. From the Americas, Ecuador, and Costa Rica debuted, and from Asia, Thailand made their first appearance. North Korea was banned, and failed to appear for the first time since 1995, and Equatorial Guinea was also absent. The magnificent seven—Brazil, Germany, Japan, Nigeria, Norway, Sweden, and the USA were there again. It is astonishing to note that North Korea was absent for the first time since 1995 given the politics of the country, and is a notable example of international sports diplomacy. Also worth pause for thought, Spain was at its first World Cup in 2015, and they would go on to win the whole tournament only two editions later.

It was also evident that FIFA had creatively calculated the overall number of fans attending to be 1.3 million, with an average attendance per game of 26,000 spectators. The games were held as double-headers, due to the logistics of the scale of the undertaking. In Group A, for instance, Canada opened the tournament in Edmonton winning 1–0 over China, kick off time was 4pm; while at 7 pm, in the same stadium, New Zealand lost 1–0 to the Netherlands. The crowd was recorded at 53,000, almost a capacity for both matches in spite of there being visible rows of empty seats in the stands. Canada, China and the Netherlands progressed to the next round. Christine Sinclair's converted penalty for Canada against China in the 92nd minute was her 154th international goal, and her eighth in a World Cup.

In Group B, Germany topped their group with a 10–0 win over Côte D'Ivoire, a 1–1 draw with Norway, and a 4–0 defeat of Thailand. The double-header format was not used on the 15 June when Germany played Thailand in Winnipeg in front of 26,000 fans, but only 7,000 spectators saw Norway defeat Côte D'Ivoire 3–1 in Moncton. Germany and Norway progressed.

In Group C, Japan, Cameroon and Switzerland went through to the next round with three, two and one wins respectively, leaving Ecuador to exit without getting a point. Ecuador's coach Vanessa Arauz was just 26 years of age—the youngest in World Cup history. For Japan, Homare Sawa made history on 8 June by playing in her 6th World Cup, to be followed on 9 June by Formiga.

Switzerland made their own records when Fabienne Hamm scored first in the 47th minute with one foot, second in the 49th minute with the other, and thirdly with her head in the 52nd minute for a perfect hat trick in 277 seconds!

It was a torrid tournament for Ecuador as Gaëlle Enganamouit had already scored a hat trick against them in a 6–0 defeat by Cameroon, in which the captain, Ligia Moreira, had been sent off with a red card. Enganamouit (who had probably the best hair at the whole 2015 tournament) was a CAF Player of the Year in 2015. In the 10–1 defeat against Switzerland, Angie Ponce had her own mixed fortune, becoming the only player to score two own goals before converting from the penalty spot to register Ecuador's first (or was it third?) in a Women's World Cup.

The USA headed up Group D, drawing with Sweden 0–0 in their second game, who had already drawn in their first, 3–3 with Nigeria, and would draw with Australia 1–1 in their third. Therefore, by dint of a 2–0 win over Nigeria, Australia went through second, sending the Africans home with one point. Abby Wambach scored her 14th World Cup goal in the group game against Nigeria, for a 1–0 win. She missed a penalty later in the tournament against Colombia, and hence did not join Brazilian Marta on 15 goals.

Brazil started brightly in Group E with goals from both Formiga and Marta against South Korea 2–0, and the defeated team would finish runners-up to progress. I am duty bound to report that Marta's converted penalty broke the World Cup scoring record she had shared with Birgit Prinz to go to 15 goals. It was one of history's poetic bookends. Her first World Cup goal had been in 2003, a penalty against South Korea. Costa Rica held Spain to a 1–1 draw for a point, and South Korea 2–2, for another—but it was not enough. The future world champions had won a single point on their debut.

In Group F, France beat England 1–0 and Mexico 5–0 to top the table, but suffered a shock 2–0 defeat to Columbia—largely due to the force of nature that is Lady Andrade who scored one goal and made one for Catalina Usme, with keeper Sandra Sepúlveda maintaining a clean sheet—in spite of France's star-studded squad. This avenged the 2012 Olympic loss to France.

When France met England in Group F, it had been 41 years since they had been beaten by one of their earliest international opponents. France extended that tradition with a Eugénie Le Sommer strike for a 1–0 victory, and it would be Euro 2017 before

THE ARTIFICIAL WORLD CUP, 2015

England would beat them again.

There were just 11,000 spectators in Moncton. But Colombia beat France 2-0 a few days later to spoil the party, with Lady Andrade and Catalina Usme the dominant strike force. Mexico, who had held Colombia to a 1-1 draw in their first match, suffered a 2-1 defeat by England, with goals from Fran Kirby and Karen Carney, and a 91st minute consolation from Claudia Ibarra. They then suffered a 5-0 defeat by France to finish fourth in the group with a single point. In this very tight group, England then outdid themselves to defeat Colombia 2-1 thanks again to Karen Carney, and a Fara Williams penalty—and a 94th minute last-ditch effort by Lady Andrade. France and England advanced with six points, and Colombia with four.

In the round of 16, Colombia faced the USA, ranked 26 places ahead of them in the FIFA rankings. Their keeper, Sandra Sepúlveda, was suspended, and in her place was 20-year-old Catalina Pérez who kept a clean sheet for the first half, denying Tobin Heath, Alex Morgan and Abby Wambach. But Pérez bought Alex Morgan down on the edge of her area for a red card offence, leaving 10 players for Colombia. This left Morgan and Carli Lloyd to score 2-0, but Fabián Taborda's team had caused some upsets in an impressive campaign before their exit.

The Steel Roses of China sent the Indomitable Lionesses of Cameroon home with a 1-0 win. Germany cruised 4-1 past long-time rivals, Sweden, while France exposed South Korea's relative inexperience in big tournaments with a 3-0 victory. South Korea had not appeared at a Women's World Cup since 2003, but Yoon Deok-yeo's squad had seven players in the squad who had performed so well at U-17 level to become world champions, and in the recent U-20 tournaments. The Chelsea star, Ji So-yun was amongst these important players, but she was benched for this game due to a knock against France.

Super sub, Kyah Simon's goal for Australia forged history as the first men's or women's senior squad to win a World Cup knockout match. Last time Brazil had played Australia in 2011 in a five-goal thriller, it had been in South America's favour. Coached by Alen Stajcic, Sam Kerr had almost scored before Simon, while keeper Lydia Williams had maintained a clean sheet against the likes of Formiga, Cristiane, and Marta for this historic victory.

Previous World Cup winners Japan eased past the Netherlands 2-1, with Norio Sasaki still in charge of the reigning champions as coach—the only man to have coached a victorious side since Tony DiCicco in 1999. Saori Ariyoshi scored the first, and Japan combined fantastic back heels, feints, and quick passing to set up Mizuho Sakaguchi for the second. Kirsten van de Ven managed to get an extra time reply for Roger Reijners' debutants, but it was not to be.

John Herdman's Canada then despatched Switzerland 1-0. The Swiss coach was none other than Germany's World Cup veteran and four times European champion,

Martina Voss-Tecklenburg, who insisted her team had exceeded expectations as first timers to the tournament.

In Norway's game against England, Solveig Gulbrandsen almost completed the mother of all comebacks by scoring in the 54th minute. She had retired as an international in 2010, but returned in time to help Norway to the final of Euro 2013. Now with two children, she gave Even Pellerud's side the lead with a glancing header, her second goal of the tournament. But captain Steph Houghton responded in the 61st minute, and Lucia Roberta Tough Bronze scored one of the goals of the tournament from 30 yards to give England their first knockout victory. And so, to the quarter finals.

The US beat China 1-0 on Carli Lloyd's 200th cap, and the captain made the day even more memorable with a winning header. Germany versus France was 1-1 after added extra time, and so went to penalties which the previous world champions won 5-4. Nadine Angerer launched herself at 21-year-old Claire Lavogez's penalty, saving it with her knee. England sent the hosts out of the tournament with a Jodie Taylor strike, followed only three minutes later by a Bronze header, and even a Christine Sinclair goal could not inspire an equaliser. Her ninth World Cup goal in four tournaments, Sinclair's side would be the fifth nation in seven World Cups to go out at this stage. It took until the 87th minute, but Japan expelled Australia with a single Mana Iwabuchi goal.

In the semi-finals, the Germany versus USA fixture had a goalless first half, but in the second, both sides were awarded a penalty only six minutes apart. Célia Šašić missed hers, in spite of being the tournament Golden Boot with six goals. Carli Lloyd converted hers, before assisting substitute Kelley O'Hara with a square pass for a tap in her first goal for her country.

As someone who had written on player migration and professional playing conditions, I found Célia Šašić fascinating. She was born in Bonn to a Cameroonian father and a French mother, but took German citizenship after being approached by the German football association, and joining their U-19 2004 championship winning squad, scoring three goals. Her maiden surname Célia Okoyino da Mbabi was featured on her shirt when she made her senior debut soon after, although because of its length, she only used her first name on her shirt in the women's Bundesliga. She had to wait for a decade until the World Cup in 2015 shone a light on her abilities. By this time, she had married the Croatian football player, Marko Šašić, whose father, Milan, coached in the 2. Bundesliga—the German second division. Célia Šašić scored a hat-trick in Germany's opening game against Côte D'Ivoire on 7 June 2015, and a brace against Sweden in a 4-1 victory in the Round of 16, along with a penalty against France in the quarter-finals. Although Carli Lloyd would match her six goals and one assist, the shorter playing time of Germany's elimination gave Šašić the Golden Boot.

In the Japan versus England semi-final, the captain Aya Miyama put the reigning world champions ahead with a converted penalty in the 33rd minute, to which Fara

THE ARTIFICIAL WORLD CUP, 2015

Williams responded again from the spot seven minutes later. Tied, and looking like going into added extra time, defender Laura Bassett tried to clear a ball from the Japanese attack, but sent it into her own net in the 92nd minute. The Notts County captain was inconsolable. But England recorded a new tournament high by winning third place in added extra time over Germany. The previous 20 match-ups had seen 18 England losses and two draws, so this was a pioneering achievement and their best finish in a World Cup until being defeated finalists in 2023. A Fara Williams penalty 18 minutes into extra time saw previous champions, Germany, finish fourth and it was the end of an era with Nadine Angerer retiring, along with coach Sylvia Neid standing down after the Olympics the next year. Šašić also announced her retirement from international football, welcoming her daughter into the world a year later.

You will be relieved to hear, I have now probably run out of gas on the symbolism of grass! 'OK Jean, we get it. FIFA trialled a new surface for a senior World Cup at a women's tournament and it didn't work,' I hear you say. But here a parting gift. On shade.

The final in Canada of 2015 was played on 7 July. The Women's World Cup final wasn't even given its own spotlight in the news cycle, as World Cup hosting confederation, CONCACAF scheduled the men's Gold Cup to kick off in Canada and the US on the same day. Victor Montagliani, the President of Canada Soccer for the 2015 World Cup (and now President of CONCACAF), considered this was merely a scheduling mix-up. The South American Football Confederation (CONMEBOL) had scheduled its Copa America final also on 4 July. So, there was a lot of football going on at the same time in the region as well as the women's championship.

The final itself between USA and Japan was a 5–2 goalfest. Golden Ball winner, Carli Lloyd led from the front as captain, scoring her first two goals in the third and fifth minute, before Lauren Holiday added to the tally in the 14th minute. Lloyd then completed her hat-trick two minutes later by lobbing the Japan keeper, Ayumi Kaihori, from the halfway line. Yūki Ōgimi offered hope for Japan with a 27th-minute strike, followed by an own goal from Julie Johnstone, but Tobin Heath scored the fifth for the USA to put the game beyond doubt. It was the third World Cup for the USA, won with the first hat-trick in a final.

Coming on as a substitute, the final earned veteran Homare Sawa her 205th cap. Christie Rampone, a veteran herself of 1999, was substituted on, aged 40 years and 11 days. Rampone earned her third World Cup medal, to add to two Olympic golds, one World Cup and one Olympic runner's up medal, and two World Cup third place medals. The total prize money was $15 million, of which the USA won $2 million.

The Rio Olympic Games which followed in 2016 was notable for the absence of Japan who lost in the qualifying rounds to Australia and China. As late as March 2016, it was agreed that the competition would be part of a FIFA trial to allow a fourth substitute to be made during extra time. Thanks to the men's 2014 World Cup played in Brazil, men's and women's matches at the 2016 Brazil Olympics took place on perennial ryegrass turf, useful for when grass is more dormant in the winter months. But I digress...

Brazil, China and Sweden progressed from Group E, leaving eliminated South Africa in fourth place. Canada, Germany and Australia made the quarter-finals from Group F, but Zimbabwe did not register a point on their Olympic debut. In Group G, the United States and France made it through to the next round with seven and six points respectively, leaving New Zealand and Colombia homeward bound.

In the quarter-finals there were two penalty shoot-outs with Brazil defeating Australia 7-6, and Sweden, who were tied 1-1 with the USA after added extra time, winning 4-3. It was the first time since 1991 that the United States had not progressed to the semi-finals in a FIFA World Cup or Olympic tournament.

Canada despatched France 1-0, and Germany by the same margin over China. But Brazil's hopes of home advantage finally bringing them a major tournament simply was not to be. In the semis, in another penalty shoot-out, Sweden won 4-3, and Marta was again distraught that perhaps her last chance of an international title had expired on home soil. She had lost to the country where she also held citizenship, having played much of her club football in Sweden.

Germany then defeated Canada to meet Sweden in the final. It was a fitting end to Sylvia Neid's career that she added an Olympic gold as coach to her previous accolades, when a dominant Germany finished 2-0 ahead. This was a clean sweep of Olympic, World Cup and European titles. It was also Sweden's first Olympic medal.

Poor old Marta. Canada won the bronze medal match 2-1 with Deanne Rose the youngest scorer in Olympic history, at 17 years, 169 days. Rose's 25th-minute strike was complemented by (who else?) Christine Sinclair's just after half time in what would be the veteran's 250th cap. Beatriz pulled one back for Brazil, but even though banners were held aloft around the stadium proclaiming, 'Marta, We Love You!' the hosts could not confound John Herdman's Canadian squad. Cristiane, then 31 years of age, had 14 Olympic goals by the end of this tournament, and Marta, 10.

On grass. Now that is poetic, and neat.

CHAPTER VI
THE WAGE THEFT WORLD CUP, 2019
Storied Objects

After getting up at dawn and attempting to eat a fried egg with chopsticks at a formal breakfast banquet, I was on the bullet train from Zibo, China to Beijing. Travelling with Kevin Moore, David Hassan, Stefan Jost and Matt Taylor, I was officially the third-ranked British/ Irish person there. Kevin, in 2016 still CEO of the National Football Museum where he had been since 1997, was obviously the most important, and Stefan, the Managing Director of the FIFA Museum, was second in charge. I knew my place. Some of our Chinese hosts accompanied us on the bullet train as we whizzed through the countryside at speeds up to 350 kilometres per hour. You never know where an email from Kevin is going to lead, but in October 2016, just before I left De Montfort University, it took me to China as a guest of President Xi Jinping.

My application for redundancy had been approved but it wasn't public news, and I was effectively on gardening leave for September and October 2016 as I had some annual leave still to take. I wouldn't be teaching in the 2016/17 academic year at De Montfort, but that suited me because on 26 August I had already obtained a 0.6 (three -day) Chair at The University of Wolverhampton, as their first female Professor of Sport.

I would start at Wolverhampton on 6 December. Because I was job -sharing with a 67 -year -old male Professor who was high up on the salary scale I would take home from my part time job a similar amount as I had full -time in Leicester.

I went straight from the interview in Wolverhampton to London to do a live media roundtable on the history of women's boxing with Lauren Laverne who was hosting *Late Night Women's Hour* on the history of women's boxing. The other guests were Maggie Alphonsi, known for her incredible career in and around rugby, and boxer Cherelle Brown: both fascinating women and I learned a great deal.

The email inviting me to China had pinged in as I was walking along a country lane with Simon, midday on a Tuesday in mid September during the period of gardening leave. Might I be available to go to China in a week or so, to speak about women's football at a conference at the Linzi Museum in Zibo? The conference was the outcome of a State meeting between Xi Jinping and Prime Minister David Cameron hosted at the National Football Museum in 2015 and the City of Manchester Stadium. Facilitated by Kevin Moore, football was being used as a form of soft diplomacy. Kevin had quite rightly hailed Chinese ball game Cuju, (pronounced shoo-joo,), as an ancient antecedent of the modern association game. To mark the first anniversary of this State Visit, Linzi Football Museum in Zibo connected with the National Football Museum to hold the First World Football Culture Summit beginning 22 to 25 October 2016. We would be the guests, keynote speakers and representatives of the UK at the conference.

Having obtained the necessary visas, we faced the challenge of deciding our order of eminence, as we were to be given a Chinese colleague of the same rank with whom we would primarily socialise. Kevin was clearly chief. Stefan Jost, who had the unenviable task of opening the FIFA Museum soon after the 2015 scandals was second in prominence. I was number three. Number four was David Hassan who had written extensively on football governance, and disability sport history while working at Ulster. That hardly does the magnitude of David's publications and grant-capture justice, but trust me, —in real life he would not normally have been ranked fourth to my third. We just made it up and he was very gracious and humble about it. Matt was fifth. We had learned that there was a drinking culture at such conferences where our Chinese counterparts might encourage us to consume too much alcohol as a form of hospitality. However, women could sidestep this invented tradition by effectively saying they were too delicate to compete. Yes, I know. There is no need to pull that face!

Food and lodging were provided but we had to get our own flights. Although De Montfort was represented twice, they wouldn't pay my flight (understandably) as I was leaving. I'd also have to get from the airport to the hotel and back. Fair enough, I had my redundancy money. BA didn't exactly cover themselves in glory on the flights, changing the configuration of the flight so that my superior economy seat no longer existed and I was downgraded to economy, with no concession to customer care other than being told to complain once home.

When we all met up at the hotel, we found that the original plan to take the two-hour bullet train from Beijing to Zibo in Shandong East China, had been changed in favour of getting a minibus, due to cost. The 430-kilometre journey would be a minimum of five hours, stopping once at a service station. This was a horrendous experience as we were speeding along the motorway when animals would cross and get stuck in the central reservation unable to complete their journey. Panicked and with no end in sight of the speeding traffic the animals would cower in terror. Animal rights were just non-existent. I saw many horrific things. Upset, I looked out the other window so as not to witness this for the five hour drive.

THE WAGE THEFT WORLD CUP, 2019

The service stations were unsanitary, with toilets like things I had experienced back in the day as a student travelling in Paris: holes in the ground over which one was supposed to hover and hope. Fellow travellers in their urgency had somewhat crashlanded on the foot plates leaving debris of the most unpleasant kind and I couldn't even go in. I opted instead for Zen-like bladder control and dehydration.

Once in Zibo, the scale of the Linzi Museum was huge, almost 12,000 square metres, and a cost of $22 million. It traced the ancient development of Cuju, as a non-contact sport of individuals of high status to team games with nets, changes of rules and so forth. There were five academic speakers who specialised in Cuju, matching our five papers on modern association football and its status in museums. Visiting the museum was the first time I had seen bronze statues of women football players, which I tapped to hear the sound of the metal. There was a representation of Marta, Kristine Lilly, Nadine Angerer, and other stars. The bronzes were actually pretty good. However, the quality of the exhibition varied, with some plastic characters representing the Men's World Cup mascots, and a very odd representation of David Beckham where he was followed by female fans in tight t-shirts and hotpants. The Cuju sections were much more serious.

Sepp Blatter had told the Chinese museum folks that they had invented football, and this was a story that the Linzi exhibitions wholeheartedly reinforced. Xi Jinping, President of the People's Republic of China since 2013, kept saying he used football as a diplomatic tool because he wanted to host a World Cup. PR China has held two World Cups, in 1991 and 2007. Having held both summer and winter Olympics and Paralympic Games in 2008 and 2022, the Men's World Cup would be another important milestone in international sport hosting. It has yet to happen, but as we have seen with Qatar and Saudi Arabia, there is likely to be a future bid.

Because our visit in 2016 was a form of soft diplomacy, we were accompanied by a member of staff whose role it was to monitor our whereabouts. This was all very subtly done. When meeting foreigners, officials present name cards with government titles but stay quiet about Communist party positions which are undoubtedly important. The young man in his twenties attending to me asked me to call him 'Dumbledore': he was a Harry Potter fan. I naively thought he was just being friendly accompanying me from my hotel room to every event each day until I nipped off to the gym at 6am one morning due to jetlag. I returned to find a very fraught Dumbledore outside my room with no glasses on, and his hair sticking up obviously having been roused from his bed, as he had been made aware I had left my room without informing him. I was asked very, very seriously not to do that again. And one would not wish to disappoint a magical wizard by disappearing unexpectedly more than once.

Each social occasion was formal. Kevin always had to enter first, and to respond on behalf of our party. But breakfast was the most hilarious. Instead of the usual Chinese food, some of the Linzi academics had spent time in England where they had learned that a fry-up was the favoured start to the day. Hence, we were presented with vast platters of fried eggs, with runny yolks, virtually impossible to eat with chop sticks without decorating yourself or your neighbour. I'd practiced at home with peanuts for goodness' sake!

Since I was by now pescatarian and couldn't eat any of the meat dishes I had little choice but to set about the eggs. Those greasy ovules were slippery little suckers. Most mornings therefore began a bit 'Jackson Pollock', bearing in mind I don't actually eat breakfast, and could hardly stomach the food at 7am. I managed to dodge the more competitive drinking aspects in the evenings, though it was a funny spectator sport, watching people get drunk seemingly from the legs up. I have to say the hospitality was superb. All very jolly.

When it came time for the conference itself, we knew that it was very serious because it was televised and also shown on a big jumbotron outside the museum for the public. We all had to do a red carpet walk when our names were called and take our places in order of speaking. I nearly had one of the most embarrassing incidents of my whole career when the two Chinese speakers who were ahead of me went over on their timings, talking about very obscure aspects of Cuju. This combined with jet lag. I began to fall asleep when I was the next name to be called. Try as I might, I could not stop myself falling asleep. I was just about to stop fighting and have my name called out mid-slumber, probably open -mouthed for all to see on the jumbotron, when the organisers actually called a break because the papers had taken so long. I got some fresh air, drank as much coffee as I could and was able to give my paper while awake. Phew.

On the bullet train journey on the way back from Zibo to Beijing, I had mentioned to Kevin and Stefan that I would like to work with the newly opened FIFA World Football Museum in Zurich. A project initiated by Sepp Blatter in 2012, the $22 million museum was controversially a move into hotels, apartments and restaurants that seemed at odds with FIFA's mission to develop world football. There were interactive stations, and a family feel to the museum experience, but many critics questioned how a heritage attraction would handle the recent scandals. Stefan Jost said it would be covered when the full details were known.

I spent the two-hour train journey chatting to him about how we could develop content in the approach to the forthcoming 2019 Women's World Cup only to find that Stefan and the museum had parted ways the day after our trip concluded. Those comments about the scandals had clearly not been welcome. Had I wasted my time? It was very difficult in the first year of the consultancy getting any work, as we were a new entity. What would my career goals become now? And how could I monetise my academic expertise in other fields? It was both scary and exhilarating to find out!

We also visited the Beijing market with Rowan and Keith, two guys who were trying to develop football as a sport in China. They both had Chinese wives, and were fluent in the language. After entering the main concourse of the market, Rowan and Keith guided us beyond where most of the tourists spent their money to the levels below where Chinese speakers had access to a much better quality of knock-off goods. Some makers were said to have actually worked for Louis Vuitton or whomever, and had this sideline of designer copies, with printed branded receipts, dustbags, tissue-filled branded boxes, the lot.

The women who ran the stalls were crazy for Rowan and Keith because they were Western, and spoke Chinese. Stroking their faces, the women would tell the two Englishmen how tall and handsome they were, and offer refreshments. We filled our empty suitcases with gifts and presents for a few pounds an item, and had an insight we would not have had, were our hosts not so generous. Rowan and Keith explained that it was difficult to spread football in China because the State usually offered sporting provision and there wasn't the amateur culture of parents and volunteers that there was in the UK. Again, fascinating and I'd have liked to spend more time, but the trip was very tightly scheduled and choreographed.

I should also say, it wasn't exactly a smooth transition to working at Wolverhampton. I had made Dave Day aware at Manchester Metropolitan University (MMU) that I had taken voluntary redundancy from De Montfort. Dave was trying to set up his own research centre in sports history. He and his Dean had persuaded the Vice Chancellor at MMU that a senior female appointment would strengthen the group. In due course, an advert went out that looked like it had been written just for me, —a Professor of History specialising in women's sport, particularly football. I applied and gave dates when I would be available around a forthcoming operation Simon was due to have. Sure enough, they picked the day after his operation when I would still be his primary carer. I had to get a family member to take Simon to hospital for his hands to be dressed, drive to Manchester early that morning, do the interview and get back again same day.

As it was a Professorial post there had to be a six-person panel, including an external Chair from another university. I have to say although Dave and his Dean asked reasonable questions, the Manchester Met VC made quite a different impression on me. Think Monty Burns without the humanising effect of Wayland Smithers. As the interview began, the VC instructed me to take off my coat, which I declined to do as it was cold in the room, and the thing went downhill from there.

Suffice to say, I didn't get the job. The job description was specifically written for me, and I was the only person interviewed. Quite the professional feat. I subsequently heard from a female Professor of Fashion who had worked at MMU, and then gone elsewhere, that she had been invited back with a bespoke job description, and also failed to obtain the post after her interview. I don't know if the VC at Manchester Met only uses this process with potential female Professorial recruits. Perhaps the governing board of his university should ask him? As Monty Burns would say over tented fingers, 'Excellent.'

To Wolverhampton then.

The purpose of accepting the part time job in the West Midlands was to keep a hand in academia, and a steady income to pay off the mortgage, while I built up the consultancy business. I really enjoyed working particularly with colleagues and supervised the MSc work of Coza (Corinne 'Coza') Mitchell and Martin Harrison on football coaching -related topics, and taught on undergraduate modules, as well as final dissertations. As well as supervising two PhD students from De Montfort, Amanda Callan-Spenn and Jo Halpin, there was an Arts and Humanities Research Council (AHRC) cohort through the National Football Museum. With the Hockey Museum, I was able to win a funded £70,000 AHRC -funded bursary on the oral history of England and Team GB hockey internationals from 1945 onwards. It was a prestigious award since the Faculty had not received funding from that particular research council before.

After a glitch, David Lewis-Earley got the hockey post and has written a fabulous thesis, also becoming a parent and surviving COVID-19 to submit his work. I had written the project bid due to my oral history expertise, and it looked at Team GB and England women hockey internationals. You can read about our work with Katie Dodd, Chair of the Board of Trustees at The Hockey Museum and a former England player, on their website.

Lizzie Richmond, Archives and Records Manager at Bath University special collections was also very helpful to David, Jo and Amanda, featuring their work on the website as profiles.

I was told however, that, as I was serving my probationary year, there was no provision to reward such entrepreneurship in my year-end review. Charming! It was a reminder that research culture at Wolverhampton was even less developed than at De Montfort, being a heavily vocationally oriented institution for whom most of the students would be the first generation of their families to enrol at university. Obviously, I was very committed to this broader social and educational project. But building a research culture was slow work.

The School of Sport at Wolverhampton was probably the strongest team, research-wise, in the whole university. I wasn't sure about how life in a Sports Science department would turn out, but the wider vocational aspects at Walsall campus where a lot of nurses and teachers were trained was sympathetic with my wider interests. It was three days a week, and I was used to working full time. What else was I going to do?

In December 2016 I attended a football and art event at the National Football Museum, where a number of important sculptors and artists, like Michael J. Browne, spoke as part of a four-year project, 'The Art of Collecting Football' led by academic input from Professor Mike O'Mahony of Bristol University and supported by a Heritage

Lottery Fund grant of £199,900. This was a fantastic project to join, and it was very kind of Mike to invite me.

My last visit to the museum had been in the middle of another academic conference on 23 June 2016, when the Brexit referendum vote was announced. We had gone to bed the night before about half ten, when it seemed like the British public still had their marbles. By the time we woke up at 6am, it was clear that, overnight, said agates had been misplaced.

Thank goodness for art.

The Art of Collecting Football project sought to develop the NFM art collection through the acquisition of priority works that have been wither inspired by, or depicting, football and its wider cultural influence. I particularly loved Browne's *Transfiguration of George Best*, and other pictures such as *The Art of the Game*, 1997.

The exhibition was a mix of new acquisitions and existing works owned by the NFM, ranging from Aardman animation house, to Banksy, and a £40,000 sculpture, *Footballeur*, by Pablo Picasso, who was famously a Barcelona fan in the 1960s before moving to Paris. Equally proud of his heritage, Bradford-born David Hockney, featured football in many of his paintings. Different forms included posters, sculpture, fashion, multimedia collages and Batik work. Contemporary artists and illustrators feature strongly in the exhibition including Stanley Chow, Jill Iliffe and Marcus Marritt. Gary Armer, who has previously been an artist in residence at the museum, was represented by *Not a Penny More*, featuring in the 'Despair' section, a portrait of a dejected Blackpool FC supporter under the Oyston family regime.

A recent acquisition, *Mid-week Practice at Stamford Bridge* by Lawrence Toynbee, was originally submitted as part of the Football and the Fine Arts exhibition in 1953, where it won one of the main prizes, alongside L.S. Lowry's *Going to the Match*. Many people are unaware that in 1953 the Arts Council funded a Football and the Fine Arts competition, which led to a touring exhibition of paintings, drawings, and sculpture organised by the FA. It was unlike the FA, perhaps, to act as curators, but work included Peter Perri, George Fullard, Bernard Dunstan, Claude Rogers, Robert Tavener, David Sylvester. As part of its 90th anniversary celebrations, it was intended to bridge the gap between football as 'low' culture, and art as 'highbrow'.

In this, the Arts Council was itself new, and part of post-war reconstruction to open up art to new audiences. Gerald A. Cains' *Saturday Taxpayers* was a case in point. The oil on canvas painting of crowds relaxedly filling a stand was entered just before the competitions closed, after the picture apparently came to the artist in a dream about his local team, Portsmouth. He was the youngest artist to enter, aged just 22. The title refers to the fact that Entertainment Tax had first been levied on professional football since 1916 as a wartime measure, and werewas still in place, although protests had taken placearisen. Hence, perhaps, the tone of reflective anticipation. The tax was finally abolished in 1960.

Another standout piece of the Football is Art and the Fine Arts exhibition was Jean Cocteau's disarmingly simple line drawing, Football Annonciation, 1923. The National Football Museum already owned influential British surrealist Ithell Colquhoun's The Game Of The Year, created in 1953. The title probably refers to the Blackpool vs Bolton Wanderers FA Cup Final, but there is no record of the painting being entered into the FA art competition. Very new in 2016 was Google's VR project, @tiltbrush Virtual Reality in the Score Gallery, a digital creative tool with many options, including DISCO which sent pulses of light along the lines drawn by the operator. It was fun to have a go.

The December 2016 workshop on public monuments set their relatively recent rise as a widespread phenomenon in this historical context, not least thanks to the groundbreaking work of Chris Stride, Ffion Thomas, and John Wilson and their comprehensive database, From Pitch to Plinth: Sporting Statues Project —www.offbeat.group.shef.ac.uk/statues. As public confidence in politicians and other figures was historically commemorated by public statuary, sports stars have more recently been commemorated due to public fundraising, and civic projects. These works are, by their very nature, outside of the walls of institutions such as the National Football Museum, and in the public domain at specific sites of memorialization.

I had worked with Kevin on a Walk of Fame outside the museum so knew this kind of 'ambient memorialisation.' That is, you take in the history as you walk past the art almost unconsciously. Of the 24 steps in the Walk of Fame, we got readers of the *Daily Mail* to vote for two women, hence Marta and Lily Parr are in the display. Simon and I were invited to the Hall of Fame dinner where I met one of my heroes, England captain Deborah Bampton, for the first time. Frank Lampard did not attend, but Roger Hunt, Bob Wilson and David Seaman were very charming. A fantastic ally, Kevin left the Museum shortly after to lead the Humber Bridge project but we continued to work together at Silverstone.

I was fortunate to be in the right place at the right time, at the National Football Museum in 2016, as Carol Aiken, former goalkeeper of the Manchester Corinthians women's football team was handing in family scrapbooks that she had to the National Football Museum archive. We met, and she talked me through her career, and that of her mother and father managing the team. Although Carol was giving part of the story, it was a subject that had always interested me and I have gone on to work with the Corinthians team ever since on a number of reunions, including linking them up recently with a documentary filmmaker. The team went on to travel to South America for three months in the 1960s, avoiding the FA ban and becoming internationally famous playing games for the Red Cross, a global charity.

I've written articles and blog posts on their history and had the great good fortune to connect players, like Margaret 'Griff' Griffiths, with their Australian counterparts.

Griff went over to Australia as a £10 Pom in the 1960s, when the emigration of Europeans was especially encouraged. She was very young, only just 18, and played football in Australia just as she had in the UK. Showing me pictures of her antipodean teammates, I was able to connect with some to reunite them over 50 years later as Griff stayed just a couple of years in Australia. Another player, Dorothy Barnett, who emigrated to Canada, did an interview with me and I met her niece and brother in Manchester also at the reunion. Jan Lyons played over in Italy, and I was able to connect her with Rose Reilly and others from that time. That's all been a huge privilege in what I get to do.

Then, in September 2017, after returning from the beautiful city of Malmö, where I had examined Matthias Marshick's PhD thesis on Scandinavian women's football, I was appointed as Academic Lead for the Hidden Histories project at the National Football Museum, an Arts Council-supported initiative. I worked with my business partner, Joanna (the other j in our company, jjheritage) who managed the project. I had by that point been studying the topic for 20 years and worked with the Museum since it had opened in Preston, especially since Kevin Moore, Jeff Hill and Jason Wood had pulled together a network looking at sport in museums from 2006--8, with AHRC funding.

Furthermore, through my links with Andy Gray, the sports law specialist, we had been commissioned by the Supreme Court to write an exhibition for the 2012 Olympic and Paralympic Games in London. So, I had over five years of experience of curating an exhibition to diversifydiverse audiences, along with a schedule of public events, and of organising international conferences over several days. This was the brief of the academic position at NFM.

I worked with Belinda, and cataloguers Kate Turner and Chris Stoker who was digitising the Chris Unger collections. I went through every box. Twice. I knew the women's football collections almost by physical memory of where I'd seen an item, and in which box. There were important transgender items in the collections, such as early magazine covers of fashion model, Lea T, assigned male at birth, the daughter of well-known former Brazilian football player, Toninho Cerezo. There are probably more LGBTQ+ items to be found by a discrete project, but time was against us on this first venture.

The painstaking research meant staying frequently in Preston. There was a rather quaint-sounding hotel just outside a service station nearby called The Tickled Trout. But that's where the charm of the place ended. It was cheap, and the walls were so thin I would regularly have to move rooms if a couple were having a domestic next door, or had lots of children in one room. A ticklish quandary in Preston: how noisy were tonight's neighbours?

We also had a reunion couple of days, just for women players, which had a dramatic effect on all involved. The new National Football Museum CEO Tim Desmond, who moved over from the National Justice Museum, came along to support the drop-in day we held when England players—the 1971 Harry Batt team—and Manchester Corinthians attended. It was a very good job he did because he stayed in the room when we went to lunch, and when we came back one of the Corinthians thought she had her medal stolen. It was, in fact, in her bag in a pouch which held two medals, but Tim's steady presence assured everyone the medal could not have been stolen, and it wasn't!

Belinda Scarlett, the Women's Football Project Manager at the NFM, was present as was Joanna. Also, at this meeting I met Chis Lockwood, Leah Caleb and Gill Sayell from 1971, as well as Welsh historian John Carrier, who had travelled with England international, Elaine Badrock. The first English woman to 100 caps, former captain Gill Coultard came along, as did England keeper Sue Whyatt, and Kerry Davis. Belinda and I also did schools outreach work with groups at the archive.

I was to work with all of these women players more closely after 2018, in the lead up to the women's Euros, and help raise their profiles. Leah, in particular, had just retired from the NHS and her brother Derry had read an article I wrote with Bill Wilson of BBC Business for International Women's Day 2018. The article was *A History of Women's Football in Ten Objects* and I was asked to interpret the context suitable for a business report. One of the items I chose was a poster for the unofficial 1970 World Cup, and Leah decided to get in touch.

We would have more reunions at the football museum, working in February 2018 also with Hispanicist David Wood when he had Silvana Goellner and Verónica Moreira over to talk about women's football in Brazil and Argentina respectively. David has always been a great ally and a first class academic, with whom I also share interests in sport and literature. He had won funding in February 2018 to host an event at his university at which two undergraduates got interested in the topic, and Julie Welch, the well-known journalist, covered the story of the unofficial World Cups. We have a great photo of David at an event at the National Football Museum wearing a Xochiti t-shirt made for him by Chris Lockwood. It's a lovely moment of synchronicity. David was one of the first people I invited to speak at the academic conference on women's football I organised with Joanna as part of the project in 2018.

Seventh of March 2018 was quite a day! In the morning, Formula One giant Ross Brawn spoke at the inauguration of the hangar in which the Silverstone Museum would be housed. It was a great support to the project to have such a well-known figure in international motor sport draw in press attention. Prince Harry was in attendance as the museum's Royal trustee, so security was tight, and it was only then I found out he was a complete petrol head.

After a light lunch I then drove to Joanna's from Silverstone, picked her up and drove to Manchester to co-host with Belinda the largest academic conference on women's football which was scheduled for International Women's Day, 8 March, 2018.

THE WAGE THEFT WORLD CUP, 2019

On the way to Manchester I received a phone call from the Manchester City press office, asking would I speak at the fan zone that night about the Hidden Histories project in exchange for two VIP hospitality tickets to the Champions League fixture against Basel. Initially I declined, as we'd quite enough on, —but had a change of heart, only to screech into the carpark with about five minutes to spare, do a quick presentation in the fan zone, and then get whisked into the hospitality where Joanna and I were directed to very nice seats on the front row. The stewards then returned, as one of us had been invited to sit in City's injured captain Vincent Kompany's seat. We made our apologies to Kompany and were then re-seated two rows back. It had been quite a Tuesday.

And we still had a two-day international conference to run!

In spite of a ridiculously tight budget for the conference, we had managed to obtain £1000 sponsorship beyond the original brief; £500 from Wolverhampton, and £500 from the British Society for Sport History. This enabled me to bring Jen Doyle, Josh Nadel, Lindsay Sarah Krasnoff, and Brian Bunk over from the US, and Shireen Ahmed from Canada. Rob Hess travelled from Australia. I'd like to have brought more African and Asian academics over but the budget would just not allow it.

As well as the UK academics too numerous to mention here, European colleagues were Torbjörn Andersson who I had met in Malmö, Sine Agergaard with whom I had worked previously at Aarhus University, Denmark, and at the women's Euros 2013. Dr Bente Ovedie Skogvang, Associate Professor Inland Norway University of Applied Sciences, Elverum, Norway, had refereed the first women's football final between China and the USA in the 1996 Olympics. A pioneering figure for female referees in Norway, Bente is a fine academic and coach. I didn't know I wouldn't see her again until the Women's Euros in 2022. Guy Oliver from the FIFA museum and David Goldblatt dropped by.

There was a civic reception and each participant was given a token, which was a well-replicated item from the Chris Ungar collection of which there were multiple copies (a ticket stub, a pin badge) as a memento. I don't think the museum has been able to hold another conference on women's football on the same scale since, and Belinda left soon after. Although a curator of women's football post was advertised, it has since become a general curatorial role. Dr Alex Jackson is digitising much of the collection, which is a great initiative. The NFM now has National Portfolio Organisation status, and so access to more financial aid.

However, increasingly museum staff began to use a new narrative about 'football people' and 'museum people' as if it were a binary model and an individual couldn't be experienced in both. Given that I have donated my material from the 1999 World Cup onwards to the museum as one of the leading collectors of women's football history, I had expected a bit more respect. If a museum specialist is able to learn a bit about football on the job, it is reasonable to expect that a football specialist can develop their applied knowledge of museology. That insularity again—people building needless silos. The Hidden Histories project exceeded its aims, and was a collaborative example of how deep expertise in a topic can be mutually beneficial.

But I stayed very loosely in touch with the museum. A few years later I curated the core content for all the museum and archive offerings across ten host cities for the Women's Euros in 2022, including the picture research based at NFM. In 2023 I was awarded an Art Fund Jonathan Ruffer curatorial grant to go to Australia for the World Cup on a contemporary collection fandom project for the National Football Museum, and particularly LGBTQ+ fan items.

Having listened to the 'football people'/'museum people' narrative, it was a funny moment a week later in March 2018 when I was at the FIFA World Football Museum in Zurich, having breakfast with Guy Oliver and museum staff at the FIFA-run Ascot Hotel which is just over the road. Tim Desmond walked in for one of his early meetings in Zurich, and looked over, completely nonplussed. Our family have a phrase, 'face don't fail me now,' when it is impolite to crack up at a given point, but I did inwardly chuckle. You could see poor old Tim do a cartoon double-take, having met me only once, 'Who on earth is this woman? What is going on? And why is she sitting there having breakfast?' However, we later connected again when I helped his daughter, Tabitha, with her dissertation.

Each time you stay at Hotel Ascot in Zurich there is a complimentary rubber duck by the bath with a different coloured cap. I have the complement of red, white, and blue capped rubber duckies and have given a few away from my visits. I was there often in 2018 because the staff of the FIFA World Football Museum had a bit of dilemma. That quandary was a blight on the orderliness of their day. Lunch was very Swiss, 12 noon on the dot, preferably at a local restaurant and a full three courses if available.

The museum had published an official history of the Men's World Cup ahead of the finals in Russia. Authored by journalists and museum staff, *The Official History of the FIFA World Cup* was billed as the definitive inside story of the 21 FIFA Men's World Cups to have taken place since the inaugural tournament in 1930. It has now been updated for Qatar 2022. In a sense, the contents advertise the permanent collections at the museum as much as they tell the story of the World Cup, and this object-based approach was part of the process of putting together a coffee-table-style publication.

But within FIFA there are some contested histories. Certain voices did not like that the book explained about World Cups emerging from Olympic football competitions, which, since the FA took control in London, 1908, had become increasingly important. As inaugural World Cup hosts in 1930, Uruguay had already won the 1924 and 1928 Olympic football competition gold medals.

Consider then that FIFA had ignored women's football until the late 1960s. There had not been a Women's World Cup for another 20-odd years. How could the FIFA museum write an official history of the Women's World Cup, without mentioning its own neglect? What stories about which objects could be used to trace that history? How to explain the recent nature of the Women's World Cup with just eight editions, including France 2019? Then, of course, the difference in Olympic competitions, when women's football was not included until 1996?

I cannot comment further on consulting for the FIFA Museum, but I can give my opinions of reading a book, *The Official History of the FIFA Women's World Cup* and seeing the related exhibition in person in Paris. The history section of the book is, to use an academic technicality, a work of genius. As such, the first quarter of the book covers events from 1881 to 1991, which is pretty good in a volume that is 240 pages long. Objects in the FIFA collections tell the story, pushing back the dating of women's football in the book to 1881, which would be contentious in FIFA. Hence the importance of a museum view. There were images even earlier, in 1869, just six years after modern football was first codified.

The book also covers the history of women's football that had been neglected by the governing body, including the unofficial Women's World Cups of 1970 in Italy, and 1971 in Mexico. The narrative of both the book and related exhibition, in that sense, speaks the truth to power and reverses a trend of FIFA claiming that women's football was in any way new, just because their own interest was recent. Having unprecedented access to the National Football Museum collections no doubt helped the historical content, based on the storied objects that formed the illustrations.

But as a reader, I could not find the names of the authors of the book. Who might have written such great work? I'd really love to be in touch. Instead *The Official History of the FIFA Women's World Cup* is registered as authored by the FIFA World Football Museum. It's pretty impressive for a non-human entity, like a museum, to write a book. Of course, as a licensed official product, it has to align with the brand architecture of the world governing body. Speaking purely hypothetically, the work of human writers should not be erased in this way, especially if they were, for instance, women authors. The gender politics of a male-run museum retelling the history of women's football while omitting the female author voice could be perceived as deeply problematic, were that to take place.

It's still a great book, with more than 800 photographs, full of statistical details and a serious look at the overall patterns in elite tournaments. It's important that it was written and published.

The temporary exhibition was, however, compiled at speed and appeared to be without subject specialist knowledge. Although lots of items were displayed in well-lit Perspex boxes, there had been more thought into the transportation and logistics than connections between the objects. There was no curation, and as such there was no storytelling, or context. The relationship of the objects to one another was not articulated. The historical display was actually too underwhelming to call an exhibition but it travelled across the host cities in France 2019 anyway.

However, I continue to resist that static portrayal of history where women's football has recently arrived.

Still today, I am still refining what we think we know about international women's tournaments, such as the Taiwan 1978 Invitational which had three further editions in 1981, 1984 and 1987. I could write more about this now, largely thanks to help from Alex Jackson, as I did not have the material before. It was an important precursor to the China 1988 invitational tournament. As part of the 'two China's' issue, Taiwan sees itself as independent and democratically run, while China considers the island a breakaway province. FIFA's support for mainland China in the form of funding through Women's World Cup hosting reflected this wider diplomatic conundrum.

I would also have liked to get more acknowledgment for women like Tun Sharifah Rodziah of Malaysia, and Veronica Chan of Hong Kong, founding the Asian Ladies Football Confederation in 1968, because the male-led confederation would not countenance women's football at the time. These pioneers deserve wider recognition for their tireless efforts. It's not that any of my previous work was wrong as such—and here is where amateur historians who like to look for 'facts' in historical work often come unstuck. It is just that as more information becomes available in the public domain, we can refine and revise what we think we know. It's an ongoing, growth mindset.

Back in the UK, there was a lot of oral history research also at Silverstone where we were trying to improve the representation of diversity across the planned exhibitions at the museum. What audiences were we seeking to engage? There is an academic analysis of sporting museums that suggests often they are unlike other gallery experiences. If one goes to the Louvre, this logic goes, one is improved by the great art whether or not an enthusiast of the painter in question. But in sporting museums, one individual is often a fan of the sport, and another accompanies them out of duty. So how were we speaking to people who were not fans of motor sport? By telling stories imaginatively for fans of fashion, of social history, of technology, of local or British history, and so forth.

One such oral history interview in late March 2018 was with Christabel Carlisle, the racing 'Mini Virtuoso.' A striking figure even in her late 70s, she had appeared in Vogue in the 1960s as a young woman in a *People And their Cars* feature. Carlisle first took up racing in 1960, entering a club race in a Mini. Don Moore built an Austin Mini Cooper for Carlisle, with which she proved to be a race winner at the second race of the year, beating male drivers all driving factory Mini Coopers at Goodwood. Two serious crashes ended her career in 1963, but her many activities included rallying, salonsaloon car events, hill climbs and sports car track races.

She married Sir James Andrew Watson in 1965 becoming Lady Watson. The Mini was a model of car known for its democratising influence, with interiors designed by great women drivers, like Canadian Kay Petre. Carlisle's immaculate overalls were made especially for her, because of her slight frame, as no male driver's uniform would fit. We put the pale blue overalls and her autobiography in the museum display. I had already done oral histories of other women racers, on two wheels and four, so it was part of an ongoing schedule that was very rewarding.

In April 2018 I travelled to Duke again, at the invitation of Laurent Dubois, to talk to his soccer politics class as part of a one-day symposium on gender equity. Other speakers included Jeffrey Gerson, Dan Levy, Carla Overbeck, Anson Dorrance, Shireen Ahmed, Gwendolyn Oxenham, and Grant Wahl.

Of course, in women's football circles, Anson Dorrance is legendary. I was excited to meet the man who had been the head coach of the North Carolina Tar Heel women's soccer team since 1979. His contribution to women's football has been world class. When the National Collegiate Athletics Association (NCAA) began conducting national championships in women's soccer in 1982, Carolina won the first three titles. The Tar Heel women had won at least 17 national championships, and other distinctions, finishing as runners up more often than not if they didn't win outright.

Dorrance was also the first national team coach to win the Women's World Championship with the US in 1991. In his final act as National Team coach in 1994, Dorrance led the US to victory at the CONCACAF qualifying tournament for the second FIFA World Cup. In 1996, he received the Walt Chyzowych Award for lifetime coaching achievement. His teams are known for their aggression and physicality. As an example, Dorrance would rival players head to head against one another in a training drill called, 'the cauldron' or 'the pit.'

Dorrance had certainly earned his reputation and I was pleased to have the chance to meet him. What I took exception to, was his depiction, in the middle of a long anecdote, of knowing a 'chubby little' Lucy Bronze when she was younger. I bided my time. Bronze's mother, Diana Tough, persuaded the young Bronze to attend summer training camps in North Carolina. After impressing Dorrance, Bronze earned herself a scholarship in 2009, aged 17, moving to North Carolina. I thought that was amazingly brave at such a young age. Bronze has credited her time with the Tar Heels for her world class mentality and she would be voted Best FIFA world's best female player Women's Player in 2020.

At Duke, Anson had been holding forth for some time before dropping this casual insult to Bronze into the monologue. He had not heard me speak so was not aware I was English. Suddenly he was talking about Bronze in a Cockney accent reminiscent of Dick Van Dyke. 'Who were you playing against,?' I interjected, 'Mary Poppins?'. Of course everyone laughed. It was a terrible English accent. Anson was not amused. Many people were startled and when they caught one another's eye, that got a second round of laughter. I had interrupted the great Anson Dorrance at my peril! My countrywoman was not there to defend her younger self though. Everyone thought I was in for a hairdryer telling off from the coach, but it never materialised. Those chuckles at Anson's expense are dedicated to the sleek goddess that is Lucia Roberta Tough Bronze, MBE.

This minor incident takes nothing away from the esteem with which his players held Anson Dorrance at the conference. Although they occasionally rolled their eyes at his more interesting opinions, the greats of women's soccer at Duke clearly had a great deal of affection for their coach and his reputation. Apart from that I had a fab time and was given copies of Grant's and Laurent's new books. I had a lot of fun messing about with Gwendolyn's kids, talking with Shireen and meeting Laurent's lovely family.

In spite of my initial concerns about how precarious freelancer life would be, I also picked up some fantastic media work. One of my favourites was working with poet, author and musician Benjamin Zephaniah on *Treasures of the British Library*, in which he was keen to showcase Rebels. His donation to the library was a rare handwritten copy of his poem *What Stephen Lawrence Taught Us*, on display in the Sir John Ritblat Gallery. I was delighted, having taught his poetry in both further education and higher education, to meet Benjamin and also to find out that he was a petrol head. He had a classic car that he loved, a TR7, which he had owned for the past 23 years. He had stripped down the TR7, and fitted a 4.6-litre V8 engine, upgraded the brakes and had the interior reupholstered.

Zephaniah had become very interested in the struggles of women football players during the 50 years FA ban in England, hence my role. It was a real honour to meet such a hero of mine and to find him such a lovely man. A vegan and animal rights activist, I would recommend his *Talking Turkeys!* or some more serious work like the novel *Refugee Boy*. We covered his interest in the rebels of women's football in the programme and I was onscreen as one of those white gloved historians you see on TV. Sadly, Benjamin died on 7 December 2023, aged only 65, from a brain tumour diagnosed eight weeks previously.

My other developing media, presenting and events work led me to work with the FA at St George's Park and Wembley as the organisation realised it had its own history as a resource to brand more of the estate it owned. We themed changing rooms, public spaces, exhibition content, also inaugurating a caps wall in which those who had won 50, 100 and 150 caps were celebrated. I was particularly pleased that it integrated men, women, futsal, and disability team members in a single list. A Stanley Matthews area was particularly satisfying, and there were plans to upscale over the whole of the Hilton hotel at St George's. There were other history events for the technical directorate, because not everyone who worked at the FA knew the history of the England (men's and women's teams), and it was powerful to deliver that work to eminent manager Gareth Southgate and also to Phil Neville.

Along with elite coach education sessions, there were inspirational storytelling opportunities on which we collaborated. The fantastic Paul Wells, Professor of Animation and Director of the Animation Academy at Loughborough helped, as did his students, with images of everything from Henry VIII in his football boots, to profiles of Lucy Bronze. As 2019 rolled around and I realised a lot of the US and Canadian academics I knew would be in France, we began to develop plans to meet up in Paris at the opening ceremony for the Women's World Cup 2019.

Chicks' Football France 2019

Gonzesses is a French vulgar derogatory term for chicks or birds as it pertains to women. It can also mean sissy. '*C'est ma gonzesse*' is basically 'she's my girlfriend/bird/bitch.' Worryingly therefore, a bird is the single most used animal for a Women's World Cup mascot since Ling Ling, the phoenix, graced China in 1991. Some commentators misunderstood the phoenix motif and called Ling Ling a golden pheasant but my point remains. Big boned Shuéme, a great white owl, so homespun in design that the mascot looked like it had been knitted at speed by someone's cataract-inflicted grandmother, had represented the Women's World Cup Canada in 2015. If Shuéme was women's football's version of Big Bird, she now gave way four years later to a chick in 2019, little Ettie.

It was as if the organisers wanted to diminish women's football at every turn. France did not much care that it was hosting Women's World Cup in 2019. It made that patently obvious in the nine host venues Paris, Rennes, Reims, Valenciennes, Grenoble, Le Havre, Montpellier, Nice and Lyon. Most of the tournament took place outside Paris, although the opener featured a 4-0 win for France v South Korea, and France played their 1-2 defeat to the US in the quarter-finals in the capital. Parc de Prince had a capacity of 45,000 for the opener, and the final in Lyon at Parc Olympique Lyonnais, had 58,000. No double header matches were staged. The smallest stadium used, Grenoble, had capacity of just 18,000, while Nice was the largest (apart from Paris and Lyon) with 35,000.

There were no matches at all at the Stade De France (80,000 seats), the national stadium, although music concerts went ahead during the tournament. Another big symbolic omission in downgrading the Women's World Cup to a petite affair, as the national stadium is the largest in France. The organisers didn't even attempt to fill it. Although the men's national team is associated with the Stade de France, the women's team is not so closely allied and this tournament reinforced that pattern.

Instead, we were meant to be distracted by the tournament's official mascot, Ettie, a young Gallus domesticus. Or a domestic hen chick to most people. She is the daughter of the famous and successful 1998 Men's World Cup mascot, Footix, a cockerel. I think the thing that still really ticks me off most about Ettie, is that someone had really thought about her back story. I'll leave you to judge the wisdom of their endeavours. Bear with me.

First, please put Footix into your search engine. As a comic strip character Footix has exaggeratedly anthropomorphic features, so that his disproportionately large beak has a permanent smile. His white eyes, both on top of his head, are cartoonishly large and looking at us, inviting us in on the joke. His eyebrows are often raised in humorous surprise. The cockscomb on his head and wattle below his beak are bright red, the comb slicked back like an '80s mullet hairstyle. He has a jaunty red tail. HIs overall stance is vigorous and dynamic. Instead of wings, Footix has anthropomorphised hands with three fingers and a thumb: the left points to the future and the right holds a football. Across his chest in white are the words, *France 98*. The traditional French farmyard cockerel therefore became a muscular, playful and perkily confident cartoon mascot for an urban audience.

But the image is also strangely subversive. Firstly, Footix was not young or slender like Kylian MBappé, instead having a physique more like a stocky, middle-aged Cantona. Having a sporty cock strutting around is not the most subtle of football mascots, nor was it intended to be. Eric-style, if the rooster had a collar on his football shirt, it would be up. But Footix is not in football kit or even shorts and shirt. Instead, he is dressed in a blue bodysuit blending seamlessly with matching studded boots. Even if we take Richard Giulianotti's concept of carnivalesque from his book *Football: A Sociology of the Global Game?* as a starting point, I have rarely seen fans of football so body-confident they would wear a one piece bodysuit with integral cleats.

Practically speaking, the body stocking is obviously a graphic designer's cartoon solution to two particular problems. First a rooster's legs are slight compared to its body shape; and second, there are no comparable knee joints in the right place. But surely this could have been anthropomorphised. The design also allows the use of as much blue as possible in characterising Footix with a palette of just five colours, red, white, blue, yellow and black. So, it's very simple.

But using a body suit creates a French frisson compared with previous world cup mascots including 1994's Striker, the World Cup Pup. All wore some form of shorts and shirt, apart from stick man Ciao in 1990, and he is entirely made of cubes so presumably had no need of either clothes or a bathroom. Everything on Footix from wattle to toe, including both hands, and except the red tail, is covered in one continuous blue garment incorporating studded boots. What is the unitard-boot attire referencing? Is Footix living his best life in fetish-gear when not mascoting at a World Cup?

It's a good job I do not spend over-much time analysing World Cup mascots; it could lead to a dark night of the soul. But before we move on. Footix and his flamboyant bodysuit had a direct influence on Ato, Kaz and Nik for Japan/Korea in 2002, three genderless Spheriks—alien-like characters, head to toe orange, purple and blue. Ato was the coach, Kaz and Nik players. For FIFA the gender-fluid designs were all a bit too much. What was needed was a very clear return to gendered mascots and family values. For heaven's sake, these designs were meant to sell things to children.

By the time Goleo VI graced Germany 2006, it was perceived as a return to more traditional masculine character values. But he was no eagle, no bear, no little boy. Instead Goleo ('goal' and 'leo', the lion) was a hirsute biped lion, as World Cup Willie had been in 1966. Willie, as we know, was the original World Cup mascot where all this began. Goleo did wear a football shirt with the number six on it, for 2006. But, like Disney's articulation of the fictional bear Winnie the Pooh, Goleo has no undercrackers or shorts. Just the shirt and some boots. All a bit free and easy breezy. And Goleo's best friend is the other mascot of 2006, a talking football, Pille, to whom he soliloquises Hamlet-style. Perhaps he is asking where his shreddies, shorts and socks are? Pille's responses are not recorded. But now I really do digress. Back to Ettie and Footix.

However Footix chose to dress, there is considerable historical authenticity in using a sporty rooster as a symbol of nationhood in France. The cockerel has been part of French culture for thousands of years; famed for its sexual prowess, it is also the bird that announces the dawn, so embodies rebirth. Historically complex, moving from the icon of Royal to Republican sympathies, from rural to urban contexts, the cockerel had been taken on by several 19th Century French national male sporting teams, such as in rugby and football.

Resurrection was part of the story that Fabrice Pialot, his creator, used to launch Footix on television. In a sequence entitled Les Années buts, The Goal Years, Footix was introduced, first in picture form, then live to a studio audience including ex-footballers from France's 1984 European Championship winning side, plus legends such as Michel Platini, as well as the late Claude Simonet, President of the French Football Association.

A national poll to name the mascot chose overwhelmingly 'Footix', the winning name announced on children's television. With obvious links between football and Asterix the Gaul, Footix recycles embodied nationhood and the essential qualities of hospitable and virile French hosts. So, the idea of the French cockerel has layer upon layer of meaning, and was used to sell all kinds of merchandise while France won in 1998 on home soil 3-0 against Brazil, the defending champions. Therefore, Footix gained legendary status. Twenty years later, France won for a second time in Russia, 2018. Could Ettie the daughter of Footix inspire the women to victory on home soil in 2019?

There is no historical authenticity whatsoever in using a chick to represent women's football in France. Unless you are Le Benny Hill. In many ways, Ettie, as the daughter of Footix, used many of the same anthropomorphic techniques of cartoon graphic design, such as hugely enlarged eyes, a beak large enough to hold a permanent smile, and legs leading to football boots. But she is also a feminised poussin with arm-like wings, hair-like feathers that can be pulled into a ponytail on her head, eyelash extensions, manicured eyebrows, and face jewellery that resembles coloured freckles. Ettie's eyes are baby blue and she is often depicted as winking at us. Her white shirt with red and blue stripes says France 2019 and her feathered legs are revealed between her shorts and her socks so we do glimpse her knees. But what's in a name?

We are told by the FIFA marketing department that 'Ettie', from the French word 'étoile', means star. The French men's shirt bears two stars for the two World Cups won in 1998, and 2018. France women's national team has yet to win a World Cup and so has 'pas d'étoile', no star. Was the name Ettie meant to inspire or console for that lack of a star? The tournament motto, Dare to Shine is practically an oxymoron, while Ettie's character was described as gregarious, social, cheeky, cute, warm and fun. Really?

I don't know that the French ex-captain, the indomitable Wendie Renard particularly self-identified with these values although she reclaimed the star motif for her autobiography, released in December 2019 with the title Mon Étoile. An utter warrior who drank in the arrogance of the US team in 2019 in the same way that lesser sporting mortals drink Gatorade, Renard walked onto the field of play in her home tournament like she really, Really, REALLY wanted to win football matches. Her passion was so electrifying it made you really, Really, REALLY need her to win. Everything. And then make her President the day after the final. Instead, it's almost as if the mascot to their own tournament symbolised to the French host national team that taking part and making friends was more important than coming first. Bless.

French girls may think of themselves as chic, but how many think of themselves as aspiring chicks in football boots with Daddy issues? The borrowed history of the cockerel just didn't square with a tournament that said it sought to bring the same success to the French women's national team as the men in 1998 and 2018, but didn't put them on the same stage, with the same resources to do so. I won't go into the posters, the overall brand architecture or any of that, because you've been patient enough to read this far, but the whole messaging was off, and Ettie was a patronising symbol of failed ambition.

France 2019 should have been bigger. Les Bleues deserved so much more than to be undercut as fledglings. Current players like Wendie Reynard, Amandine Henry and Eugénie Le Sommer merited more respect, and a global stage. Retired legends like Sandrine Soubeyrand on 198 caps should have been celebrated for their pioneering service. None of these women struck me as being like a baby bird. All mascots are, of course, consumerist inventions aimed at children to sell everything from keyrings to travel packages, but Ettie felt more fake than most. Sorry chick.

France had been awarded the hosting rights to the Women's World Cup in 2015. But the French Football Federation (FFF, formed in 1919) didn't formally recognise women's football until March 1970. Sports journalist Pierre Geoffroy writing for *L'Union* was a key figure in changing governance, working with a team at Reims which became the de facto French women's national team for almost two decades. Having failed to qualify for the first three Women's World Cups, largely because the French Football Federation provided no support, Élisabeth Loisel took over as head coach of the national team and technical director, establishing the women at the Centre National de Formation et d'Entraînement de Clairefontaine, the national training centre. Qualification for the 2003 Women's World Cup finals followed. But 2007 was not a success.

However, it was largely as a result of club football professionalising that the national team benefitted. First at Montpellier under Louis Nicollin, then at Lyon, with Jean-Michel Aulas forming OL Féminin in 2004. Cue Wendie Renard who left her native Martinique in 2006 to try out at Clairefontaine for the national team, and failed, before getting the train to Lyon aged just sixteen. She arrived just in time. Aulas was the one to persuade the FFF to issue 'federal contracts' of fixed salaries, enabling players to train full time from 2009/10. The change was dramatic, with France losing to the US in the 2011 World Cup at the semi final stage, finishing fourth overall. In 2015 Germany defeated France in a dramatic quarter final match on penalties.

Since France's men had a really difficult World Cup in South Africa in 2010 with their own industrial dispute, the semi final achievement in 2011 showed how quickly even small investment could return dividends in women's football. What became known as L'Affaire des Quotas in 2010/11 season also revised notions of how successful the men's Black-Blanc-Beur diverse team winning the 1998 world cup on home soil. It would seem that a quota system was debated at Clairefontaine to limit the number of black and north African-origin male players on the national team. Although this wasn't actioned, the women's team benefitted from increased fan support, with its multi-racial composition a strength, especially the likes of Renard, Laura Georges, and Louisa Nécib of Algerian descent.

But Corinne Diacre, the head coach of France women's national team had dropped Wendie Renard from the captaincy in 2017, favouring Amandine Henry instead. Also controversially she left out Kheira Hamraoui and Marie-Antoinette Katoto from the 2019 squad, the latter the French league's top scorer. In some senses Wendie Renard's stoic silent tolerance of Diacre's disciplinarian regime and the FFF's handling of the situation in 2019 was the bookend to Megan Rapinoe's vociferous critique of US Soccer.

Although Renard would be invited to retake the armband in 2021 by Diacre, the unpopular coach could not unite the squad due to a lack of communication skills, and a draconian regime. So although France 2019 was hailed as a chance for the women to replicate the feat of the men in 1998, the conditions were very, very different. It was a missed opportunity, with average attendances at club games still below 1,000 fans after the world cup left town. By 2023 Renard knew she had a bigger reputation and fan base than the coach, refusing to play for France while Diacre remained. The captain of French women's club football's most winning team would go to Australia 2023 and Diacre did not. Wendie had the last word.

France 2019 would be the second and last of the 24-team World Cups before the tournament expanded to 32 teams in Australia. France was the third European country to host behind Sweden and Germany. Beside the hosts, there were eight European squads, England, Germany, Italy, the Netherlands, Norway, Scotland, Spain and Sweden. Oceania had a single representative in New Zealand. The Asian confederation had five national teams, in Australia, China, Japan, South Korea and Thailand. Cameroon, Nigeria and South Africa represented Africa. The South American sides were Argentina, Brazil and Chile. The remaining spots were taken by Canada, Jamaica and the USA.

Chile, Jamaica, Scotland and South Africa were debutants. This reflected the lack of support in the national associations for the women's team often citing financial reasons to cut the women's programme but not the men's.

I have outlined in a previous chapter how I felt academia inflicted wage theft upon marginalised academics in particular who were required to do a great deal of academic citizenship, as it is known, in order to obtain promotion. Academic citizenship often involves 'acting up' to the next level for quite some time before a person is promoted and paid for doing the work that they have already been doing. I've shown I was at Professorial level for quite some time before being paid at that level, and of course people don't talk about money so you are never sure how much your male colleagues are being paid. So it's a kind of wage theft. You are persuaded by the system to defer the gratification of actually getting paid for working by labouring towards something that may, or may not, be conferred. But at least in academia you do get paid something, eventually.

Women's football remains much more precarious than academic careers, and often teams were not paid by the national association because they are told they do not deserve recompense, representing their country should be enough. The professional footballer's union, FIFPRO conducted a survey which revealed that almost a third of female players did not receive payment from their national teams over 18 months after big tournaments, with two-thirds reporting having to take unpaid leave from their main day jobs to play for their national teams.

There's a brilliant detail in Megan Rapinoe's *One Life* where she finds out the men are on $75 for incidental purchases a day from US Soccer, and the women $60. That male daily bits and bobs cost $75 and women's $60 is not, I would argue, scientifically or economically evidenced. Male players were paid $5000 if they lost a match, but the women got no bonus for loss or draw. Paying male players more in bonuses to lose than women to draw is discriminatory and intended to be so.

And it can be more subtle. Famously when Japan won the Women's World Cup in 2011 they were flown home on a regular flight while the Japan men's team had chartered planes to their matches, and won nothing. So although wages might get paid, they are not at the same rate of recompense because Women's World Cups are valued as less important, and stealing the limelight of successful women's teams by sending them home in coach class is part of the layered larceny. It's not necessarily market value that is operating as the key economic driver, but perceptions of female player value.

In the case of Jamaica, the team had been disbanded in 2008 after a disappointing failure to qualify for the Olympic programme, mainly because the national association had not resourced the women's programme properly. That kind of logic is virtually a mugging in plain sight. The women's national team project was only restarted in 2014 at the instigation of Cedella Marley, daughter of Bob, who used her family name and connections to fund, and raise awareness of the 'Reggae Girlz' as they are known. They would be eliminated after losing all their group stage matches in 2019, showing how lack of support from the national federation could translate to poor performances. Since any World Cup appearance money goes to the national association, FIFA considers its an internal issue to that orngaisation if that is passed on to players. Or not. It can lead to systemic wage theft from the players themselves and by extension their supporters like Marley. Why are entrepreneurs required to get involved when there is a national football association whose remit it is to develop its national teams?

The opener in Paris was at the Parc de Princes Paris on 7 June 2019. I make no bones about the fact I was contemplating all this at Mollitor, the Paris hotel where the lido opened in 1929 and popularised the bikini with French women in spite of the Catholic church's reticence. In 2019 it was a very arty Parisian hotel with installations in the old changing cabins. People have had a lot of fun at Mollitor, and joy seeps through the walls. Olympic swimmer Jonny Weismuller had been at the launch and was a life guard for the 1929 season. Another fabulous pool for the collection, and an historic facility right by Roland Garros. Because, why wouldn't you?

We had managed to get seven 15 euro tickets together, which was not difficult and I met up with my friends from Leicester, Rachel and Louise Rawding, aka 'the lioness who Rawd.' Tying in with Lindsay Sarah Krasnoff and Erin Twohig, Rachel Allison, Grant Wahl, Jen Doyle and Jonathan Johnson, French football correspondent for CBS Sports, we met at a restaurant ahead of the game. Having connected with Gwendolyn Oxenham and her family we very slowly made our way into the stadium. Fans were corralled and funnelled into limited spaces in ways that made our progress unpleasant. I am not particularly claustrophobic but others were uneasy. Not great for children anyway as an experience of a match.

There had been new ticketing systems, and we were required to print out tickets ahead of the match with QR codes. But at the last minute the FIFA systems had reissued tickets, which prevented us from entering through the turnstiles when we had already queued for half an hour. Families realised they would not be sitting together as the tickets were renumbered.

It was ridiculously policed, and over-zealous security bag check staff confiscated personal items like lip gloss, and mascara which stewards said could be used as missiles. I don't know how much the stadium steward had ever spent on a lip gloss, but mine had cost £20. I wasn't going to lob an expensive shade named Tangerine Dream from Row Z in the general direction of Eugénie Le Sommer with any great conviction that it would influence her decision-making. It wasn't her shade for a start!

When personal items such as this were summarily binned, and drinks were taken off children, which incensed everyone even more, we merely walked around the truculent security guard in question and retrieved them. The process achieved nothing apart from further alienating the crowd. Like many, I may have picked up an extra bottle of water or two. Why pay the exorbitant stadium prices to FIFA sponsors when we were being treated so disrespectfully?

Worse still, the majority of male security staff searched the minority of men spectators, and the few female stewards rummaged slowly around long queues of women and girls. We then had to re-queue at customer services for them to re-issue tickets. Hence in spite of getting there an hour before kick-off we missed the opening ceremony and the first few minutes of the match. It was a joyless, designedly inefficient, unfair, upsetting shambles when we had hoped to be dancing in celebration.

Upset a group of feminist football academics at your peril! At least one will bear a grudge and write the hell out of it for posterity. We did find a lone Korean student to whom we gave our spare ticket. Her reaction and interaction with her countrywomen in the stadium bought us back some joy. The Korean student literally walked up to us and said do you have a ticket, to which I replied yes. She may have paid me for the ticket, she might have bought me a beer. I can't remember and it doesn't matter. That one interaction sums up my experiences of following women's football internationally.

But what I did see and hear, unusual in French football, was gangs of young men in the seats in front of me at the Parc de Princes with chants they had made up for specific players, especially stars like Kadidiatou Diani, Henry, Renard, and Le Sommer. Travelling as an all-male group, in their late teens, to early twenties the fans had adapted standard English 'She's here, she's there' chants for their chosen favourites which they sang in French. This was a new kind of masculinity, perhaps priced out of men's football or alienated from the likes of Paris Saint-Germain and its Qatari owners.

The performance of Disco Foot by Ballet de Lorraine in which mixed teams wearing gold lame hotpants (yes, really) improvised a dance-off led by a DJ was pure delight. The dance-battle is entirely an artistic one. Both those young men on the terraces, and Disco Foot gave me gladness. If you are ever hosting a Disco Foot event, I am here for it.

In Group A, France went through on nine points having won all their games, Norway progressed second on six, losing only to the hosts, and Nigeria defeated South Korea 2-0 to secure progression. In the process of being eliminated, South Korea scored a lone goal. One of the world's most gifted women players, Norway's Ada Hegerberg had made herself unavailable for the national team from 2017 to 2022 in protest at the poor conditions for women players. This was hardly commented upon in the media. But it was a sign of player power, and of bitterly contested gender relations that would spread by the time of her return in 2022.

Hegeberg was criticised for this act of industrial action, withdrawal of labour, which some commentators argued was antithetical to 'growing the game' another form of unpaid labour that female players are obliged to perform. Hence, promoting women's football as a whole actually encourages female internationals in colluding in their own financial exploitation. Do a bit more, love, unpaid work after playing a 90 minute match. Sign autographs, smile for selfies, make yourself available for an extra half hour to the fans and then get into the ice bath. That one of the world's most gifted players would choose to miss out on the largest tournament for women, which only came around every four years while at the height of her game to make a case for structural discrimination seemed beyond the comprehension of many media folks. So wedded were they to the progress narrative in women's football, many have said to me that 2019 was a breakthrough event. I can't share that view.

In Group B, Germany topped the group with three wins, Spain had one win and a draw as runners up, and their draw with China earned the former double hosts their access to the next round. South Africa, like South Korea, registered a single goal and conceded eight as bottom of the group.

In Group C, Italy won two matches, as did Australia and Brazil but conceded fewer to top the group. Jamaica was eliminated with a single goal, thanks to Havana Solaun. In Group D, England won three matches, narrowly missing a perfect record due to a Claire Emslie goal for Scotland. In spite of a six-goal thriller against Argentina at the Parc de Princes on 19 June, Scotland's only draw was not enough to save them. Thanks to Argentina also drawing with Japan, they progressed third, behind Japan, with one win and one draw.

In Group E, the reigning European champions, the Netherlands, advanced to the knock-out stages with three wins. Canada won two matches to progress second, and Cameroon, by virtue of defeating New Zealand 2-1 earned the final spot, although

Marie Aurelle Awona helped the Kiwis with an own goal. In Group F, the US won without conceding a goal, including a 13-0 drubbing of Thailand. Sweden also progressed, while Chile and Thailand exited at this stage.

The round of 16 saw Norway go through against Australia to meet England in Le Havre. France had to go to added extra time to defeat Brazil 2-1 to rival the US in Paris. The Netherlands defeated the previous world champions Japan 2-1 to play Italy in Valenciennes. Germany and Sweden respectively won their matches to kick off in Rennes for their quarter final.

Different But Equal?

I was back in Lyon for the two semi-finals. England lost 2-1 to the USA on 2 July and the Netherlands defeated Sweden the next day in the same stadium. I couldn't get excited by an England team coached by Phil Neville. I wasn't surprised by captain Steph Houghton's missed penalty, although I admired the instinct to lead from the front.

I had greatly enjoyed audacious Alex Morgan winding England up with her 'cup of tea' gesture in celebration of her goal. It was witty and had the desired effect. I wished someone had thought of how to inspire a bit more grit in the England performance all round, but Neville was too busy eyeing up a new contract in Miami with his old friend to properly concentrate. Millie Bright earned a red card against the US, having been somewhat challenged to lose her cool by the experienced American players, especially Morgan, whom she clattered twice. More tea Millie? Christen Press ran riot around Houghton. That winner mentality was not there yet with England, and the US was fighting against Trump, not just lining up for a game of football.

This was an England team of huge potential, and of achievement—Bronze Boot Ellen White on six goals, midfield wraith Fran Kirby, and Silver Ball winner, Lucy Bronze. The Neville effect had at least been to get the FA to invest more money in the technical directorate, which paid off as gifted players were able to perform at higher levels than before. I just didn't know what England, the Netherlands and Sweden stood for, whereas the US left us in no doubt.

Nor did Brazil, as they exited to the hosts 2-1 in the quarterfinals. Cristiane scored the headed goal of the tournament versus Australia. Marta ended up scoring at five world cups, and exited the tournament with seventeen world cup goals in all. As Brazil lost to France she gave her now legendary speech (well it is in my house), which translated roughly as:

'I mean you have to treasure this. We demand so much, you know? We demand support but it needs to be appreciated. I would have liked to be here smiling but here I am crying with joy. That's the most important thing. It's wanting more. It's training more. It's taking care of yourself more. It's being ready to play 90 plus 30 minutes or whatever it takes. This is what I ask of the young girls. You won't have a Formiga forever, you won't have Marta or Cristiane forever. So women's football depends on you to survive. So think about that. Appreciate that more. Cry in the beginning so you can smile in the end.'

Crikey, there's not going to be a Formiga, Cristiane or a Marta forever? That's about as existential as it gets.

On 7 July, USA won 2-0 against the Netherlands. Sarina Wiegman got everyone's attention and I cheered on my favourite Dutch player, the number 7, Shanice van de Sanden who was subbed on after 72 minutes. Two female coaches at the final. There was lots of very cool styling in the US victory parade, where the players looked horrendously hungover. And, err, that's it.

The public transport systems to the matches were hopelessly crowded and suffocating. In both Paris and Lyon, crowds of families with children were crammed into dangerous situations, both confined into underground stations, and onto trams. The fan festivals were, mainly closed, full of the usual FIFA sponsor hoardings and, when open, meh. You wouldn't have known Paris was being inconvenienced by a world cup. We got more excited finding the coffee shop that England used in Lyon and going there. I met Sean Ingle from *The Guardian* on one such outing.

Fan marches, which the organisers wanted, were impossible because the stadiums were so far from the centre of town. Most Dutch fans didn't come along for their semi-final which was played in a half empty stadium. So, there was a great deal of window-dressing by FIFA media to show a celebratory atmosphere. We sat around chatting about various issues with Portland Thorns supporters at USA v England, and we could not even give away 15-euro tickets to the Netherlands v Sweden semi-final on the street.

It was entirely the case that those of us who travelled to France made our own fun, because the assumptions of the organisers were so wide of the mark. I saw FIFA documentation that said as a mainly family audience, fans of women's football did not want to be near bars, because they preferred coffee shops. This enabled the owners of *buvettes*, essentially a bar in a backyard with a barbecue, to make an absolute killing with both families and those who travelled as adult groups. Trust me, fans of women's football like beer and a burger. FIFA, you can have this observation for free.

This was the real fun, because it felt underground and marginal which is where women's football had always been. As well as the *buvettes*, there were festivals by LGBTQI+ groups and inclusive kickabouts. Hanging out, chatting, and arsing about in glorious July sunshine.

It was incredibly social, hilariously chaotic and a perfect antidote to the anonymous, anodyne fan zones. Presumably, the final in Lyon and third place playoff in Nice were scheduled so that folks could follow the sun. It was anticipated that US families would take off the summer to come to Europe to attend France 2019. FIFA was more interested in saying that media audiences were huge, which was good because there were plenty of spare seats in the actual stadiums.

The overall star of 2019 alongside Morgan, Megan Rapinoe, had also played in Lyon at a crucial stage in her career. Rapinoe became the first white professional athlete to kneel during the national anthem in 2016 at an international match, in support of NFL player Colin Kaepernick who has been protesting racial injustice since 2016. Rapinoe had also campaigned against US Soccer for equal pay for a similar amount of time. Her autobiography *One Life*, published in 2020 is compelling, about the extent of the personal risk she undertook. That said, subsequently under a Trump presidency, Rapinoe was the most high-profile campaigner in the US women's national team, embodied by her pink, blue or purple hair, and the gladiatorial stance she took while VAR decided if a goal was valid. Alex Morgan was a huge presence, and again even from row Z I could feel the charisma. I wouldn't feel that again until Alexandra Popp swaggered into the stadiums of women's Euros in 2022 with a confidence that sent shock waves into the stands.

The use of VAR robbed the women of a spontaneous goal celebration, and to regain her joy Rapinoe stood like a gladiator, arms outstretched in a pose now often replicated by male players in major tournaments, which said, 'Are you not entertained?' It was powerful. Not least she was challenging a sexist, conservative, narcissitic president while trying to win a World Cup. He tweeted she had better shut up and win first. While she won, she did so loudly, proudly, and confidently. A grown up gay athlete with pink hair was using a World Cup to scold an orange toddler in the White House. Imagine playing at that level while protesting at that level. Hence by winning the tournament, the Golden Ball and Golden Boot, Rapinoe refused Trump's terms of reference.

But there were ambivalences. Having dared to shine, Rapinoe's taking the knee was halted by US soccer because they changed the rules so that her protest was modified to not singing the national anthem. Although coach Jill Ellis made comments of support for Rapinoe after an earlier recording of her saying, 'I'm not going to the f***ing White House' if the US won the tournament, she did not play in the England game in Lyon. While some said this was a hamstring injury, and Hope Solo also offered the view that the 34-year-old did not have the stamina to play for 90 minutes, it also followed a public rebuke by Trump that she should, to use his capitalisation, WIN first before he would consider inviting the team.

So, she did not look very happy having scored the two goals that secured the US the semi-final place. There were rumours that she had been required from the highest level to be dropped. In the event, the Trump Twitter spat unified the US team and lifted their game. Of course, Rapinoe scored in the final, in this case from the penalty spot, and

Rose Lavelle, whom everyone loves because she is Rose Lavelle, was a popular scorer of the second goal.

'Equal pay, equal pay, equal pay' the crowd chanted in unison in Lyon on 7 July 2019. But US Soccer at one point claimed that if the women were paid equal to their achievements it would bankrupt the federation. When this was not convincing as an argument, the President of US Soccer, Carlos Cordeiro, suggested that equal pay was not required because women have less ability than men. Players like Alex Morgan were repeatedly asked if they played against men's teams would they, could they, win? After he resigned in 2020, Cordeiro's LinkedIn profile suggests he became a Senior Special Advisor to the FIFA President.

A settlement was reached in December 2022 incorporating $22 million in back pay and $2 million for US women's players' service on retirement, but it remains contested whether it constitutes equal pay. Especially by Hope Solo. You may want to watch her version of events on the Neflix documentary, *Hope Solo vs US Soccer*.

Although the winners in 2019 celebrated like the rockstars they are to millions of fans, for those of us who write about the structural inequalities of sport, the victory in France was nowhere near as optimistic as it had been in 1999. How could it be with Trump in the White House, Gianni Infantino heading up FIFA, and the wealthiest and most well-resourced women's team in the world having to become a walking protest at the same time as winning a World Cup?

The portents for Australia 2023 were that by the time we reconvened in four years, every women's national team would be fighting against their own federation for their right to decent working conditions and better pay.

This would make 2023 the Industrial Dispute World Cup.

CHAPTER VII
THE INDUSTRIAL DISPUTE WORLD CUP—AUSTRALIA, 2023
The Night Soil Man's Granddaughter

I was inspired to go to Australia by the romanticism of a seed drill. Some British people might say they were motivated to go Down Under by Charlene marrying Scott Robinson on *Neighbours* in 1987—which was a big deal in the UK; or there is the more nebulous draw of a large country with a relatively small population; and of course, the sunshine. All very valid points. In my case, it was not so much the scarlet Massey Harris seed drill used on the farm to plant corn *as such*, but what it represented.

My Grandad, William, was one of the most important people in my life. He was given to travel, but had little chance to get beyond France, Scotland or Ireland. Grandad established his smallholding piecemeal, ostensibly in order to keep the horses for the haulage business established by his father, Edwin.

William never sold a piece of land, and slowly bought enough ground to establish Little Fields Farm, eventually 200 acres of mixed arable use. Having first been a market gardener, using an allotment to grow produce sold at Leicester market, his main business became hauling—anything and everything. He would cart people in charabancs going on holidays and celebrations, once receiving a speeding fine for going 22 miles per hour down the high street after the local cricket club won a hard-fought match. He had two horse-drawn hearses but only one black horse for funeral processions. Sometimes he had to dab black shoe polish on a white dobbin to draw the cortege as etiquette demanded.

William had also been one of the local night soil men. 'Night soil' was a polite term for human waste retrieved from earth closet outhouses before flushing toilets (water closets) were invented. Collected in a variety of buckets and pails, sewage was usually harvested from domestic and industrial properties after dark, and sometimes then used in agriculture as a fertiliser.

Once late at night outside the local pub a drunk man dropped all the lamps used to light Grandad's night-cart into the contents by way of a jape. When found, the jester was invited to retrieve the lanterns and illumination was restored.

Grandad wore a white shirt, waistcoat and flannel trousers as his work uniform. Rarely was he seen in public without his cap. He was always referred to locally as 'Mister' as a mark not just of respect, but admiration. A holiday was something people valued, saved up for, and looked forward to. A funeral retinue required trust and humility. William was a man who conducted his professional life with the utmost discretion, even when publicly disposing of the most intimate business of his customers. He took shit seriously.

By the 1940s, most houses thankfully had an outhouse or, by the 1950s, an indoor bathroom featuring a flushing toilet. So, by the time I arrived, night soil as an income stream in Grandad's haulage firm was long gone in favour of farming. If the management of effluence had not immediately conferred affluence, (sorry), as his family we basked in the glow of Grandad's elevated standing in the community. It was a good start in life. I was very proud to be his granddaughter.

Grandad, although a very stalwart and steady man, sometimes 'went walkabout' as he put it. He would go to Scotland, France or Ireland on his own. He would literally walk miles in fetching or dropping off a cart. After World War One he had intended to emigrate, with Canada we think his preferred destination, but the Great Depression and the difficulty of his own business prevented that from happening. Having gambled on Sentinel Waggons, the first steam powered trucks, to carry freight instead of using horse-drawn vehicles, the industrial landscape changed to make them obsolete in less than 20 years. Sentinels were not like a steam engine, and more like a conventional truck, but were nevertheless heavier than internal combustion engines and so not great on tarmac roads. By the mid-1930s a range of taxes on motor vehicles, coal and so forth put many steam hauliers out of business.

Grandad diversified from haulage into farming, developing a milk round, and keeping cows for the purpose. My Uncle Ted, a technophile who loved the Sentinels, could never quite reconcile the move from lorries to bovines. Uncle Ron, much given to Westerns at the cinema, was much more at home on the range.

The story of the seed drill was one that I had grown up with. Grandad had bought the Massey Harris from Australia, and it had come over lashed on the deck of a ship covered in layer upon layer of grease so that the sea water could not perish its working parts, or the smart red finish. It took months of the destined equipment enduring the thrashing of briny waves before it reached us. Not actually manufactured in Australia, the Massey Harris had at least been there. As farm machinery went, it had the exotic distinction of being better travelled than its new owners.

Quite why a Leicestershire farmer would bring a seed drill over from the other side of the world made no sense unless you understood that my grandad had not been able to emigrate, would travel vicariously through the farming machinery catalogues to see what others in far off lands were using as new technologies, and loved a bargain at an auction. We think he must have seen it in one of the many directories he studied, or liaised with one of the local agricultural suppliers. What it represented was that if he could not make it to Australia in this lifetime, a piece of something from the antipodes would make its way to him. The difficulty of bringing it over was part of the charm.

There are Cine 8 films of us kids jumping on and off the seed drill. The Health and Safety people would be appalled, but they were not around to ruin our fun! It was, to us, a plucky little red chariot: we had seen Charlton Heston in *Ben Hur*. There was a board on which to stand and a hand rail, which for practical purposes was meant to be leant on while the operator sowed corn. Because it was towed relatively steadily behind a tractor and the earth had been ploughed and then tilled to a fine powder finish for corn, the Massey Harris allowed us to die dramatically, falling off the back onto the soft earth, before being resurrected and scampering after the receding drill; only to hop onto the footplate and perish all over again.

Sometimes we were charged by other chariots in the Colosseum and crashed; other times we were shot; sometimes our demise was an arrow to the eye. Whatever fanciful way we had been despatched we usually expired with a theatrical cartwheel off the back onto the soft earth. The hand rail also allowed for decease by drowning, as we could hold on, feet flailing behind us only to declare it was impossible to endure, and pass into an imaginary watery grave.

The Massey Harris was a convivial vehicle for the imagination, if not particularly practical as an item of farm machinery because it only had a four-metre span for drilling, meaning we had a lot of journeys on which to give up the ghost, even while not much corn was being sowed. It was eventually replaced by eight-metre seed drills, or larger, and I found other pastimes. But essentially, that's why I had always wanted to go to Australia. I knew that if I did, I would be very fortunate indeed. So, 50 years later how did it come about?

After seeing so many academic friends at the Women's World Cup in France in 2019, I was by then frustrated by a lack of progression (again) at the University of Wolverhampton. I went for Faculty Head of Research, which went to a guy who had worked there for 20 years. When I asked for feedback the next day, I was told by the interview panel Chair she couldn't remember why they had preferred him for the job.

A rather crude experiment linked colleagues from the discipline of Psychology with the Institute for Sport to form a new centre in Health and Wellbeing. I went for Interim Head of the new Centre, which instead went to a male Senior Lecturer of Psychology who had been there for 20 years. Having been declined for the Interim job there was no point in going for permanent Head, and it went to a different guy who had been there for 20 years who was very good at massaging National Student Survey (NSS) scores, and hadn't researched or published much. If it was his reward for manufacturing satisfactory metrics, it didn't do the institution much good as he left soon after to repeat the feat at a nearby rival.

I took the Athena SWAN gender equality academic role across the University, reporting to the VC, and could see that my frustrations were nothing compared to what female colleagues were experiencing across the institution. Athena SWAN was originally a scheme to promote women in Science and Technology but now had a wider gender equity agenda. The University had lost its classification of a bronze award, as it was so poor in regards to gender equity. The gender pay gap was much worse than sector average. My brief was to regain the bronze award. It was a big ask.

On my case load, returning mothers were being invited to use cleaning closets to breastfeed, the nursery didn't open in time for parents to drop off their children and teach or attend a 9am lecture, and the male to female ratio in the Professoriate was shocking.

The VC was a nice guy who once announced at a dinner he had ordered French wine, as there was a Professor from France present. It was actually a very flinty Sancerre, but since we were all driving to the dinner it was a moot, and untouched, point. Fine detail not his strong point then, the VC didn't seem especially across the business model of the institution.

I had by now finished the *Britain's Olympic Women* book with Routledge, finally, and although the institution had agreed to pay the indexing fee to expedite it for the REF 2020, any purchase over £500 had to be signed off by the Chief Financial Officer. That indicated a level financial difficulty, and caused considerable delays. The e-book and hardback eventually came out in July 2020, by which time everything had changed. For everyone.

Having recruited David Lewis-Earley to the AHRC-funded Doctoral position on the oral history of women's hockey internationals, I also began to work with Helen Cromarty, the archivist of the Much Wenlock Olympian Society, on a biography of its founder, William Penny Brookes. Helen is very impressive, professionally as well as personally, and she recently completed her PhD viva voce examination, as did David, in 2024. Amanda Callan Spenn and Jo Halpin also completed their PhD examinations with me at Wolverhampton, so it was a very rewarding experience from that point of view. I took on the role of Faculty Postgraduate tutor at Wolverhampton, as I had previously at De Montfort, enjoying this kind of work enormously.

However, I was getting more fulfilling work as a consultant than as an academic. There were several player reunions in 2019, both with the National Football Museum and independently. The team managed by Harry Batt from 1968-1972 continued to meet up, facilitated by lunch provided by Joanna and I, and similar events with Manchester Corinthians with whom we held another Mayoral reception in Manchester.

By now I had built trust with several players who were initially reluctant to tell me their story, and I plan to write about this in forthcoming work, so will not repeat here.

One new area of work was extending the previous England technical directorate, to help them understand the FA's history. Not all of the male players and coaches knew the story of Bobby Moore, and why his 1966 victory was such a personal triumph. Fewer in the FA knew about Sheila Parker, England women's first captain in 1972, whose son was just nine months old when she led out her country for the first time. I had begun this work in 2018 and revisited it a couple of times in different ways during the next twelve months. This culminated in an October 2019 event at Wembley for an international game when previous England women's team members were invited to reunite in the Lioness bar.

Gail Emms, the Olympian daughter of one of the 1971 Harry Batt players, Jan, had written to Baroness Sue Campbell who was head of women's football at the FA, to ask why her mum was not being recognised. By now, publicity on the BBC and more widely was causing an embarrassment for the FA, so the Harry Batt players were invited, but kept in a different room than the 'official' Lionesses from 1972 onwards. While the official players were invited to parade around the pitch at half time, unintroduced to the crowd, so they just looked like older women in rain macs wandering around, the Harry Batt team were treated to a well-meaning pep talk by Sue Campbell. I'll leave that there.

While the football yearbooks give every male player a legacy number, so that Kalvin Phillips became the 1250th male player for England in September 2020, no such research had been done on the women. September 2020 marked the 1000th men's international for England, but how many games had the women's team played?

This became a major line of work for me from 2019 to 2023. It helped in doing player interviews that most people were at home during lockdown. My network of football historians in a range of countries also sent me programmes and line-ups, to help. I also won funding from Football Against Racism in Europe (FARE) to look at the history of England women's Black and Asian players, again made visible on the website. I began to circulate the information for free on my website at jjhertiage.com both to stimulate other players to get in touch and to disseminate the findings. My academic book with Palgrave Macmillan, *Legendary Lionesses: a History of the England Women's Football Team, 1972-2022* came out in early 2024, summarising the findings. I intend to develop another public history version of the work with more player interviews for 2025.

Due to various confidentiality agreements, I cannot comment on the specifics of the projects related to the Lionesses, unless already in the public domain. But it is worth saying here that many people misunderstand history to be about facts, rather than interpretation. Actually, what constitutes a fact can be an interpretation. Here is a good example.

THE INDUSTRIAL DISPUTE WORLD CUP—AUSTRALIA, 2023

What is a full international match in football? Can it be different in men's and women's football? Does it have to be played for 90 minutes? Does it have to be between representative sides, and if so, who do these sides represent? Who decides?

So, the well-known historians at FIFA have decided retrospectively that the first ever women's international was the club side, Stade de Reims Féminines, who played against the Netherlands on 17 April, 1971 as a qualifier for the unofficial Women's World Cup in Mexico later that year. The match took place in Hazebrouck, France, and resulted in a 4–0 defeat for the Netherlands, organised by the Algemene Nederlandse Damesvoetbalbond, rather than the KNVB.

So, although it was with players from a club side from France who played a Dutch eleven not recognised by the national association in a World Cup organised by FIEFF, which was not ratified by FIFA, the world governing body decided some years later that this was the first official women's international. It is not logical, let alone decent history. But its disregard for the women's game is the point—FIFA does not care, even about its own unreasoned arbitrariness.

Although France, as Stade De Reims, had played since 1968 in European competitions, their players were not told it was a world cup qualifier until after the game. The Dutch considered it a friendly, and lodged a complaint when they were expelled from the world cup. The remainder of France's games in 1971 are not considered official by FIFA. Which is absurd. Of course, the incongruous nature of the judgment is part of the violence to women's history that FIFA has metred out by casually discarding female players' efforts as 'unofficial' and beneath public record. Hence why the work is so important to challenge both the FIFA narrative as in any way plausible, and to recover a more complicated, lucid history.

My approach was always to side with the players. That is the ethical and epistemological stance of *my* historical interpretation. Others might do the work differently. And some have.

By October 2019, the fit out at Silverstone Museum was completed and we held a 'soft opening' for friends of the project. What a challenge opening at *all* had been. The main contractor went bust just as we were moving to an important phase of construction. There were insurance claims and counter claims, but the National Heritage Lottery Fund was steadfast in their support for the venture, and somehow Sally Reynolds held it all together.

Renovating the World War Two aircraft hangar in which the museum was housed had its own charms. In the days before latrines, pilots would pee on the metal stanchion in the corner of the hangar. Presumably it was a convention that the same upright would be used by everyone because the acid in the urine had corroded the metal. However, it wasn't to such an extent that it was unsafe, and the relevant sections were replaceable. Amazingly rewarding after working with the circuit for so long to see this project fulfilled, and the archive secured in a purpose-built facility rather than in the old farmhouse.

As January 2020 rolled around, we went to Barbados for a holiday. The cat's heart had crashed, he died quite suddenly at the end of November 2019, and we were bereft. A week in the sun was consolation. At the beginning of February, we went to London where people were talking about this new SARS virus, but it seemed to be happening elsewhere, and we were not unduly concerned. At the end of February, we went to Center Parcs for half term with the family. On 6 March, Silverstone Museum had its grand opening with Prince Harry and Sir Lewis Hamilton as patrons. A fantastic occasion! We went out for an Italian meal on 16 March for our niece's birthday, and on 20 March pubs, restaurants and bars were asked to close.

Following soon after, the first British COVID lockdown took place. Some called it "the greatest peacetime challenge to society since World War Two". Myself, I thought the Johnson Tory government handling of the situation was more of a trial. Doctors and nurses at risk from insufficient and not fit-for-purpose PPE. But let's not go there. For many people close to me, a lot was lost.

It was certainly odd sending money for Easter eggs to my family through the post. We were advised to shop weekly and I did that, otherwise not venturing out unless it was for exercise. Simon and I walked for about six miles a day in glorious sunshine, and I often contravened the rules to go out again in the opposite direction on my bike for another hour or so. Not commuting to Wolverhampton was so freeing. I also had a raft of work either by post or electronically to trace the England women's history, and wrote a great deal so was never short of challenge.

We also used technology to continue the reunions we had begun. Online in May 2020 we recoded sessions of the Manchester Corinthians reuniting with Dundalk Ladies whom they had played 50 years ago in Wales, a story that journalists then picked up afterwards. In what was a de facto England v Republic of Ireland fixture, Paula Gorham remembered Stella Clarke, nicknamed Eusébio, carrying another player on her shoulders and singing their heads off in joy after a 7–1 defeat to the much more experienced Manchester side.

As this work continued during lockdown, it again was picked up by the media as a powerful social tool to counter isolation, loneliness and the effects of a pandemic. It also countered digital isolation as the families of players helped them to learn to use iPads and WhatsApp. We also did international sessions bringing together Scottish and Italian striker Rose Reilly, with Brazil coach, Sweden's Pia Sundhage, England's Kerry Davis and Gill Coultard online.

In 2020, we also reunited the Harry Batt 1970 England team online, along with the archivist of the Martini Rossi aperitif company who provided the *Coppa del Mondo,* the Martini & Rossi Trophy. The lack of previous recognition caused some tension between the 1970 England squad for the Italian FIEFF Women's World Cup and the 1971 players, who got more media attention. For instance, Angie King and Barbara Dolling, both prolific strikers in 1970, didn't get to go to 1971 but teammates in Italy, Louise Cross, Val Cheshire, Paula Rayner, Jill Brader (nee Stockley) did. So, it was a way of allowing the women to tell their story. There was some sensitivity on behalf of the sponsors because many of the women players were too young to drink. This work was recorded and broadcast online so we celebrated in a very lockdown fashion.

Most university undergraduate teaching was over for 2020/21, and postgraduate work was manageable. So, Lockdown 1 was not too difficult, although it was alien not to be with family and friends. We stuck rigidly to the rules, apart from my rogue additional solo bike rides which were a pleasure on empty roads. Leicester, I am afraid, bore the brunt of the pandemic, facing extended lockdowns.

In June 2020 when restrictions on outdoor sport were lifted, I started swimming at Mallory Park race circuit in the pond with my niece Kelly, organised by a triathlon company. The idea was to complete an open water event, as I had already done two pool sprint triathlons in 2018 and 2019.

Just as things began to get back to normal, or so we thought, the Vice Chancellor at Wolverhampton called an online meeting of the Professoriate in June, 2020. At the time rules were that up to six people could meet at a distance of two metres apart. It was envisaged that this would enable universities to return to in-person teaching in the autumn. All the work for the research exercise framework, or REF 2020, was completed, the VC informed us, and the university had managed to increase its return of research staff to 75%.

There was more good news, he continued: students could now return to in-person teaching. So, our research time and money would be cancelled in favour of the Professoriate becoming an extra undergraduate teaching resource. We would teach five repeated sessions to six socially distanced students instead of one 30-person seminar, in order to try and shore up the metrics of student survey reviews.

The plan for the repeated small sessions to replace one larger seminar was a huge over-reaction, even in June 2020. Information gathered at a number of English universities found the risk of viral transmission to be greater in residential settings, such as halls and student houses, with minimal evidence found of the virus being spread in face-to-face teaching settings such as classrooms. To say nothing of the loss of morale.

We were being asked to be good team members, in a policy that did nothing to recognise or reward our previous efforts. The experiment to host five in-person seminars of six socially distanced students was eventually short-lived, but much discussed. Clearly large lectures would have to remain online. A whole raft of work on space and time was being undertaken to facilitate timetabling. I found this so disrespectful to the Professoriate that it was difficult to articulate. In the end most of this proposal did not take place due to the Omicron variant spike in November 2020 which meant that a travel window had to be organised for returning HE students from 3-9 December.

That was the Christmas where Boris was warning us all not to go out unnecessarily as it might cost the life of an older relative. As we later learned, he was not much given to taking his own advice. A further resulting lockdown meant that face-to-face teaching was again suspended in the winter of 2020/21 term.

A Mutually Agreed Resignation Scheme (MARS) existed for professional services staff at Wolverhampton. Exploring this, I found that if I negotiated, they would consider my case. I left at the end of November 2020 in what was a very depressing winter lockdown. The university has never really recovered. In May 2022 the institution halted recruitment to 138 undergraduate degrees for the 2022/23 intake, cutting further Masters courses the following year. By July 2022, a £20 million deficit was reported in the public domain, and 250 jobs put at risk, more than a tenth of the workforce. Obviously COVID-19 was unusual for all involved, but the University of Wolverhampton leadership team did not much help the long-term viability of the organisation.

Education was not the real reason why in-person teaching was so much of a priority. Both in 2020, and 2021 when commercial direct flights to China were suspended, over 50 UK universities collaborated to charter flights for Chinese students. During times when minimum periods of isolation ranged from two weeks to 10 days, the Chinese students were provided with accommodation and food, before being allowed to continue with their studies. About one in 10 students at Russell Group universities were Chinese, providing an important income stream for the most prestigious institutions. Paying four times the fees of UK students, the overseas market was at risk. To further reinforce the point, many domestic students pointed out, why were they being charged the same level of fees for accommodation when the learning had to go online? The "student as consumer" was more important than learner-centred experience, and ultimately this was unethical in my view. There were also the mental health consequences of flying in students who could not easily get home again.

Meantime, I had picked up some fantastic media work, recording *You're Dead to Me!* With Greg Jenner on football, and Dan Snow on mega events in times of crisis. By May 2021 there was an event to connect the people behind New Black Films with the women from Harry Batt's 1971 Mexico team. There had previously been a meeting in my kitchen before COVID with a BBC producer to discuss the project, but he was not convinced of the urgency. Strictly speaking, May 2021 was a carvery that meant a lot of people were touching the same cutlery at a time when we were just re-emerging from lockdown. It is now known in my house as the COVID Carvery. It was in that weird time when things were reopening and people could eat outside, but not inside. But

Lincolnshire seemed to have missed the memo. Thankfully the vegetarians were given their food on plates, and so Jo and I dodged the COVID Carvery.

The Harry Batt players bought lots of memorabilia and it seemed likely the film would get made this time around. And sure enough, it did, although it would be September 2023 before its release as *Copa 71* at the Toronto International Film Festival (TIFF). The designer Martine Rose also wanted to create a bespoke football fan shirt (rather than a replica) for the group called the Lost Lionesses and Chris Lockwood of the group featured in a campaign. I was pleased that the group was finally getting recognition. They had, after all, waited 50 years, and had some very savvy businesswomen in their number, so were well equipped to handle the issues.

As things began to open up more at the beginning of December 2021, we returned to Center Parcs with the family, just glad to be in one another's company again. On my return, Jo and I organised an event for the FA technical department at Warwick Castle, which is where I first met Sarina Wiegman, Anja van Ginhoven and Arjan Veurink.

We had dinner afterwards in the Great Hall. Joanna's organisational skills pulled off a triumph, and Stuart Wilson as A licence coach working for a long time in women's football helped the scripting. After a dinner involving two knights slogging it out in a choreographed fight, Sue Campbell strutted her stuff to a DJ, surrounded by suits of armour, all kinds of weaponry, and life-size models of horses in full regalia. Even before COVID it would have been an unusual Monday evening!

We reprised the session again in February 2022 in quite a different setting of Rockcliffe Hall and Spa, Darlington, ahead of the women's Euros for the senior England squad at Sarina's request. I would normally keep this kind of work private because of client confidentiality but Beth Mead wrote about details, including her own reaction to the session, in her autobiography in some detail, so it is already in the public domain. Lucy Bronze already knew the history. Stu Wilson was again pivotal in the organisation, although it was difficult to manage the session under strict COVID conditions, and I was very grateful for his continued support.

I have been asked a lot about this work, which can be adapted to a number of elite coaches and technical directorates, as more sports and disciplines understand that their sport is also a heritage brand. If a team intends to make history, then it needs to understand what its past achievements and challenges have been. I have also had the good fortune to work with leaders who understand how to change workplace culture—the behaviours, habits, attitudes and mindset which will bring about improved performance, regardless of a specific aim. Culture amplifies more than a strategy alone because a team environment is required to realise that plan.

The Sarina Wiegman revolution was a short, sharp shock to the FA that had employed her. Wiegman was the first head coach of the England women's team appointed with proven international experience when it was announced, in August

2020, that she'd take over the role in 2021. Let that sink in a moment. The first coach with proven international experience of winning tournaments. Having taken the Netherlands to its first home Euros win in 2017, and the World Cup finals in 2019, could she recreate this feat with the England women's team?

World Cup-winning teams like the US Women's National Team (USWNT) had foreign coaches in the form of Mike Ryan in 1985. Since FIFA competition, USWNT foreign coaches included Pia Sundhage since 2007, and Tom Sermanni in 2013. It is a mark of the lack of opportunities in the UK that Jill Ellis would finally take over as US head coach in 2014.

Created in 1972, the England women's national team was managed by part-timers until 1998 with the full-time appointment of Hope Powell. Having played but never coached at that level before, Powell served for 15 years until the disastrous Euros performance in 2013, followed by successor Mark Sampson who had never managed internationally. His successor, Phil Neville, had played but not coached a national side at senior level, but did have FA links with the men's under-21 side. Phil served for three years before departing for Inter Miami CF II, owned by David Beckham, his ex-teammate at Manchester United.

Wiegman, in using the session on history, was changing a 50-year-old culture where England women players were infantilised, and expected to conform. I remember the captain of the first team to attend a Women's World Cup in 1995, Debbie Bampton, telling me a story about how she had fed back to Ted Copeland that the US Women's National Team was improving its strength and conditioning regime even then. A noted coach in her own right, Bampton had offered the view, as leader of her team, that if England did not match this effort and investment, the US would outstrip their performance quickly. Although she was right, she never played for her country again.

Having a view, even as a trained and qualified coach, was anathema to how England women were expected to behave. There are lots of other stories in my previous work of adult women with 9pm curfews, players sent home for wearing the wrong tracksuit bottoms, and being told that they should 'count their blessings under these working conditions' to represent their country. Most were given pocket money of about £15 a day while on England duty. No wonder it was not always a happy camp.

What Sarina changed in the culture of England women with the history work was that the players were now trying to stand for something larger than themselves. I particularly refer to Chris Lockwood, as part of the LGBTQ+ community and the challenges she had faced since the late 1960s, since a large number of England women are part of that group and understood Chris to be a pioneer. Gill Sayell had a 37-year-old daughter, Courtney, to whom she had not spoken about her experiences in the Mexico World Cup of 1971 because she had been made to feel ashamed. Leah Caleb had more success with her hockey career, although continuing to play football. Carol Thomas firstwoman to 50 caps and Kerry Davis the first mixed heritage player, with Caribbbean descent, also told their stories. I wanted the young women of England to see what a footballer in her mid-60s looked like, and what a love of the sport had cost. 'Don't wait 50 years to tell your story, the time to do it is now,' I told the group. Many of them now have, writing books for adults and children. And I suppose I should have taken my own advice earlier too, shouldn't I?

Having worked across different age groups, sports and into the arts, this disruptive storytelling is a powerful range of work. I was fortunate to meet with England women's Olympic gold medal-winning hockey coach, Danny Kerry, at an elite coach event, have heard Emma Hayes present on several occasions, and been inspired by Charles Hazlewood of Paraorchestra. The conscious disruption of a prevailing culture requires progressive change. When Sarina was told the closest pitch to the main building at St George's Park was 'the men's pitch' she used it for England women's primary area of play. The area was the same, only its meaning changed.

By August 2023, in two short years, she had replicated her previous feat with the Netherlands of winning a Euros on home soil and being losing finalists at an overseas Women's World Cup, England women's highest international victories to date.

But I hadn't got to Australia yet.

British Judo had at this point commissioned me to write a history of the organisation. With the impending Commonwealth Games in Birmingham 2022, their archives were in need of some organisation in Wolverhampton, as they were moving on-site to the university campus in Walsall. Having supervised Amanda Callan-Spenn's thesis and discussing a number of articles with her, this was a history that was rich and very rewarding to research first-hand.

Beautiful minutes in the handwriting of Gunji Koizumi, or 'GK', also known as the Father of Judo in the UK, dated back over 100 years. Having trained in jiu-jitsu, GK made several trips to England in the early 1900s, participating in the Japan-British Exhibition as a martial arts demonstrator. After settling permanently in London, he established the Budokwai, the UK's oldest judo club, in 1918.

The Budokwai is also the oldest Japanese martial arts club in Europe, making a massive contribution to internationalising the sport. For over 50 years, the Budokwai put on an exhibition of judo at the Albert Hall in London, and there is a fascinating social history of who is drawn to martial arts more generally, and to judo, which first took place as an Olympic sport in 1964 at the Tokyo Games. It has since been contested continually since 1972, with the first women's medal event added in 1992. I also visited the Budokwai in London and discussed the social make-up of British judo, which was again fascinating.

By March of 2022 I was working across all 10 host sites for the women's Euros as heritage and history consultant. I had separate arrangements also with Southampton, and Gunnersbury Park, but by far the best organised and creative exhibition was curated with Jody East at the Royal Pavilion and Museums Trust in Brighton. Jody had the foresight to come to our conference in Manchester in 2018, and when a new head of the Royal Pavilions and Museums Trust wanted a major exhibition to celebrate the women's Euros for 2022, we had already been planning it since 2021.

The other host venues for women's Euros were Sheffield's Bramall Lane; Stadium MK in Milton Keynes; Old Trafford, Manchester; Brentford Community Stadium; New York Stadium Rotherham; Leigh Sports Village; and Bradford's Academy Stadium. Several players and commentators criticised the small size of the last three venues in particular, less than 12,000 capacity and further restricted due to rules preventing standing fans, and there were no Midlands host between Milton Keynes and Sheffield, and none at all in the North East.

England had been the only country to bid for the women's Euros, winning the hosting rights in 2018, so it was a knock-on effect of COVID that it took place in 2022 rather than 2021, as it should originally have been. Michel Platini's vision of a European-wide men's Euros to mark the 60th anniversary of the first competition should have taken place in 2020, but was postponed to 2021, so the women's tournament was rescheduled. By then, of course, Platini had long gone as president of UEFA.

It is worth pausing to consider how much women were affected by the COVID pandemic in the UK, and how gendered the experience generally was—not just in sport. Because this had a direct outcome on the joy that gathered momentum as the women's Euros progressed. It is not just that the caring professions, in which women tend to outnumber men, were particularly vital in the national story of handling the virus, and then mitigating its spread; but that educating children at home, and looking after elderly and vulnerable people who were shielding also disproportionately affected women. We know before COVID hit that women are four times more likely to be affected by dementia in the UK than men—as sufferers, paid and unpaid carers, as economic support, and so forth. With the advent of increased social isolation and loneliness, the figures rose even more. So, in wider society, women were impacted in far more ways than men.

In sporting terms, the economic and legal differentials in elite male and female sport were starkly evident. Top-flight women's football in the UK was more of a casualty of COVID than the men's game, due to the immediate suspension of the WSL in May 2020 for which the championship was decided on 'sporting merit.' Chelsea won £100,000 on an algorithm and donated it to charity. Liverpool men's team won £175 million for winning the Premier League in 2019/20, while Liverpool women were relegated the same season. Similarly, the women's FA Cup was suspended because as amateur athletes, players could not compete under social distancing restrictions, whereas male amateurs could compete in the FA Cup, as it was against elite athletes, under different professional rules. There was very little brotherly love extended for women's football by the historically wealthy male clubs.

Although men's Premiership teams playing the subsequent season behind closed doors reportedly cost as much as £3 million a game in lost revenue, with fewer resources on which to draw, women's football was again trivialised. The game's elite millionaires could train in a home gym, or argue that they were going about their work which required travel in isolation. In contrast, Welsh international Angharad James was prevented by police from doing practice drills on her own on a public pitch in a local park for her daily exercise during the first lockdown.

This was symptomatic of how women were treated differently in public throughout COVID lockdowns on the UK. In 2021 there was an example in Derby of two women walking with a coffee and being fined £200 for having an illegal picnic. There were no rules in place which said they couldn't drive five miles to exercise together, and the fine was later withdrawn because it was shown to have been discriminatory. After driving 264 miles from his usual residence in London to Durham with COVID symptoms, Special Advisor to the Prime Minister, Dominic Cummings made a subsequent speculative 30-mile round trip from Durham to Barnard Castle to test his eyesight in preparation for a longer drive home. The police found no wrongdoing and nor did the Prime Minister. This sparked widespread public anger at the lack of impartiality of the police force. Worse was to follow.

Heartbreakingly, in March 2021 while trying to get home in London after leaving a friend's house Sarah Everard was detained by a serving police officer in plain clothes under what he argued were COVID powers, using his warrant card as proof of identity before handcuffing her in a false arrest. He later drove her around 80 miles, raped and murdered her, an innocent woman. A known serial offender, the man in question was vetted several times by the police and issued with a firearm. The subsequent heavy-handed Metropolitan Police handling of the vigil for Sarah on 13 March, which criminalised grieving women who were not protesting but marking her memory, is one of the most shameful things I witnessed during lockdown, even with a chaotic Johnson government at the helm, and Tory Partygate scandals.

In contrast, the absence of sufficient numbers of police officers at the Men's Euros final at Wembley, 10 July 2021, when violent ticketless fans stormed the entrances was in direct contradiction of how large groups of peaceful women were policed in public. Unfortunately, the fact that a minority of the England men's fans were nasty, short of intelligence and brutish was entirely predictable. Only 86 were later arrested and media outlets called it a day of national shame. Certainly, booing the national anthem of opponents as hosts at Wembley in 2021 showed elements of the crowd to be chauvinistic, boorish and unsophisticated. The opposition are essential co-creators of the game, lads.

I have covered this in some detail because what happened a year later at Wembley when England won the Women's Euros in the July sunshine, in a peaceful, happy, celebratory, capacity crowd, with lots of children present, can only be understood in this wider context. One, the sadness and loss represented by Sarah Everard's murder by a serving police officer whom people should be able to trust; and two, the rehabilitation of national pride which was lost at the men's Euros final.

You can call it gendered sportswashing if you like, but the women renewed and reorientated the FA's dented image, after several UEFA fines for poor hosting in the men's Euros, some as large as £100,000 and a two-match stadium ban for the England fan behaviour at the final. Whatever England women earned, the redemption they provided for the FA was priceless.

On 30th July 2022, when England women won, everyone was in tears—not just Alexandra Popp and the German fans. Never mind 30 years of hurt in football. The Sarah Everard story became linked with the hashtag, She Was Just Walking Home. The victory at Wembley was also for every woman who has heard a noise behind her and grabbed her keys to defend herself walking on the way home in the dark. We had taken over Wembley stadium and conducted a final as it should be played, standing next to German fans in the same row and commiserating with their loss. The victory was for generations of women and girls who had refused the misogyny of male-dominated institutions of power like the Metropolitan Police, the government, and the FA. For one day in the sunshine, all together in the light, in peaceful celebration, we won. It was never just about the football.

But before all that, there was a lot of work to do. Led by FA Arts and Heritage director, Caterina Loriggio, £3 million worth of activities promoted community engagement, cultural leadership, supported health and wellbeing initiatives and supported local economies after the pandemic. We hadn't even got to the football yet! Host partners included the local authorities of Rotherham, Sheffield, Trafford, Wigan, Manchester, Milton Keynes, Brent, Hounslow, Brighton, and Southampton to engage with tourists and inspire their residents.

I had helped Caterina to secure significant Heritage Lottery Funds in designing activities and bids. We also held an evening to celebrate International Women's Day 2022 at the European Parliament where Pia Sundhage joined us on a zoom from Brazil, and reunited with her old friend, Rose Reilly, who joined in the banter. Kerry Davis and two of the Manchester Corinthians, Margaret Whitworth or 'Whitty' and Margaret Shepherd or 'Tiny' also spoke.

The cultural programme for the women's Euros was the first time since 1953 that the FA had backed an arts and culture programme, although quite a few of us academics also did FA 150 in 2013. In 1953, the FA offered £3,000 prize money in celebration of its 90th anniversary, for works of art that would depict the game of football or anything connected with it, supported by the recently founded Arts Council (inaugurated in

1946). Open to all, 1,700 professional and amateur artists submitted entries. In the end, 32 prizes were awarded, and 127 additional paintings, prints, sculptures and drawings were chosen for a touring exhibition called Football and the Fine Arts.

In 2022, there was much less of an emphasis on the fine arts, and more on community engagement. I presented to the Football Supporters' Association, young people, and to all host city staff, on the background to this tournament. The feedback from each session was that they could not get enough history. You can imagine having worked for so long as a lone researcher, what a relief it was to finally have some significant resources, and an attempt at a national programme, although with the caveats above that it missed historically significant areas for women's football by ignoring the Midlands, North East and South West. By far the biggest problem was getting new partners to engage with rigorous history. Many enthusiastic amateurs were repeating factoids, and escalating Wikipedia mistakes without checking their accuracy. The quality of what was produced varied enormously as a result.

In all, I wrote the core content for eight museum/archive indoor exhibitions, and eight outdoor exhibitions. I also wrote the geographically specific content for eight host city outdoor exhibitions. Heritage outreach programming included 'Wikiathons', gallery talks, hosting school groups and writing education resources. I conducted many of the oral history interviews for 45 memory films and wrote new online content covering the history of the women's game. Oral history was a very important part of the Euros heritage and history strategy because so few of the museums we worked with had archival items of women's football. Doing the oral history work brought memorabilia out of lofts, back bedrooms, and from the back of drawers. With Gunnersbury for instance, I suggested the museum interview Pat Gregory, and Kerry Davis. They had already linked with Rebecca Edwards and a young player for a Muslim local girls' team. For Brentford at Wembley, I suggested Rachel Pavlou, and the brilliant Co-President of the Gay Games, Joanie Evans. The museum already had links with League representative, Gill Jones, so those interviews are now available online as legacy films.

Again, I regretted not being able to do more because local history enthusiasts either didn't know the history of football, so missed out on important questions, or were generalists who had covered women's skateboarding, say, and worked with the local authorities on other projects, and had not had oral history training. At Rotherham we filmed conversations indoors and outside, and I loved that some internationals, like Kathy Bird, came in their kit. It gave a dynamism to the interviews that brought out the players' passion.

We had particularly strong media coverage at Brighton, which was in many ways the national exhibition. Because we featured Rose Reilly, three of the Harry Batt team, and Petra Landers of Germany's Euro winning team in 1989, the national and local media turned out in force. Landers had loaned the Brighton exhibition the coffee set awarded to her by the Deutscher Fußball-Bund as part of the winning squad of the 1989 women's Euros. She had been so disgusted by the patronising gift that it had sat under the bed for over 30 years so was in pristine condition for exhibition display. Landers was interviewed by two young footballers, Caitlin and Lili, and the outcome promoted on the website, so really interesting cross-generational work.

Brighton was also a really intriguing example of how to balance public history, as two opposing versions of who was the first local women's team were offered by very different groups. The historical challenge of, when is a fact an interpretation, again. We decided to place the two interpretations side by side, and not privilege the authenticity of one or the other but let people make up their own minds. I also especially loved working with Rotherham, Gunnersbury and Southampton because the curators there were so enthused by the project: new fans of women's football. The whole programme of work has subsequently been publicised by the FA, the British Library and the UK Web Archive.

As well as the photographic research, which was supplemented by the National Football Museum and Getty Images, there were online digitised exhibitions developed across many sites. Proving the significant appetite for history and heritage entertainment, it was estimated that 405,000 visitors went to museum exhibitions and over 3.9 million people saw the outdoor exhibitions, while the programme exhibited 1,450 objects. To give an indication of how hectic the schedule, I would be up at Rotherham one day, down in Brighton the next, across to Southampton, calling in at Brentford and Gunnersbury on the way home, before speaking in Sheffield—all in one week! So, it is hard to summarise all that went on without it reading like a diary.

Without going into details of all the events, one highlight was presenting with the Royal Philharmonic Orchestra, on an outreach programme in Sheffield and Brighton. I'd pick this particular highlight as an event in Brighton where I was on a panel with the composer, conductor and violinist of Jamaican descent, Shirley Thompson OBE, and the great Rose Reilly. This was because the Royal Philharmonic Orchestra was another cultural partner of the Euros, and their musicians engaged with community choirs across host cities, where we also held public events to invite discussions about the connection between football, dance and music. Shirley loved the Scottish striker's story and I joked we must write Rose Reilly: The Musical with myself providing the libretto. We must still do that!

I attended the opening match at Old Trafford as a guest of Hisense, one of the new Chinese electronics and appliance manufacturer sponsors of football. The largest Chinese TV manufacturer since 2004, Hisense had moved into football in more recent years. It was a great opener, with a celebratory crowd of 69,000 and we could tell that the whole thing was going to be a seismic shift in PR for the England team, even while the effects of austerity and lack of access for girls would continue to limit who got to

THE INDUSTRIAL DISPUTE WORLD CUP—AUSTRALIA, 2023

play football for the foreseeable future.

Alongside the work with museums and the FA, Nationwide Building Society put up a series of plaques to important women players and I was historian to the campaign, filming with Gill Coultard, the first English woman to make it to 100 caps, and others. There were elite coach development events in August, and it was at one of these that I connected with a young woman who had remembered my handing out my questionnaires all those years ago when I was collecting data for my PhD. She had been out in America and football had literally opened up her professional horizons. Finally on 30 August, along with select others, I was invited to St George's Park to see the European Cup and meet Sarina and the squad. I was able to buy the legendary striker, Beth Mead, a coffee of her choice, and all were very kind with their time in making the case that it had been won for more than just the squad.

To round out what had been a memorable set of events around the Euros, a couple of months later, Rose Reilly had a pub named after her in Glasgow, as well as being inducted to the Scottish Football Hall of Fame, a portrait hung in the National Gallery, the Scottish Sports Hall of Fame and made an MBE! There is a planned film of her life with Chris Young the Director from the Inbetweeners movies, and scriptwriter Lorna Martin. Recognition long overdue.

An idea for a fan-based project was percolating in my brain during the Euros that came to fruition at the World Cup. By attending the majority of England matches at the Euros 2022, and quite a few randoms by intention, I gradually became aware of how fans of the England women's team were becoming more visible to one another as the tournament progressed, and as the national team continued to win, which in turn was creating a distinct aesthetic. But how to mark that particular moment in history in an artistic and engaging way? Not easy if you have a drawing age of three, can't sew, don't have any equipment to make items of clothing, and no brand.

Obviously, I knew about the fantastic England touchline coat made by Jacqui McAssey and Paul Robbins which featured far and wide. Jacqui's pin badges, basically a cheap, flexible way of narrating the tournament, were also very popular and appeared in Vogue. The McAssey-Robbins touchline coat was actually inspired by Arséne Wenger, when he was manager of Arsenal for 22 years (1996–2018); he wore what was basically a King-sized duvet as a side-line jacket to keep out the cold of North London. The poor man looked like he would rather be in the South of France and frequently wrestled with the zip to the amusement of the media. For 22 years. But hilariously, the day of the women's Euros final was 26° at Wembley, and fans were still wearing Jacqui's coat. The scarves it used were recycled, and that was quite rare in women's football before the Euros, when merchandise flooded the newly created markets. Most of the merchandise was cheaply produced and of little aesthetic value. Could I do something that was the antithesis of mass-produced, cheap copies of men's football fan merchandise, and more thoughtful?

In 2022, Paul Robbins and Jacqui succeeded in making an iconic garment. That coat was everywhere! There were, of course, consequently rip-offs and replicas—even some of the big companies like Nike using the idea in their own designs. This, and the clothing strategies of ordinary fans, which Jacqui had been documenting in the Girlfans project since 2013, also combined with a new move after 2019 for more fan groups of women's football to formally join the Football Supporters' Association, the FSA.

I began to notice a change in how fandom was being performed at women's matches, and began to plan to make items based on my historical knowledge and contacts. There were others doing the same thing of course. The very generous Nico Tuppen at Homeground London created a 1st class stamp with Sarina's face instead of Queen Elizabeth's after the Lionesses won, and he allowed me to use the image in Australia. It was one of the ways that 'cultural cool' was reflected onto the young women of the football team. The Queen would pass away shortly afterwards, in September 2022, ending the 70-year longest reign in British history, second only to Louis XIV, (depending upon how his accession in 1643 is seen). But the same long-serving and widely respected female monarch who had handed Bobby Moore the World Cup in 1966 at old Wembley Stadium lived to see England women become European champions in 2022.

Calling the brand, 'Jeanola FC' after my old football nickname, I wanted it to look hand-made, and create low numbers or one-off pieces, to critique the adoption of shirt-wearing as a monoculture within football fandom. The replica shirt industry is an historical change I had documented with Chris Stride and other colleagues. I knew from my own family history that before the adoption of shirt-wearing as the main uniform of fandom during the 1980s, supporters had made much of their clothing and accessories themselves.

Though hardly important now, FA Cups were traditionally known to be carnivalesque because getting to the Final occasioned a long trip down to Wembley as part of the build-up. Scottish fans were wearing shirts in the 1978 world cup, but where from? We know that few fans were wearing football shirts to the 1980 FA Cup from photographs of the time. By the 1990 FA Cup, almost all fans wore shirts. This accelerated with the advent of the Premiership to multiple issues of club shirts, and globalised the trend through pay-to-view TV.

However, I also knew that the practical methods of producing the shirts were often unsustainable, exploiting women and child labour in the global south particularly. There was also a misperception that children living in poverty wearing football shirts denoted fandom, when actually the economies of recycling meant that unwanted shirts were often sent back to places from which they had originally been manufactured.

The scale of shirt manufacture continues to grow and become more complex. Wearable technology tracks players' physical data, which the gambling industry wants

THE INDUSTRIAL DISPUTE WORLD CUP – AUSTRALIA, 2023

to exploit for in-play betting purposes. So, I wanted a fun and engaging way to have those conversations. Bearing in mind my own complicity in those processes of lack of sustainability of course, because I had always loved sportswear myself, and I was intending to fly to Australia to deliver this critique. The contradictions are not lost on me, nor the scale of the replica shirt industry. I wrote about this most recently for a book celebrating Leicester-based Admiral sportswear as a pioneer of the replica shirt market.

I wanted to recycle clothing to produce items of fanwear that were not shirts, ideally, and to express something about the history, and distinctiveness of the women's game rather than just copying men's football fan culture. Being from a large family, I had a lot of occasion-wear that I had purchased for weddings, funerals, christenings, and so on. During COVID this had sat in large bin liners because I literally had nowhere to go. So, I dragged out those items and thought about how they could be repurposed.

My mum had been a very good overlocker and machinist, but had also made many of her, and our, clothes from a pattern and cloth. She could knit, crochet, embroider by hand, as well as modify patterns when she wanted to tweak a look. Obviously, with my dad being MD of a hosiery factory, I had seen the large-scale production of knitting, cutting, machining, dying, packaging and delivery. Dad was an early producer of branded goods endorsed by Disney or other film studios, putting 'Winnie the Pooh' or other figures on children's hose, sold in trademarked packaging at one of the big stores like M&S, or Sainsbury's. He also produced some more niche items for the likes of Pink Soda.

Chatting with Jacqui McAssey, up at Liverpool John Moores University where she works as a Senior Lecturer in Fashion Communication, they had a collection of literature called 'Femorabilia', and we thought we would borrow the name for our feminist football memorabilia, Femorabilia, and bring some of these ideas together. Which is absolutely great, but I cannot sew, draw or make anything! I once knitted Simon a jumper, and in my anxiety, it came out three sizes smaller than it should have been. To get what was in my head into garments was going to require collaboration and quite a bit of patience.

Oh, and some money. Fortunately, Liverpool John Moores had a research call out, and together we won £10,000 to go to Australia to explore how the England women's national football team became an icon of cultural cool by winning at Wembley. I was also aware of an Art Fund Jonathan Ruffer curatorial grant for contemporary collecting, and with the National Football Museum was able to secure £4,000 towards my travel. Bearing in mind that I planned to be out in Australia for the whole tournament, because I had a hunch that we would make the final, (partly because of Sarina's track record and partly because the England team was on such a high from 2022), I had quite a bit of cash still to find. It was more a case of Jacqui and I being £10,000 Poms each in 2023, than being a £10 Pom back in the day.

I managed to secure three media gigs, one with BBC Bitesize who liked the

Femorabilia concept for their young audience. I had done a couple of films with them before, including bringing together representatives of the England and Scotland players from the first ever international to film, 50 years later, at Wembley in November 2022. A smaller input was for comedian and writer, Maisie Adam, who was starting to do podcasts for the BBC. I also filmed with Chris Kamara in Middlesbrough for one of those TV history programmes where different experts pop up in successive venues to impart some nugget or other.

We had also offered a history session, an technical day in January 2023, where Jacqui also introduced her coat to the FA. More cash came in from a project with the FA working on a data collection piece of work—which I found so interesting I would have done it for free. Finally, pretty much on a wing and a prayer, I wrote to Bonita Mersiades to say I could potentially attend the Football Writers' Festival in Sydney if I changed my flights by a couple of days. She readily agreed. All set to travel, I just had to make some items of Femorabilia.

Before that though, Peter Aleggi hosted one of his Football Scholars Forums where anthropologist Hillary Haldane spoke about how FIFA chose to use te reo Māori and First Nations languages and symbolism in their branding and marketing for New Zealand, predicated on the Treaty of Waitangi. Hillary explained her research and work for a student trip to the games, highlighting important historical aspects of how indigenous and First Nations groups have been historically discriminated against. Jacqui and I presented on Femorabilia, and our project. It was a really valuable session to understand some of the sensitivities of the different kinds of racism within Australian society ahead of the trip. As part of the branding, all host cities would use indigenous names in Australia and New Zealand, such as the Turrbal Aboriginal group's word, 'Meanjin' meaning Brisbane; or Māori, such as 'Te Whanganui-a-Tara', meaning Wellington, to reflect their history before British colonisation. Aboriginal and Torres Strait Islander flags were flown in Australia and the Māori, Tino Rangatiratanga in New Zealand.

In terms of getting things made, first off was to copyright my trademark name and symbol 'Jeanola FC'. Then Millie Chesters, the brilliant illustrator, drew things for me to order at very reasonable rates, given she is such a big name. I literally could not have done the project without her. Mille is extraordinarily humble but her work is fantastic! And of course, Joanna, my sister-in-law came with me up to Liverpool when I was really quite ill at the time, and struggling to complete the work. Jo is patient, very methodical and practical as well as stylish so gave her opinions and ideas and drove me around when I didn't feel great. She learned new skills, stayed up at Liverpool for long working days, and kept me company at night. Plus, I cannot thank Jacqui enough, as she actually took garments apart, printed several items, showed Joanna and I how to use a heat press, and gave us all kinds of support.

We made two large coat pieces and several smaller ones, mainly t-shirts. The t-shirts were either old ones used hundreds of times already from the gym, and given new life, or workwear that I had used to brighten a Monday morning that was now not used, and stuck in a bag at the back of the closet. The ever adaptable Simon made some festival headdresses, and I wanted to locate the garments as something that could be worn to dinner, as much as a match. So, while summer music event clothing styles were part of the inspiration, I wanted to steer well away from the fancy dress-style used by many fans of The Netherlands.

Often swarming local party stores for anything and everything in orange, this look was highly celebratory and festival-ready, but too kitsch for Femorabilia. With its feminist sensibility, and also awareness of the need to be practical for actually attending matches, I wanted an edge, so that people would turn and ask, 'What is that?'

Thinking about all this, on 29 December 2022 two of my heroes passed on the same day. The first of those was Edson Arantes do Nascimento, or Pelé. The second was Dame Vivienne Westwood. It was Westwood's early punk aesthetic, which had a do-it yourself ethos, irreverent graphic screen printing and graffiti references. The Westwood punk clothes were designed to provoke a reaction, and inspire change.

The Jeanola FC collaboration helped to create two coats for Australia, one based on a long linen jacket I had worn to several weddings. The second was a redesigned Desigual coat in peacock colours of green and blue, in which I had once attended the wrong christening in the wrong church, and on a second occasion the wrong wedding in the wrong village! Both times I was wearing leopard print stilletoes with the coat so made quite an entrance and an exit. So I already had a history in each coat. The linen concept was 'In Queen Sarina We Trust', and the Desigual 'The Kerrminator'. As you can guess, I was hedging my bets in trying to make something that could become iconic. Would England win, excelling Wiegman's second place in 2019 with the Netherlands? Or would Sam Kerr be victorious, scoring the winning goal on home soil?

Looking back, I should have gone for a Las 15 coat for Spain, but it was a very complicated situation and remains so today. Jorge Vilda's performance as Spain's head coach in the women's Euros was so tactically naïve that 18 players, Las 15+3, publicly boycotted the national team in September 2022. Fifteen sent identical emails, while three supported the boycott but did not hit 'send' themselves. Of the 18, six were eventually selected for Women's World Cup 2023. Some of those players do not talk to one another today. Before Vilda, his predecessor Ignacio Quereda had been in post from 1988 until 2015. By 2011, players like Laura del Rio, a striker who had 40 goals in 39 caps for her country, said she would not play for Spain again while Quereda was manager. There was a long history of coercive control of women players in Spain.

So, there were deep problems in the national association that made creating a celebratory piece more difficult. That remains the case now Spain have won the

Women's World Cup. Jorge Vilda, after his dismissal as Spain head coach, was recommended by the Spanish football federation as the national coach of the Moroccan women's team. He has taken a four-year contract with Morrocco and took them to the Olympic Games in 2024. This is no coincidence ahead of the Men's World Cup in 2030 in which the two countries are co-hosts. Vilda remains under criminal investigation in Spain. In such a mess of misogyny as the Spanish situation, I suppose I would have had to look to Goya for inspiration for my Las 15 coat, and I don't know that this would have produced much in the way of warm, witty fan-wear.

As to the design of 'In Sarina We Trust', using the Homeground stamp in the back, a graphic artist who worked with Jacqui at the university did the lettering. I wanted the word 'Queen' to look like an afterthought, and the gold foil lettering to shine against the pale linen in the Australian sunshine. Which it did! Jimmy Choo and Timberland had just bought out a collaboration in which the traditional 'Tims' had four-inch heels and black and gold graffiti. A pair would have looked great with the coat, but they cost £6,000. The luxe-street look was very on trend, so easy to reference more cheaply with printed foil.

Another feature was that the England captain, Leah Williamson, had sustained an ACL injury and was not playing in Australia, replaced by Millie Bright. With her heavily tattooed left arm, and hair worn as a top-knot, rather than in a pony-tail like most of the squad, Bright reminded me of those Rosie the Riveter posters during World War Two.

Rosie was an everywoman rolling up her sleeves to do manual labour while also wearing full make up. From the Rosie the Riveter posters, she met our gaze directly in meeting the challenge of major conflict. In the image of Mille Bright as Rosie we used a bit of artistic licence, because her right arm provides the strong triangular dynamic that I wanted for the composition. Normally Rosie's hair is tied back by a scarf, but Bright's top knot of hair made the need for a fabric bow redundant. We also made her smile wider than normal, adding a cartoon 'zing' of shine to the whitening of her teeth, and also made her eyes larger than lifelike. Then I adapted the caption 'Captain Brightside' from the Killer's song. In the absence of Leah Williamson, Captain Brightside was rolling up her sleeves to lead her country into its biggest tournament since 2022. At the time of the World Cup, Bright was not Chelsea captain, but was later given the club armband in September 2023, after receiving an OBE shortly after England's final appearances in Australia. So, it was a specific moment in history for player and country.

For the 'Kerrminator' coat, it was easy to iconise Sam Kerr by giving her a halo of gold, as if she were a divine religious figure. Her regular features and parted hair when playing gave a symmetry to the design, and we also had her return a neutral gaze as if conferring a blessing on those she surveyed. The nature of the benediction was conveyed by sacred Sam's hands, which predicted she would score two goals to nil in

THE INDUSTRIAL DISPUTE WORLD CUP—AUSTRALIA, 2023

the final for Australia. Also, given Kerr's status as an LGBTQ+ icon, the fingers predicting her two goals were a sign of peace.

Mixing the sacred and the profane, I chatted to various people about what she meant to them, as a player and a person. Mille Chesters said to me, 'she's relentless, never gives up, always likely to score'. That will to win made Kerr inevitable, and I had a vision of the 1984 film starring Arnold Schwarzenegger as the T-800 or Terminator, a cyborg assassin, who regularly runs through walls in search of his victims. So, it wasn't much of a leap to get to The Kerrminator, which in a nod to the late Westwood we printed in bright pink graffiti style across the skirt of the coat, complete with intentional paint spatters, as if the spray cans were faulty when used at speed. I found a dog tag while out walking as we were making it and knowing that Kerr loves animals, sewed it on as a found item, and added 'Jeanola FC' in sequins.

I had also chatted for a time with Mizizi International CEO, Paakow Essandoh about his reimagined African diasporic football shirts, and he sent me some recycled Nigeria garments to which we added small foil kangaroos and koala designs. I'd liked to have done more of this kind of work but we ran out of time!

Finally, Simon, of course, printed t-shirts, helped design aspects, and solved making issues with his good suggestions, and made headdresses by hand, fetched, carried, organised, facilitated, the lot. We call him the 'office boy of jjheritage.com' Fighting for time before catching the plane, my tennis friends, Lynda and Penny, were also going out to Australia so we made them bespoke recycled Lucy Bronze items, printed in bronze foil on their white football shirts. The burnished foil looked statuesque, and fantastic on a white background. I'd have liked to make more items, but with my health, time, and constraints of working to fund the project I was delighted with the quality of what we had by the time I got on the plane on 11 July 2023. I quite understood that seven weeks of women's football discussion was just too much for Simon. In return, he knew I would know lots of folks in a country where I'd never been, once I got off the plane. As it turned out, he was right.

A Kiss is Just a Kiss: Australia 2023

I suppose what first struck me about Sydney was the wateriness of it. It was a bit like when I first went to Venice and expected, based on my experience of Birmingham, for there to be the odd canal. Of course, I had seen pictures and knew the geography of the wider Sydney region from maps and so on, but the sheer volume of water, the light and energy that it created coursed through me, and made me feel well. It will seem cheesy and trite, but I felt like I had been there before. As soon as I got off the plane, I knew my way round as if I already had a sense of the land. That feeling grew. By the end of my seven weeks I felt the best I had healthwise since 2011. That's quite some load off.

On the way over though, the flight had been rough. There was only a one-hour transfer at Hong Kong, so no time to shower after a 14-hour flight, and then nine hours onwards with turbulence so bad it was like being in a tumble dryer. I consumed two bottles of water and half a can of coke in nine hours. When I asked for a salty snack, the aircraft only had tomato sauce-flavoured crisps, which I found very easy to decline. Funny isn't it the details that the mind retains? So, I just tried to sleep.

In short, I was in a bit of a state by the time I landed in Australia late in the evening. The founder and curator of the Football Writers' Festival and—as it would turn out, my publisher—Bonita Mersiades had thankfully arranged for a driver from the airport to the accommodation in Milsons Point, just on the north side of Sydney Harbour Bridge. The driver was a lovely man called Geoff. I was grateful for the forethought from Bonita, and Geoff's kindness. He in turn was bemused that a woman travelling on her own to the other side of the world, to a city in which she knew no one, would be certain that she would soon be amongst friends. But that's football, or my experience of it. Absorbing the dancing light on the water, I bought another coke and some plain crisps and contemplated having made the journey that the previous November had not even been a reality. Well done old bean!

If you have left your dearly beloveds to fly to the other side of the world, are suffering from jetlag, and several months of a dodgy medication regime, I really cannot recommend my 'coke and crisps diet' as a remedy enough. It perked me up sufficiently that on Day One I tackled the Sydney Harbour Bridge. Walking, not climbing. Not a big deal for all those who are not afraid of heights, and I could see people higher up taking the actual climbing tour. But for me it was horrendous, and I knew I had to walk across on Day One or I would psyche myself out. Of course, folks cycle, run, skateboard or whatever across the bridge all the time. Security stewards ensure safety and keep the pedestrian and cycling element separate.

The worst part was being out over the open water, when the space zoomed in and out crazily like that scene in Psycho but on a much more dramatic scale. It was so big there was no point of reference, I was bound to fall because of the lack of certainty where to put my feet. Or that's what I experienced anyway. To counter the boomeranging perspective, I managed to latch my eyes on a distance of three meters, following a middle-aged woman and a young teen who were breezily taking in the sights, pointing to the Opera House, leaning on the side, and taking selfies on their phones. Not a care in the world. I was dry mouthed, terrified and weak-kneed. Making it over the bridge, and scouting out where the Football Writers' Festival would be held the next day, I knew I wouldn't be going back over the bridge, preferring instead to use the ferries. Because, why wouldn't you?

The 2023 Football Writers' Festival was held from the 15th–17th of July in Tar-Ra

THE INDUSTRIAL DISPUTE WORLD CUP—AUSTRALIA, 2023

(the Indigenous name for Walsh Bay), a few days prior to the opening match of the 2023 Women's World Cup. It was the fourth and most international edition of the festival, the first being held in Jamberoo, New South Wales in 2019. I only really knew Philippe Auclair, because I had by then served on the Football Writers' Association book judging panel, which he chairs. Everyone else I had only followed on social media, including Ciara McCormack of Canada, who played eight games for Ireland, and whom I had interviewed by phone about her professional career in Denmark, Norway, and Australia, back in 2011/12. Clare Shine, another Irish international also spoke about her memoir *Playing in the Dark*.

The headline speaker from Europe, apart from Philippe of course, was Thomas Hitzlsperger, former German international, media personality and co-founder of one of the festival's charity partners, Future4Nepal. Aboriginal-run charity, Literacy for Life Foundation, was the Australian charity partner, supporting its simple but powerful mission of assisting Indigenous adults hoping to improve their reading and writing skills.

Australian internationals who had become changemakers in their respective fields included Craig Foster, Francis Awaritefe, Andy Bernal, Jade North, Dr Karen Menzies and Elissia Carnavas. Sarah Dingle, Adam Peacock, Tracey Holmes and Murray Shaw brought media perspectives and lively debate.

There were too many high-profile journalists to name here. I enjoyed chatting to Osasu Obayiuwana of Nigeria about the situation with their women's team, the coaching staff and federation. Nick Harris is a mine of information on so many subjects. I had a coffee in Norma's Deli in Manly with Samindra Kunti from Belgium hearing about his journalism, specifically writing about FIFA.

Forgive me if I have not mentioned everyone, because it would become too list-like, but writers of all kinds from at least 16 nations also included emerging women authors published in an anthology edited by Bonita Mersiades, entitled *Hear Us Roar*, such as Olga Bagatini (Brazil) who wrote a profile of Sissi—so you can imagine we had a lot to discuss. Steffany Wangari Ndei (Kenya) wrote of her love of football, and disaffection of the organised sport on her coaching journey, and Alina Ruprecht (Germany) looked at how women investors can change the business models currently operating.

Although I was too poorly to attend some of the evening events, it was a thought-provoking and inspirational few days. The curation placed opposing views on the same panel, so that debate and discussion were amplified. This was seen in the case of Football Australia hopefully recognising the women players from 1975 as Matildas alumni, and I was glad to hear from football fan and friend of the 1975 group, Elia Santoro, that this had been rectified sometimes later. A bit like my work with the pre-1972 England players, it was fundamentally an act of illogical institutional violence not to recognise these women.

I got to meet academics like Greg Downes, whose PhD I had examined all those years ago; Kasey Symons and Kirby Fenwick, Fiona Crawford, Jorge Knijnik, and so many more, before departing Sydney for England's first match of the World Cup in Brisbane. And the commutes were a joy of beholding scintillating lights on water, by day or night.

Geoff again took me to the airport, chatting about all the cruises he enjoyed taking with his partner, and giving me ideas for return journeys. It was such a different approach to vacationing than back in the UK, and I hadn't realised Australia had so many islands to visit, let alone Indonesia and Thailand which seemed to be Geoff's favourite. We agreed he would pick me up at the airport when I came back eight days later.

I was running increasingly longer distances each morning about 5k and using the gym. I was helped also by the proximity of the hotel to The Valley Pool, in Fortitude Bay, one of the most historic swimming facilities in the city, where the manager was surprised by my interest—but very welcoming in showing me around. If you are a swimmer, you will know the slippery viscosity of buttery swimming pool water instantly. The thin flow of Valley Pool was practically frictionless, really refreshing for lap after lap outdoors in the sunshine. Another swimming pool to add to my wonderful experiential collection.

Two days into my Brisbane stay, I had an odd WhatsApp message from driver Geoff. Except it wasn't Geoff. It was Sasha, his partner, about whom he had spoken, informing me that Geoff would not be able to pick me up because he had passed away that day. I couldn't get over the shock, although we had only spent two hours in the car chatting to and from the airport. All his plans for future holidays! And his kindness. He had confirmed the return trip only 24 hours before in a jolly message. Suddenly feeling a long way from home, of course I called Simon.

But there was still some work to do! I had launched the idea of Femorabilia back in England at an event organised by the Football Supporters' Association (FSA) Free Lionesses network in Manchester. The group had been launched for the Women's World Cup in France in 2019 and was approaching its fourth anniversary, compared with the men's Free Lions project which was inaugurated for Italia '90. We joined with them to write the 'Fun History' aspects of the supporters' guide to Australia, invited to do so by Deborah Dilworth (Debs) head of women's football at FSA. So we could highlight the links between Eric Worthington, coach of the first England women's team, who emigrated to Australia soon after heading up their coach education scheme and remaining in the country.

Toyota GB has partnered with the FSA, having advocated The Automotive 30% Club, a new scheme designed to promote at least 30% of key leadership positions with diverse women by 2030, so there were key collaborators in fan provision, not least the

THE INDUSTRIAL DISPUTE WORLD CUP—AUSTRALIA, 2023

She Kicks magazine whose editor, Jen O'Neill, had been working in women's football for over 20 years at this point. These FSA fan meet-ups would be a key part in our methodology collecting data on how they behaved before, during and after games. This also helped collecting contemporary material for the Football Museum, Manchester.

In Brisbane the High Commission was also involved, and it was a great pleasure to talk with Liverpool fan, Vicki Treadell CMG MVO, British High Commissioner to Australia, and her PA, Meghan. Born in Malaysia, of Cantonese, and French-Dutch ancestry, Vicki spoke candidly at the pre-match meet up with myself and Sally Freedman (who had also been at the Football Writers' Festival) about some of the challenges of working in senior diplomatic postings.

The UK media representation was a bit hit and miss. Some BBC coverage, some Sky, and mostly syndicated pieces by freelancers. Unusually *The Mirror* was a fixture, and the journalist was clearly intrigued by the title of Sally's book, *Get Your Tits Out for the Lads*. It wasn't exactly what I had anticipated for the first game, but it was a lot of fun, and the High Commissioner agreed to wear Jacqui's England coat—in spite of the heat—for some photos, which of course the press loved. I thought Vicki Treadell was very impressive in an understated way, and her staff, especially her PA Meghan, were protective of her challenging workload.

What struck me about the media was the rehearsed nature of what they wanted England fans to do, which is not how the supporters were behaving otherwise. There was an organised fan march, which was pretty thin, on the Brisbane waterfront to the first meet and greet at the Pig 'n' Whistle Riverside, cue special guest: the High Commissioner. Mainly people were having a drink, something to eat, and chatting. It was pretty calm, mostly chilled. Supporters were interested in the Femorabilia but didn't much want to make anything, so we learned that lesson early on. They were interested in purchasing anything we had already made, so another point of feedback there.

But the media, the television especially, wanted fans singing, and shouting in a 'Come on England' vibe. It was all entirely clichéd based on how they tended to cover England men's games. Although Deb and the FSA were trying to get a few chants going which had been written and learned, it wasn't the kind of spontaneous supporter culture I had experienced before. Not wanting to crash anyone's experience, but equally not particularly keen on being on TV shouting 'Come on England', I tended to place myself on the edge of groups so I could easily be cropped out. Which I often was.

Then the next fan march, led by Debs through the streets of Brisbane from the Pig Riverside to the Pig 'n' Whistle George Square, our next venue, where we were met by Ian Wright. Debs had really done lots of work in the background to make this fun for fans. Ian was absolutely charming taking lots of time for everyone, signing and obliging with selfies. Helped by Debs to be first in the queue, I managed to get Ian to style out

Jacqui's touchline coat, Sally was having her own photos taken with him, it was a real hoot! Not least because Lynda and Penny my tennis friends were in all of it, with the former wearing Jacqui's coat, in The Mirror and in Rob Smyth's piece in *The Guardian*.

So, wearing 'The Coat', as it became known, became a theme of the trip. I had travelled Business class and Jacqui's touchline coat had its own suitcase—which was fitting as it had a life of its own. People spotted us flying The Coat across Australia at luggage carousels. Air Stewards also recognised my Sarina coat and, with it being linen, hung it up for me so I'd arrive less creased. As the fan experience went on, The Coat began to have its own next chapter, having already become iconic at the Euros. Everyone, and I mean everyone, wore it. This was helped a great deal by the number of diaspora England fans.

The official tour was very, very expensive and I spoke to fans who had individually paid around £20,000 to be in Australia for the whole tournament. I seem to remember a figure of about 12-14 people on the main England Supporters Travel Club official tour, comprised of men, women, different ages, dual heritage, at least one visibly disabled supporter—a real mix of fans. I joked with Fiona Crawford that to make this trip, each of us had to be a £10,000 Pom at least, and I think this will go into her next book.

England support was amplified hugely by Australian fans with English or British heritage, and another cohort of mainly young women from a range of backgrounds who supported the Lionesses off the back of their Euros 2022 success. I'm guessing a significant element of this was young LGBTQ+ individuals, but also England women were icons of cool by then, having appeared in Vogue, and campaigns for Prada and Burberry, let alone for Adidas and Nike.

Unlike in France, where it was assumed that we would all drink coffee, there was a real bar culture in Australia which was celebratory, occasionally loud when coordinated singing was orchestrated, but mostly pretty mellow. Curious families tended to gravitate towards us, rather than head away, and so hanging out with the England fans became a thing more people did as the tournament progressed. Snowball is probably too optimistic a way to describe it in an Australian winter, but folks could see we were having a good time, and came along to join the party. Some homesick Brits flew in from across Australia wherever England were playing, and diaspora families wanted their kids to experience football fans. After the confines of the pandemic, in particular how strict things had been in Australia, here was a group of very happy folks all sharing a common interest in the middle of the afternoon, in contrast to workaday Brisbane commuter life. Folks were curious.

Which is how I met my new friend, Burberry. As I was waiting for Ian Wright with Debs, a woman of Chinese descent came up to me and began asking, in short English phrases, what we were doing? She was dressed head to toe, and I mean trainers, socks, and hat—in Burberry, with a beautiful camel cashmere cape the standout piece of her ensemble. I tried explaining that we were football fans and had made some of our own items. I was not sure how much she was getting of what I said—and also I had one eye out for Wrighty. So, we chatted as much as we were able for about 15 minutes, and off she went.

The FSA fans then marched to Suncorp Stadium and watched a narrow 1–0 win over Haiti, with a retaken penalty by Lioness Georgia Stanway after VAR adjudged the goalkeeper, Kerly Théus, had stepped off her line too early. The attendance, 44,369, indicated that although not necessarily fans of football, the Australian public would come out for big events, and this continued with both England and Australia picking up a lot of neutrals along the way. For instance, there was no plan at this stage to light up the Opera House in honour of the Australian women's team—but that soon changed!

As well as photographing lots of fanwear for the Femorabilia project, Suncorp was a revelation for an English football fan. I had of course stood in the stands back in the day at Leeds versus Leicester matches as a teen, when the iconic Admiral smiley face had become the new Leeds badge. But safe standing being an issue in British football for a number of reasons since the 1970s, my main experience of football had been watching sitting down, and as a punter with no access to alcohol except away from the cameras.

Suncorp is mainly a 52,000-seat capacity rugby union stadium, although obviously used for multi sports. I was able to get a beer while watching the match, stand on the concourse during the game, and converse with a police officer about the action. The absolute novelty of this entertained me more than the football.

A sluggish start from England, but good tournament strategy - winning by just as much as required, and no more.

England had selected its base camp out at Terrigal Beach, north of Sydney, in the area known as the 'Central Coast' of New South Wales, where the Darkinjung people were traditional custodians of the land. Having prepared for the World Cup at Sunshine Coast in Queensland, Terrigal had all sorts of FA historically themed facilities, largely thanks to the partnership with Nike, to link the past with the present. No detail had been left to chance, including using Qantas to advise on jetlag and a range of PR, from whale-watching to meeting local communities for technical staff. Designed to create the home-based feel that won the Women's Euros, the camp minimised travel, with England importantly based in Australia throughout.

After a late start the next day, I had a coffee with Vicki's PA Meghan and discussed Brisbane's culture. I had also held back a significant portion of a writing fee for a treat, thinking I'd like to add to the Sarina outfit. There was a brilliant independent boutique which had a pair of gold Chelsea boots in my size in the window. This style, with thick soles and elastic inserts, were popular when I first stood on the terraces, and a more punky, music-fashion alternative to the lace-up Doc Martens which were often associated with violent fans in the 1970s and 1980s, like skinheads. The glam-rock overtones of the gold boots also took me back to a British band called The Sweet, who unlike David Bowie's androgynous alter ego Ziggy Stardust, looked like your average builder who on the weekend, for a bit of a change, wore a gold lamé jumpsuit, stack-heeled platform boots, and his Mum's sky-blue eye shadow! The glam in their rock tended towards butch-bubble gum pop.

With this purchase made, I was looking in the window at the Burberry store when my friend from the day before tapped me on the shoulder. She wore the same beautiful camel cape, different Burberry trainers, and a snazzy pair of Rupert the Bear-style plaid trousers which were displayed in the store windows as new season. She really liked Burberry! However, she informed me her ensemble was not complete, and she was going in to buy a hat.

About two hours later we had purchased matching bucket hats in Burberry's iconic check. I had specifically wanted a bucket hat because everyone was wearing them in Australia and the FSA had specific ones made for England fans. I'd written about how sports clothing manufacturers had often begun making them, in response to the British weather in the mid-1800s, so it appealed to my sense of humour to be wearing a rain hat in about 30 degrees, albeit during Australia's winter months. So, there you go. My new friend was a bit bemused as to why I was wearing the Kerrminator coat today but our language skills didn't allow us to quite communicate the nuances of that. After a coffee I waived her off, as she was doing more shopping but my morning had been expensive enough.

Back to Sydney then in time for the next match on 28 July against Denmark at Sydney Football Stadium, which was walkable from our hotel. A pretty lacklustre match except for Lauren James' superb sixth minute goal, and Keira Walsh stretchered off for a narrow 1–0 victory. By now Jacqui was out and reunited with her coat. It was great after all the planning to go to the match together.

As the tournament progressed the industrial relations between players, both as individuals and as squads, were shown to be problematic in relation to the national association, the confederations and FIFA. By expanding for the first time to a 32-team final tournament, the multiple and complex ways that female football's elite players were being undermined, placed at different kinds of risk, and trivialised as athletes and workers, was showcased. The trip would get more and more serious. What the 2023 World Cup would do is give a platform for the debate of workers' rights in women's football.

This seems counterintuitive, because prize money was increased by $80 million, to $110,000 which seems an enormous proportion—and it is. However, the figure is also completely arbitrary and in relation to the funds for Qatar were $440 million, up by $40 million on 2018. Of this prize pot in Qatar, the winners, Argentina, took home $42 million. In Australia/New Zealand 2023 Spain took home $4.29 million. So ten per cent. Worst still, the pay differential is escalating.

So, if the fans of the USA were chanting, 'equal pay, equal pay' back in the 2019 Final, not one women's side who played in 2023 was treated equally with their male counterparts, be that in pay, working conditions, or in prize money. Poor governance issues were highlighted in the build up across many national associations, not least tournament heavyweights like Canada, Spain, and hosts Australia. None of these were addressed in ways that were transparent or changed institutional culture.

The fish rots from the head, and FIFA President Gianni Infantino was sickeningly and repeatedly disingenuous about the issues. For instance, on 8 June 2023, a new payment model was announced which was supposed to address the problems that squads of players had with not been paid what they were due by their national associations in 2019. To quote the rhetoric: 'Under this ground-breaking new model, Participating Member Associations (PMAs) will receive record distributions to support football development in their countries, while all participating players will receive guaranteed remuneration for their achievements at the tournament.'

In an eye-catching announcement of increased revenues, almost half of the money was paid to players and the winning team taking home $270,000 per squad member. FIFPro endorsed the deal with FIFA, which President David Aganzo said would be audited, and further pledged conditions and service levels for players equal to what the men had experienced in Qatar in 2022. But this legalese did not guarantee anything. The player entitlement was downgraded, within six weeks, to a general guideline.

What had been worded as a legal condition was later revised by FIFA to be essentially unenforceable as no mechanism for audit was in place, nor was there a commitment to create such processes. By 27 July, Norway's President Lise Klaveness was criticising that Infantino could not guarantee the minimum player payment of $30,000, which for countries like Haiti and Philippines where the players are not professional, would have been a huge benefit. Given her criticisms of Qatar, which cost her at the UEFA Executive Committee vote in May 2023 Klaveness was increasingly a lone voice. While she polled just 18 of the 55 votes required for the 19 spaces not ringfenced for a woman (which went to Laura McAllister of Wales), Luis Rubiales of Spain was one of the men re-elected.

Instead of responding to Klaveness's calls for ethical distribution of appearance money, Infantino reneged on any kind of guarantee. In an article in which FIFA said it was investigating allegations of sexual abuse in the Zambian national women's team, reported on 3 August in *The Guardian* he was reported as saying 'we are an association of associations, so whatever payments we do make will be through the associations and then the associations will make the relevant payments to their own players. There are different situations in different parts of the world, taxation residence and so on.'

Before looking at the case of Zambia in more detail, it is worth noting how the idea of an association of associations was problematic in relation to women's football. Not least, many male national associations had not sent squads to World Cup qualifiers.

The sexual abuse allegations against coach Bruce Mwape had been first made in 2022, and players had reported that they had not been paid for the Tokyo Olympic Games two years before. In 2022 Mwape and the under-17 coach, Kaluba Kangwa, were referred to FIFA with the latter leaving his post. Making further sexual abuse allegations in May 2024, a FIFA contractor in New Zealand also indicated that player welfare was an issue since they did not have enough money on their days off to buy a coffee.

Mwape remained in charge of Zambia at the Paris Olympics in 2024, and with world class talent like Barbra Banda and Racheal Kundananji the Copper Queens deserve better from a national association in which the President Andrew Kamanga, and FAZ General Secretary, Reuben Kamanga were arrested in April 2024 on money laundering offences. At the time of writing, no trial has been held. FIFA investigations did not want to disrupt the Olympic Games.

It would take a chapter in its own right to detail the level of poor governance, financial and other exploitation of all 32 women's teams in Australia, but Football Association Zambia is far from a lone case. International tournaments can highlight these stories.

As Ciara McCormack has shown in relation to Canadian soccer, the situation with its own sexual abuse scandal covers women's club and international squads going back to 2005. I had first interviewed Ciara for *Globalising Women's Football* in 2010/11, and the book was published back in 2013. She had played internationally for Ireland, and professional club football for Vancouver Whitecaps Women, Danish side Fortuna Hjørring, and in Australia for the Newcastle Jets.

Essentially, any woman who wished to play for the Canadian women's national side had to play for the Whitecaps from 2006 when one of the owners, Greg Kerfoot, invested in the national team ahead of the 2007 Women's World Cup and the Beijing 2008 Olympic Games. Whether the perception was that Whitecaps fed directly to the national team, or was an actual advantage, is less important than the culture within Whitecaps: that unpaid women players like Andrea Neil, Christine Sinclair, Erin McLeod, and Kara Lang should promote the club as part of their national aspirations. This included unpaid appearances at public clinics, and when the players began to collectively meet to ask for financial reward, then-president Bob Lenarduzzi attended a training session offering three bands of pay, the smallest being $125 per month. This disquieted the players because they had planned a meeting that evening to collectively bargain and someone had evidently tipped off Whitecaps owners, which if a player was judged to be a troublemaker, could affect national team selection.

If this seems like an over-reaction, it wasn't. After Greg Kerfoot partially funded a compulsory residency programme in Vancouver at short notice in October 2006 in the approach to the World Cup, Charmaine Hooper, Sharolta Nonen and Christine Latham protested that both the time frame and enforced move across Canada were unreasonable. Of course, training camps are a routine part of international preparation. However, scheduling can affect the day to day lives of players, many of whom in 2006 were working more than one job. The three did not attend the Vancouver camp and were released from the national squad. All had been 2003 Women's World Cup players. Hooper, Nonen and Latham had a combined 243 international caps, and 87 goals for Canada. Hooper, a member of the national team since 1986, was Canada's all-time leader in caps (131) and goals (71). None of them ever played for Canada again. Hooper lost the captaincy to Christine Sinclair who supported Canada Soccer's decision.

The escalation of the situation between male coaches and players was facilitated by a few people holding multiple roles. Bill held multiple roles as Whitecaps' women's head coach, the Canadian Under-20 team and as an assistant with the senior national team, giving an undue amount of power over young developing players. This led to bullying behaviour, particularly by an individual anonymised as Coach Billy by McCormack in her blog posts.

The compulsory residency programmes became an opportunity for predatory behaviour with Under-20 players required to live in the same apartment block in Vancouver, and Coach Billy, who had family in another suburb, retaining an apartment. When reports were made by McCormack and other players to Whitecaps staff, and those in Canada Soccer, a supposedly independent mediator sought to manage the PR of the situation to be favourable to the club and national association, rather than the players.

Although not named by McCormack in her blog, Bob Birarda was eventually said to have 'parted ways' with Canada Soccer and the Whitecaps, who terminated their women's team in 2012. He was convicted in 2022 of three counts of sexual assault, and one count of sexual touching between 1989 and 2008. Crucially, Richard McLaren's review found that the policies of Canada Soccer enabled Birarda to continue coaching in the elite programme at Under-17 level with young women. Eventually he was convicted and given 16 months in jail and eight months of house arrest. However, FIFA publicly backed Canada Soccer's Victor Montagliani, the President of CONCACAF and a FIFA Vice-President, and Peter Montopoli, the Chief Operating Officer for Canada Soccer for the 2026 World Cup, who handled the case at the time.

So, to contextualise the disputes between players and Canada Soccer in the 2023 Women's World Cup, Italian international Carolina Morace followed Norwegian Even Pellerud as head coach in 2008, but with several disputes over funding and a disastrous 2011 World Cup performance, left soon after. England's John Herdman then took over, winning the bronze medal at the London Olympics in 2012, at a time of greater visibility. Hosting the World Cup in 2015, it was clear that offensively there was an overdependence on Christine Sinclair and, Canada exited in the quarter finals. After another Olympic bronze medal in 2016, Herdman moved into men's football. After a brief spell with Denmark's Kenneth Heiner-Møller, England's Bev Priestman took over, winning gold in the Olympic Games.

Ahead of the 2023 She Believes Cup, the players called a strike about both the funding for the national programme and the compensation for international duty. Sinclair said the national team had not been paid for its 2022 work, had not been told why budget cuts were happening in a World Cup year, when the team were also Olympic champions. The reasons for the budget cuts, for the men's and women's programmes, were because Canada Soccer was funding expensive lawsuits based on the wider context outlined above. Instead of responding to player concerns, Canada Soccer threatened its women's squad with legal action. That Sinclair threatened not to attend a training camp was a significant story, given what had happened to Hooper previously. Canada were the first Olympic champions to be knocked out of the following World Cup, losing 4–0 to hosts Australia in 2023.

As we now know in 2024, with Bev Priestman sent home from the 2024 Paris Olympics for the 'Dronegate' spying scandal on the New Zealand team, the players remained world class, progressing without a head coach, losing to Germany in the quarter finals. But at what personal cost? Working conditions, pay, player safety and well-being all remain much larger problems than who will replace Sinclair as the next striker. When systemic failure in governance has decades of proven cultural behaviour, it is hard to see from where change will come. And Canada is one of the better behaved national associations.

So, if there were cries of equal pay in 2019, there was not a women's team in Australia who was not in dispute with their national association. Ironically, 'player power' through representing their country has been a factor in more women's voices being heard. In the case of England, the players paused their dispute with the FA for the World Cup, not just in relation to the size of the pay each received from the FIFA pot, but in relation to commercial activities the FA benefitted from, such as links with M&S, Nike and others. Since players had agents at this stage, they were able to use PFA links and collective action to reconcile conversations about working conditions in September 2023. Scotland women had also had a pay dispute with the SFA which was resolved the same month.

Australia and New Zealand 2023 was still an overwhelmingly Eurocentric tournament—with 12 of the 32 berths, over a third of allocations, reserved for European teams. This reflects the location of FIFA headquarters currently, which may well change with more staff going to North America ahead of 2026. The Republic of Ireland attended their first World Cup, coached by Dutch international Vera Pauw. While there is an ongoing case of historical sexual abuse in the 1990s which the recent

THE INDUSTRIAL DISPUTE WORLD CUP—AUSTRALIA, 2023

RTÉ Investigates: Girls in Green documentary covered, there was also a more recent series of strikes and collective action since 2016 led by Emma Byrne, the captain.

Of the eight teams making their debut, only Morocco made it through to the round of 16, where they lost to France, ironically a country in which wearing a hijab in international sport is prohibited. Morocco did not play its first official international until 1998, and the women's international programme had been dormant for long sessions in the next two decades. It was really only after the COVID pandemic that a restructure enabled the first North African and Arab country to reach the Women's World Cup. Nouhaila Benzina became the first player to play in a World Cup match wearing a hijab, and star striker Ibtissam Jraïdi scoring their first World Cup goal. It's an indication of the situation that Jraïdi has only 60+ caps to her name having first represented her country in 2009. So, the four CAF berths in 2023 went to Morocco, Zambia, Nigeria and South Africa. Under the guidance of Jorge Vilda, Morocco lost to Zambia in the Olympic qualifying rounds for the Confederation of African Football (CAF), and so did not compete in Paris, 2024.

There were just three teams from South America in 2023, Brazil, Columbia and Argentina. Columbia, having reached their first Women's World Cup in 2011, were eliminated in the group stages. Improving to a 12th place finish in the round of 16 in 2015, they did not qualify in 2019. All the more impressive then, to win their group by defeating Germany and South Korea, to reach the quarter finals, losing 2–1 to England in Stadium Australia, Sydney on 12 August 2023. I really enjoyed this match, and it was a narrow defeat. The fans were fantastic, many diaspora migrants now living long-term in Australia. But the working conditions of the players were, again, dire.

Captain Daniela Montoya Quiroz was not selected for the Brazil Olympic Games after criticising the Colombian national association for not paying players after the 2015 World Cup. She alleged that they received $60 in a brown envelope for their efforts in Canada where they reached the round of 16 for the first time, exiting after defeat 2–0 by the USA. Again, she has only 60+ caps in spite of playing for the national team since 2010, and as the captain is a mainstay, apart from her exclusion in 2016, so this reflects the overall lack of internationals organised by the national association.

In Australia, Catalina Usme shone as did Linda Caceido, having come through the youth system, but Brenda Elsey's article, *'Café con mala leche'* explains how the development teams have historically been used for the exploitation of players.

Even the co-hosts Australia had endured over four years of controversial build up with the qualifying coach for France 2019, Alen Stajcic, sacked for controversial reasons which ultimately resulted in a Football Australia Board member forced to publicly apologise about allegations she had spread about him that were untrue. Stajcic had been in charge since 2014. Ante Milic took over as coach for the 2019 tournament before Football Australia appointed Tony Gustavsson in 2020 for the 2023 tournament.

Stajic instead went to the 2023 Women's World Cup as head coach of the Philippines women's national team, which since 2018 had been supported by entrepreneur and football club owner, Jefferson Cheng. Attending their first ever World Cup, 18 of the squad of 23 were born in the US. Tahnai Annis, the captain, epitomised the opportunities that the US offers, that perhaps the national association doesn't provide. With the support of Cheng the team defeated New Zealand 1-0 in their first game of 2023, but now that he is no longer supporting the women's programme, it is not clear how the national association will continue the women's programme.

In a similar position is Jamaica, without the support of Cedella Marley, who quit as global ambassador of the Jamaican women's national team, following non-payment for their round of 16 finish in 2023. Cedella funded both 2019 and 2023 World Cup appearances through the Bob and Rita Marley Foundation to the tune of $2.75 million, plus drawing in other funders. After withdrawing their labour in protest at the lack of payment, senior players were suspended by the Jamaican Football Association, resulting in Marley's departure as ambassador. Marley had originally appointed coach Lorne Donaldson, who led the team in France, and Australia where they lost 1-0 to Colombia. In spite of world talents like Captain Khadija 'Bunny' Shaw, the players found out that Xavier Gilbert had been appointed the new head coach by social media. Having taken 10 years to build the programme, Marley's departure leaves the players unpaid and unsure of their future.

Set in this wider context of the industrial disputes that players are having after every successive major tournament, it is clear that the narrative of progress doesn't match a pattern of development and retrenchment, and in which male-led governing bodies benefit financially from women's work as players, without necessarily passing on payments that ought to be contractually due. I could go on, on a team by team basis but it would take a book in itself.

As to my own travels in Australia, I was by now running five miles a day from my hotel to the Opera House and back after saying hello to Benny, the resident seal and at the gym first thing. We were then walking about six to eight miles a day around the city or going to the beach at Manly where the water was too freezing to surf for long. I regretted my swimming collection could not be added to because many of Sydney's iconic pools were closed for winter. I did a conference at Sydney University, meeting old friends and new, and a keynote for Jess Richards at Western Sydney which was a complete blast. I bumped into lots of people who I had not seen in person since before COVID, so that was a great pleasure.

Jacqui and I debated whether to return to Brisbane for the game against Nigeria on 7 August. Thank goodness we made the right choice. It was worth two return air fares, a very expensive one-night's accommodation in a two-bedroom apartment, and all the travelling hassle. Nigeria should have won. I kind of wish the Super Falcons had won,

THE INDUSTRIAL DISPUTE WORLD CUP—AUSTRALIA, 2023

given what I knew of their federation and the difficulties they faced in their country, but with superior game management, England held on for penalties, clearly a plan well before the end of the second half, let alone extra time.

Mary Earps was superb to win her golden gloves for the tournament, but England did not look like scoring. It was, of course, the game where a frustrated Lauren James received a red card in the 87th minute, which after her previous two goals against China on 1 August bought her World Cup to a halt for now. Having printed Sarina's image on a stamp, I was very tempted to do the same with Lauren James in view of how she came to be sent off but it was perhaps too soon. We had managed to find independent printers in Sydney where we had designed more compassionate 'The Name's James, 007' and 'Licensed to Thrill' t shirts ahead of the match, printing one-offs and sharing with fans.

The US national team went out in the round of sixteen to Sweden on penalties, a sad end for Rapinoe and co in Melbourne. This was before Vlatko accepted the inevitable and Emma Hayes went to the USA.

Back to Sydney, onto Colombia in the quarters. Again, an iconic backdrop to the fans collecting for their fan march at Syndey Opera House before moving onwards to Stadium Australia. On 12 August I couldn't help but think back to 1999. Stadium Australia was packed for the England-Colombia game, due to kick off at 20.30. However, those who couldn't make it to Brisbane for Australia versus France at 17.00 packed out the surrounding area watching on big screens. And honestly it felt like most of Syndey was there. I had never seen so many people watching women's football, as England and Colombia fans arrived for the match to find every bar, public area, café, and concourse awash with Matildas fans. I took a video of the food and beverage trucks, and it took me five minutes walking along the road to capture even a small amount. Matildas fever was more like attending a music festival. Australia went through 7-6 on penalties. England won 2-1, and so the semi final between the two was set up.

Back again for the Australia semi-final match on 16 August, where an injured Sam Kerr was able to take part for the game. It was sad to see how little she had been able to play, although it perhaps balanced the team and allowed others to shine in a more collective performance. After Ella Toone's screamer of a goal on 36 minutes, we wondered would half time help us or hurt us? The Australian captain replied on 63 minutes, not long before Lauren Hemp (one of England's most undervalued players in my view) put England ahead, with a personal favourite, Alessia Russo, finalising the score on 86 minutes. It was estimated between 7 and 11 million people watched the match on Australian television.

What a drag it was to get out to that stadium and back, what with vandals not at the game allegedly cutting the cables on the trainline, but what a joy it was to be there, and see how many fans had filled the park. We could see the momentum in the public interest, and it reminded me of Los Angeles 1999, when the women were also front page news; lots of fan swap events and discussion of relative fan cultures in between. Sweden beat Australia for third place, and that fourth place gave women's football within Australian culture a higher profile than ever before.

And so, to the final at 20.00 Sunday 20 August with 75,000 packed into Stadium Australia. I had said to Kay Cossington and Anja van Ginhoven when I did the FA event back in January that I would see them at the final in Sydney and to reserve me a ticket. I bumped into them in Sydney's Botanical Gardens and reminded them about that ticket as I did Sue Campbell when we photographed her in The Coat. After all, not many people had flown out for the entirety to support England. None was forthcoming. Instead, I was directed to the general fan ticketing site like everyone else. Bad karma. I had a foreboding that we were not going to win.

In the end I was gifted a ticket by a collegue and watched behind Millie Bright's friends and family as Spain looked technically and tactically much superior to England. Spain were the Under 17 and Under 20 women's world champions and the head of the Regional Training Centres (RTCs) in England had been studying the technical expertise of the Spanish system. Whatever I thought of Jorge Vilda at the Euros, at the World Cup Final, Spain just outplayed England. When the fantastic Olga Carmona goal went in on 29 minutes, I nipped out to buy us beer. We would need it. It was to be our only chance. Due to some ridiculously outdated licensing laws from the UK, the bars in Australia close at 10pm on a Sunday.

Without Beth Mead we didn't have the two-pronged attack, so key to winning at Wembley, and without Leah Williamson, the mood was not as relentless as maybe it had been a year before. Rachel Daly, again a wholly under-rated player in my view, was asked to play a number of roles, somewhat sacrificing her own game for the team. Spain had 60% possession, and it looked like more inside the stadium, while England were right-sided in attack. Aitana Bonmati won the Golden Ball, Mary Earps the Golden Glove, and Hinata Miyazawa the Golden Boot.

Our compassion was for the young women whose moment of victory was stolen publicly by the behaviour of Luis Rubiales by kissing Jenni Hermoso, one of the original 15, on the lips on the winner's podium.

I don't propose to spend long on Rubiales, as I'd rather talk about Aitana Bonmati and *Las 15*, including missing players from 2023, like Mapi León, Sandra Paños, and others. What must have they felt about seeing such treatment and being excluded for speaking out, while so technically gifted? Vilda's days were numbered when he publicly applauded Rubiales who publicly offered Vilda a new contract, increasing his salary from €170,000 (£145,000) to €500,000 a year. When Rubiales's mother went on a hunger strike, briefly, and his uncle Juan, who also worked at the Spanish Federation, denounced him for corruption, the absurdity of the situation took the victory of the women and made it a farce.

THE INDUSTRIAL DISPUTE WORLD CUP—AUSTRALIA, 2023

The hashtag *se acabó* (it's over), came after the speech in which Rubiales claimed that Hermoso had consented to the kiss and denounced 'false feminism.' The Spanish football federation threatened to sue Hermoso, and offered still photographs as evidence she had initiated the kiss and enjoyed a close relationship with Rubiales. Ugh.

The day before the final kicked off I was having a glass of mulled wine in 34° heat with Jacqui and Natalie Smith in the very odd fan zone FIFA had constructed, explaining that I felt more sad about the fact that I'd probably seen Marta's last World Cup than if England lost the final. But still, even with the subsequent retirement of Daly, and others, the England team of Leah Williamson's era will go onto more great things.

Other than their usual merchandising partners and sponsors, the local organising committee didn't know what to do with the fan zones, which had been similarly hopeless in France in 2019. In Australia this was reflected in the choice of music which ranged from jangling pop so loud you couldn't actually conduct a conversation and you'd have to relocate to a restaurant, to individual singers with guitars, bemoaning emo-type anxieties about their difficult lives. Not what I expected at the football. But the big screens acted as magnets for fans to collect, move away in smaller groups, recongregate and so on. Again, most of the fan culture was away from this plastic construction from the Organising Committee, with its fake organised fun.

It had been a life-changing trip. I met some wonderful people, reconnected with others, and loved Australia—quite apart from the football. In spite of the contested gender relations, racial tensions around the 2023 Australian Indigenous Voice referendum in October later that year and other societal problems, the land and sea had rhythms that made me thrive while there.

But now it was time to go home to Simon, friends and family. We had the *Copa 71* premiere in Toronto to come and I had this idea to write a memoir, covering seven World Cups at the same time as building, and exiting, an academic career.

I caught the ferry to Manly to chat to Bonita. We had a pizza in the sunshine and she said, 'Yes, why not?'

Three of my favourite words.

More really good football books from Fair Play Publishing

Encyclopedia of Matildas Beyond the World Cup 2023

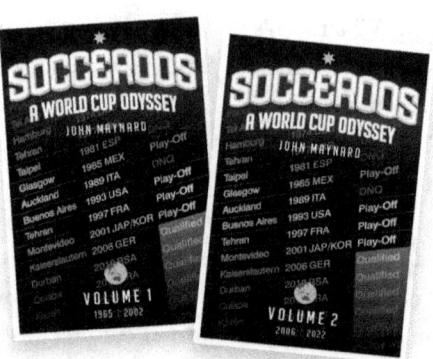
Socceroos – A World Cup Odyssey, 1965 to 2022 Volumes 1 and 2

Noddy, The Untold Story of Adrian Alston

"Get Your Tits Out for the Lads"

Hear Us Roar – An anthology of emerging women football writers

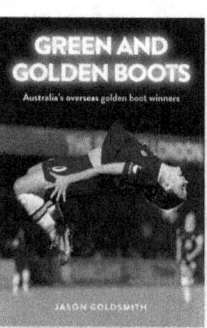
When Mum and Dad See Me Kick

Football Fans In Their Own Write...

Available from
fairplaypublishing.com.au/shop
and all good bookstores

fairplaypublishing.com.au

www.ingramcontent.com/pod-product-compliance
Lightning Source LLC
Chambersburg PA
CBHW052025070526
44584CB00016B/1899